Cases on Digital Entrepreneurship

ELGAR CASES IN ENTREPRENEURSHIP

Elgar Cases in Entrepreneurship offer an instrumental resource to fulfil the needs of instructors in entrepreneurship. Spanning numerous discrete fields, *Elgar Cases* cover state-of-the-art developments in real-world entrepreneurial endeavours, providing expert analysis with an international focus. *Casebooks* are edited by leading instructors, who bring together experienced and knowledgeable case writers to illustrate and analyse contemporary entrepreneurial scenarios. Each case offers a strong foundation for constructive discussion and includes learning objectives and summary questions to guide classroom discussion. Teaching notes for each case provide opportunities for instructors to further develop understanding and promote class engagement. An invaluable boon to course leaders and students alike, Elgar Cases in Entrepreneurship combine practicality, student engagement and international expertise to bring entrepreneurship alive!

Cases on Digital Entrepreneurship

How Digital Technologies are Transforming the Entrepreneurial Process in Existing Businesses and Start-ups

Edited by

Luca Iandoli

Associate Dean, Global Programs and Research and Professor of Computer Science, St. John's University, New York, USA

Carmine Gibaldi

Professor of Management and Entrepreneurship, St. John's University, New York, USA

ELGAR CASES IN ENTREPRENEURSHIP

Cheltenham, UK • Northampton, MA, USA

Published by
Edward Elgar Publishing Limited
The Lypiatts
15 Lansdown Road
Cheltenham
Glos GL50 2JA
UK

Edward Elgar Publishing, Inc.
William Pratt House
9 Dewey Court
Northampton
Massachusetts 01060
USA

Paperback edition 2023

A catalogue record for this book
is available from the British Library

Library of Congress Control Number: 2022950617

This book is available electronically in the **Elgar**online
Business subject collection
http://dx.doi.org/10.4337/9781802203868

ISBN 978 1 80220 385 1 (cased)
ISBN 978 1 80220 386 8 (eBook)
ISBN 978 1 0353 2920 5 (paperback)

Printed and bound by CPI Group (UK) Ltd, Croydon, CR0 4YY

Contents

Contributors

Rubén A. Ascúa, PhD, is President of the National University of Rafaela (2017–2025), Professor at the National Technological University-Rafaela and Visiting Professor at the Faculty of Economic Sciences of the University of Applied Sciences of Kaiserslautern, Germany. He is former president of the Red Pymes Mercosur, the International Council for Small Business (ICSB) and the Fundación Empretec Argentina. Prof. Dr. Rubén Ascúa has obtained two undergraduate degrees, National Public Accountant (UNL-FCE) and Bachelor of Economics (UNR-FCEyE) in Argentina; a Master and Doctorate (PhD) in Economics (PWU San Diego, USA). He has worked as an external consultant for ECLAC, IDB and IFC. His fields of research and teaching are: development of SMEs and new companies; theory of the firms; markets and financing instruments for SMEs; formulation and evaluation of industrial investment projects; clusters and industrial districts.

Cesar Bandera, PhD, is Associate Professor of Entrepreneurship at the New Jersey Institute of Technology Martin Tuchman School of Management, USA. His research interests include entrepreneurship ecosystems and pedagogy. Bandera has also launched several successful ventures in m-Health and video processing. He received his PhD in Electrical and Computer Engineering from the University at Buffalo, NY, with a specialization in biomimetics and active vision. He is recipient of four patents and Small Business Innovation Research awards from DHHS, NSF, DOD and NASA. Bandera is Associate Director of NJIT's Leir Research Institute, Associate Editor of the *IEEE Journal of Translational Engineering in Health and Medicine*, Guest Editor of *JSBED*, Senior Member of IEEE, and NJIT Master Teacher.

Maria Bogren has a PhD in Business Administration within entrepreneurship (2015) from Mid Sweden University, Östersund, Sweden. She is currently Associate Professor in Organization and Leadership at NORD University, Steinkjer, Norway, and Assistant Professor in Business Administration at Mid Sweden University, Östersund, Sweden. At NORD University she teaches courses in marketing and digital marketing. She has published articles and book chapters mainly within the field of entrepreneurship, and lately also within marketing and sustainability. Her research interest is broad, including for example women's entrepreneurship, lifestyle entrepreneurs, social capital, networking and SMEs within nature-based businesses.

José A. Borello, PhD, is a Researcher and Professor at University of Rafaela and at Universidad Nacional de General Sarmiento; he is also a Researcher at CONICET. He is the Vice-President in charge of Research at Red Pymes Mercosur and Ambassador of the Regional Studies Association in Argentina. His areas of expertise include economic geography and planning. He has undertaken sectoral, urban, and regional studies. He has also worked in projects related to the application of geographical information systems, and in science and technology planning and policy. Borello has been a consultant for a number of international, national, provincial, and municipal agencies and NGOs and private firms. Since 2010 he has been working on film and audiovisual production and consumption. Trained in geography and planning in Argentina, Canada, and the US, he currently teaches courses in economic geography, in the social and economic geography of Latin America, and in project development.

Ricky Celenta is a PhD student in Big Data Management at the University of Salerno, Italy. His areas of interest are innovation management and digital entrepreneurship. He is a member of Lisa Lab, a Research Centre on Innovative Entrepreneurship and Academic Spin-Off, at the University of Salerno.

Pasquale Del Vecchio, PhD, is an Associate Professor in Management Engineering at the Department of Management, Finance and Technology – LUM University, Italy. In 2007 he was a visiting PhD student in the Center for Business Intelligence at MIT's Sloan School of Management. His research field concerns the issues of circular economy, data-driven business model innovation and digital transformation. He has been involved in research and innovation projects focused on technological entrepreneurship for circular economy and digital innovation.

Odile De Saint Julien, PhD, is a senior strategy consultant in the field of biotechnology and a professor at KEDGE BS, France. Her expertise and research work are related to innovation ecosystems where entrepreneurship plays a key role in the design of disruptive innovations. Since 2016, Odile has been an Assistant Professor at KEDGE. She teaches strategy, open innovation and entrepreneurship.

John DiMarco, PhD, has helped people with learning, communication, and design for the last 25 years. John is Professor of Mass Communication and Digital Media Design at St. John's University in New York City, USA. He teaches, writes, trains, and consults in creativity, design thinking, new product development, digital media, instructional design, persuasive communication, and career building. John delivers seminars, creates learning products, and publishes extensively across disciplines. His passion for helping people intersects digital, communication, instructional, visual, and product design disciplines. Dr. DiMarco is a patented inventor. His product design for The SHAPE STRETCH Body Bar offers users a unique tool and educational approach to stretching and flexibility.

Michael Dominik, PhD, teaches entrepreneurship in the USA and mentors his students and those of his community in creating and maturing entrepreneurial ventures. His 35+ years of experience as an engineer, manager, and entrepreneur included leadership roles with General Electric and Lockheed Martin. He co-founded his first technology start-up company in 1999, a software-as-a-service firm which was later acquired by a publicly owned strategic partner. He also founded another technology services consulting firm, from which he continues to serve clients in aerospace, medical, and software industries.

Paul Drews, PhD, is Dean of the School of Management and Technology, Speaker of the Research Center for Digital Transformation and Professor of Information Systems at Leuphana University of Lüneburg, Germany. Previously, he acted as the president's delegate for cooperation with practice and entrepreneurship. His research is dedicated to the great challenge of digital transformation with a focus on digital strategy, digital entrepreneurship, digital innovation, data-driven business models, enterprise architecture and scaling agile. He is the co-leader of the EU-funded transdisciplinary project Digital Entrepreneurship at Leuphana University.

Gianluca Elia, PhD, is Associate Professor in Management Science and Engineering at the University of Salento, Italy, where he teaches Digital Business. His cross-disciplinary research focuses on knowledge management, technology entrepreneurship, digital transformation, collective intelligence, open innovation, and big data. On these topics, he has published more than 160 papers in international journals, conference proceedings, and books. He has also co-authored five books. He is Associate Editor of *Computers Application in Engineering Education* (Wiley), and *International Journal of Knowledge and Learning* (Inderscience). He has had scientific responsibility for several R&D projects, and been reviewer of innovation and research projects. He is co-founder of the TIE Living Lab (Technology Innovation Ecosystem Living Lab), which is part of the European Network of Living Lab (ENoLL) to promote and support open innovation and user-driven innovation approaches for the development of technology entrepreneurship. In 2014 he was a visiting researcher at Peking University in Beijing (China), and in 2014–2015 he was research affiliate at the Center for Collective Intelligence at MIT in Boston

(USA). Since 2001, he has been teaching in academic and corporate programs. He is also supervisor of graduate projects and PhD theses.

Rosangela Feola, PhD, is Assistant Professor of Management at the University of Salerno (Italy) and Affiliate Research Fellow at IPAG Business School (Paris, France). She is member of Lisa Lab, a Research Centre on Innovative Entrepreneurship and Academic Spin-Off, at the University of Salerno. Her research interests are mainly related to entrepreneurial processes, technology transfer and innovative start-ups. She is co-author of several publications on national and international journals among which are *R&D Management, Journal of Small Business Management, Small Business Economics, Journal of Cleaner Production* and *Journal of Small Business and Enterprise Development.*

Davide Gamba is a PhD student, and a teaching and research assistant at the Center for Young and Family Enterprise (CYFE) at the University of Bergamo, Italy. He holds a Master's degree in Industrial Engineering. He also serves as Business Analyst Leader at MEI Srl, an Italian manufacturing company in the optical industry. His research interests include the management of servitization strategies adopted by small and medium enterprises.

Carmine Gibaldi, EdD, is a Professor of Management and Entrepreneurship. In addition to serving as a professor, he has worked in a consulting practice that addresses issues related to organizational change, leadership, training and development, and executive coaching. He has delivered over 60 papers at international conferences addressing issues related to management and organizational behavior, higher education, and college teaching. His most recent papers address applying neuroscience to management and using trans-formational learning with adult learners. His present research includes fear in the workplace, examining cultural implications and organizational behavior, the impact of COVID-19 and working remotely, and fears related to returning to the workplace post-COVID-19.

Luca Iandoli, PhD, is Associate Dean for Global Programs and Research and a Professor in the Department of Computer Science at St. John's University, New York, USA. Luca was a Fulbright Visiting Scholar at the MIT Center for Collective Intelligence and served as Associate Professor at the University of Naples Federico II, Italy, and as Visiting Professor at Stevens Institute of Technology, USA. His research focuses on collective intelligence, interaction design, and product aesthetics.

Marco Valerio Izzo serves as CFO and Board Member at Buzzoole, an end-to-end influencer marketing platform that connects brands with the right influencers on the web through a data-driven, automated and scalable technology. In 2014 he founded Volano, a corporate financial advisory firm consisting of professionals experienced in management and strategic consulting, supporting different Italian start-ups in fundraising strategy and business model validation.

Matteo Kalchschmidt, PhD, is Professor of Project and Innovation Management at the University of Bergamo, Italy. Matteo Kalchschmidt conducts research in the field of innovation and management of production and logistics systems. His commitment to scientific research is focused essentially on the topic of supply chain management, with specific attention on demand management, sustainable supply chain management, global supply chain management and manufacturing strategies. He is currently Co-Editor-in-Chief of the international journal *Operations Management Research: Advancing Practice Through Theory*.

Dmitry Katalevsky, PhD, has 20+ years of teaching experience in strategic management, innovation management, systems thinking and business simulation courses in the leading Russian business schools. He combined an academic career with working experience in business (consulting & financial services, project management, R&D management) both in Russia and the EU. Dmitry has more than 30 academic publications in the area of strategic management, R&D portfolio, business simulations, managerial & systems thinking, and global value chains management. He is an author of a business simulation textbook (in Russian), several book chapters and the highly successful interactive business simulation "StartUp: the Limits to Growth." As an entrepreneur, he co-founded recently an international digital start-up in machine vision with application for healthcare.

Alessandro Margherita, PhD, is Associate Professor at the Department of Engineering for Innovation (DEfI) of the University of Salento (Italy) and Research Partner at ENGIN/UFSC Federal University of Santa Catarina (Brazil). Professor Margherita is Innovation Manager at the Italian Ministry of Economic Development (MISE), Scientific Committee of the Italian Association for Total Cost Management (AICE) and Academic Editor of *PlosOne*. Professor Margherita has twenty years of teaching, research and consulting experience at national and international level in academic and industrial contexts, and expertise in human resource and business analytics, digital organizational transformation, and technology entrepreneurship. Professor Margherita has published more than 90 research works in international conferences and leading journals and is the author of five manuals on business engineering, process and project management. Professor Margherita is also scientific coordinator of the MUR-funded (Italian Ministry) research project HUMANWISE on human resource analytics to face the pandemic emergency;

visiting scholar at the Center for Digital Business of MIT Sloan (USA), research affiliate of the Center for Collective Intelligence of MIT Sloan, and visiting researcher at PKU – Peking University (China).

Andrea Minetti, Lic, is in charge of the Entrepreneurial Development Department of the National University of Rafaela, and Doctoral Student in Administration (National University of Rosario, Argentina). Minetti graduated in Industrial Organization (National Technological University, Argentina) and is a teacher and researcher.

Tommaso Minola, PhD, is co-founder and Director of the Research Center for Young and Family Enterprise (CYFE) of the University of Bergamo, Italy, where he is a tenured professor in the fields of technology management and entrepreneurship. He has been TOFT Visiting Professor at Jönköping International Business School (Sweden). He has also been Technology Manager and Director of Technology Incubator at Politecnico di Milano. He is a member of several academic and professional associations on entrepreneurship and family business, and reviewer for major international journals in the field. His research and teaching is focused on entrepreneurship, family business, technological innovation, and technology transfer.

Roberto Parente is Founder and Director of LISA Lab, a Research Centre whose main topics are: science based start-up; student entrepreneurship; and finance for innovation. Through LISA Lab he regularly organizes Labs and Acceleration programs on the issue of new business creation. Roberto is the Head of Student Entrepreneurship policy of his university, actively promoting the culture of innovation and entrepreneurship among students and researchers. He is a member of the Italian Association SIMA, and Facilitator of the "Entrepreneurship" group. Roberto is an active angel investor contributing to the development of many science-based ventures, mainly in healthcare and biotechnology industry. On the other side he is involved in social innovation projects helping local communities to develop micro and SMEs for sustainable growth. The most recent one has been focused on the Cilento National Park, an area in the south of Italy that is known worldwide as the home-base of the "Dieta Mediterranea."

Katia Passerini, PhD, is the Provost and Executive Vice President of the Seton Hall University, USA. Prior to Seton Hall, Katia was the Lesley H. and William L. Collins Distinguished Chair & Dean of the Collins College of Professional Studies at St. John's University, where she also held a Professor appointment in the Division of Computer Science. From 2003–2016, she was Professor and Hurlburt Chair of MIS and Dean of the Albert Dorman Honors College (2013–2016) at the New Jersey Institute of Technology. She holds MBA and PhD degrees from the George Washington University. Prior to academia, she worked as a management consultant for Booz Allen and Hamilton in the automotive and telecom industries. Her research spans knowledge management, entrepreneurship education, technology management and computer-supported learning. She has published over a hundred peer-reviewed journal and conference proceedings articles and has received numerous teaching, research, and service recognitions.

Katia Richomme-Huet, PhD and HDR, is a Senior Professor in Entrepreneurship at Kedge Business School, France. She currently leads the Department "Strategy, CSR and Entrepreneurship", after holding the positions of Director of Entrepreneurship and Coordinator of the Center "Entrepreneurial Diversity." Her research focuses on social and sustainable entrepreneurship, women entrepreneurs, small businesses transfers and family businesses. She led the "iBlue" project for France (European project ERDF, Interreg Med) and held the Research Chair "Visible and Invisible Disability Management" (supported by Société Générale).

Ada Scupola, PhD, is Professor at the Department of Social Sciences and Business, Roskilde University, Denmark. Ada Scupola has extensive experience in managing and participating in international and Danish research projects on value co-creation, innovation, and digitalization. Funding bodies include the Horizon 2020 Program, The Danish Council for Independent Research, The Danish Industry Foundation, The Strategic Research Council, and The Nordic Council of Ministers. Her research counts over 170 publications. She serves on the editorial board of several journals and has been visiting scholar in several universities including University of Texas at Austin, USA, University of Michigan, USA, Queensland University of Technology, Australia, and University of Maryland, USA.

Giustina Secundo is Full Professor in Management Engineering at Department of Management, Finance and Technology University LUM Giuseppe Degennaro (Bari, Italy). She is Rector's delegate for innovation and Third Mission, Scientific Director of the Master's degree in Digital Transformation of the Public Administration and of the Executive Master's in Cyber Security Management at the LUM School of Management University. She serves as co-editor of the *International Journal of Entrepreneurial Behavior & Research* and she sits on the editorial Board of Management. With more than 20 years of experience as researcher at University of Salento (Italy), she published 190 international papers appearing in *Technovation, Technological Forecasting & Social Change, Journal of Business Research*, and *Journal of Intellectual Capital* on the topic of academic entrepreneurship, intellectual capital, open innovation and digital transformation. She managed several R&D projects in collaboration with companies in the sector of new product development and technology entrepreneurship. She received several awards for her research activities, including the Emerald Literati award, the best papers award and the highly commended award from Emerald. From 2014–2015 she was visiting researcher at the Innovation Insights Lab at University of the Arts London (UK).

Anna Sörensson has a PhD in Business Administration within international marketing (2014) from Åbo Akademi, Finland. She is currently Assistant Professor in Business Administration at Mid Sweden University, Östersund. She has published articles and book chapters mainly within the field of marketing, entrepreneurship, tourism and sustainability. Her research interest is broad, and also including for example nature-based businesses, sustainable development and entrepreneurial education.

Jan K. Tänzler, PhD, is currently project manager of the EU-funded transdisciplinary project Digital Entrepreneurship at Leuphana University, Germany. He primarily conducts research on the topics of digitalization, family businesses and corporate governance.

Nils J. Tschoppe is PhD student at the Institute of Information Systems at Leuphana University of Lüneburg, Germany. As a research assistant in the EU-funded, transdisciplinary project "Digital Entrepreneurship," he works on technology-related challenges of (fast-growing) SMEs in the digital age. His research focuses on digital entrepreneurship and the digital transformation of SMEs, as well as enterprise architecture.

Acknowledgments

This book is the result of several months of work during which we received encouragement, ideas, suggestions, constructive criticism, and support in various forms from many colleagues, students, and friends, including Almerinda Forte, Jerry Cusack, Joan DeBello, Glen Gerstner, Kevin James, Bill Reisel, and Charles Wankel.

A special thanks go to Gohar Aznauryan for her help with the editing of the volume and to the students on our courses "Creativity, Innovation, and Entrepreneurship," "Social Entrepreneurship," "New Venture Initiation," "Invention, Innovation & Lab to Market" at St. John's University, and "People Management" at University of Bologna Business School with whom we have experimented and discussed many of the ideas and materials contained in this book.

We also want to thank the case authors who patiently worked with us through the editing process. We have tapped into our networks to scout for great cases, and we wish to express our gratitude to several colleagues who helped us to spread the word or put us in touch with potential contributors such as Eileen Figueroa, Geralyn Franklin, Agnieszka Kurczewska, Eric Liguori, Ria Slingerland, Silke Tegtmeier, the Association for Information Systems, and the European Council for Small Business and Entrepreneurship.

Thanks to our publisher Edward Elgar and our editor Finn Halligan for believing in this project and for their support, guidance, and patience. We are grateful to Stephanie Mills and the anonymous reviewers for their suggestions.

Finally, much gratitude to our families for their love and support.

Companion materials for this book can be found online at: https://www.e-elgar.com/textbooks/iandoli

Introduction to *Cases on Digital Entrepreneurship*: digital entrepreneurship as digital transformation

Luca Iandoli and Carmine Gibaldi

DEFINING DIGITAL ENTREPRENEURSHIP

Digital entrepreneurship (DE) is a term that describes how entrepreneurship will change, as business and society continue to be transformed by digital technology. Digital entrepreneurship highlights changes in entrepreneurial practice, theory, and education.

The digitalization of entrepreneurship affects virtually all the activities needed to launch, grow, and manage new ventures, providing entrepreneurs with new ways of finding customers, designing and offering products, and services, generating revenue, and reducing costs (Lyytinen et al., 2016; Marion and Fixson, 2020), as well as with new opportunities to collaborate with partners and new sources of opportunity, risk, and competitive advantage (Steiber et al., 2021).

On a *practical* level, DE opens new possibilities for anyone thinking of becoming an entrepreneur. Some opportunities are more technical, but many others are within reach for anyone who learns the basic skills of digital entrepreneurship. These basic skills include finding new customers online, prototyping new business ideas, and improving business ideas based on data (Nylen and Holmstrom, 2015).

Beyond learning new practical skills, DE is also about new ways of thinking about entrepreneurship itself – which is another way of saying it offers new *theories* of entrepreneurship (Nambisan, 2017). DE creates further questions about strategy, opportunity, and risk (Kolk et al., 2018; Tapscott, 2015).

In terms of *education*, digital entrepreneurship opens new possibilities for training the next generation of entrepreneurs (Millman et al., 2009). The best way to learn entrepreneurship is to do it and reflect on that experience. Starting a new business, or launching a new product, in the everyday world is costly and risky for beginners. The digital world not only lowers the barriers to starting something new but offers a variety of pathways to success. It is just a different world educationally from case studies, simulations, and business plans.

Finally, on the *contingent* level, the COVID pandemic greatly accelerated digitalization trends and forced many small businesses that had been left behind to quickly adopt digital solutions to stay afloat and even innovate during the economic crisis that followed the epidemic (Chesbrough, 2020).

The exact definition of digital entrepreneurship is still being debated, partly because it is in its early days and partly because it is a moving target. As digital technology evolves, what is new about digital entrepreneurship will change over time. One day, most entrepreneurial ventures will be born-digital, and digital entrepreneurship as a separate topic will cease to exist. Today, however, there is a real need to better prepare entrepreneurs for the digital transition and give more people a new path to entrepreneurship.

In the existing literature, DE is defined based on two different perspectives (Sahut et al., 2021):

- Entrepreneurship generated through digital technological innovation and new venture creation taking place in the digital industry (digital entrepreneurship).
- Or DE as the digital transformation of the new venture creation process as we know it (digitalized entrepreneurship).

In this book, we will adopt both definitions and include case studies of pure digital startups and gazelles along with cases related to the digital transformation of businesses operating in non-digital and mature industries.

Digital Entrepreneurship as Digital Value Creation: A Framework

In this book, we look at DE as a process of entrepreneurial creation of digital value using a variety of digital enablers to support the effective acquisition, processing, distribution, and consumption of digital information. Such a process is modeled according to the framework illustrated in Figure 0.1 (Sahut et al., 2021), which shows that:

(i)   each phase is characterized by information needs and wants that can be specific to the industry and the business
(ii) frictions can be present between phases
(iii) digital enablers are digital technologies that help a company reduce conflicts and fulfill the information needs
(iv) feedback obtained by customers consuming the digital value created by the company can be used to revise and improve enablers and needs.

The creation of digital value overlaps to a greater or lesser extent with the value chain of the core business and should be integrated with it. The best-case scenario is when the digital and the core business value chain are strongly aligned and synergic. For instance, Domino's pizza was among the first fast-food companies to adopt digital technologies to transform the experience of ordering a pizza for its customers. The company enhanced the customer experience by increasing customization and improving delivery while collecting a massive amount of analytics to optimize its physical value chain.

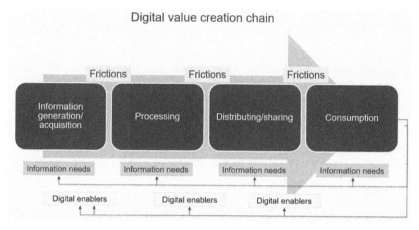

Figure 0.1   *Digital entrepreneurship as a process of digital value creation*

The digital value framework is general enough to be applied to the analysis of a given business to identify whether and how a company creates digital value, the points of strength and weakness in the company's digital chain, and the enablers a company needs adopting, and the information needs that are not fulfilled.

Let us consider a quick example of applying the digital value creation framework to a traditional brick-and-mortar business, e.g., a restaurant. Restaurant entrepreneurs can exploit digital technologies for multiple purposes, including establishing an online presence, creating additional revenues via online ordering and home delivery, and promoting events and the business through online advertising, to name some typical applications. In the information generation/acquisition phase, the company needs to create appropriate online content via enablers such as social media and a well-designed website. In the processing phase, the restaurant needs to rely on digital infrastructure to transform digital information, content, online orders, customer feedback, etc. Given the difficulty for a small brick-and-mortar business to support such an investment, the typical choice is to rely on external providers such as food delivery apps. In the distribution/sharing phase, companies like these can leverage digital advertising, using some analytics and enablers such as Google analytics. In the consumption phase, the company should manage its online reputation and improve customers' digital experience by employing tools to analyze online reviews or UX design.

This quick example shows that the digitalization of a small business comes with many opportunities and challenges and requires companies to identify ways to create digital value and align digital value and core-business value creation while acquiring the necessary skills and technologies.

The cases presented in this volume offer concrete examples of how small businesses in different industries and countries face the digitalization challenge. In the following section, we use the digital value creation framework of Figure 0.1 to introduce the case studies contained in this volume. Our framework provides a way to classify and index the cases collected in this book and help readers focus on recurring challenges and emerging opportunities that entrepreneurs face in creating additional business value via digital technologies.

Presentation of the Cases

This collection includes 12 cases selected from eight different countries and three continents. Five instances are related to pure digital companies, i.e., companies designing and commercializing digital products, services, or technologies. In contrast, the remaining cases focus on the digitalization of entrepreneurship in traditional industries and the public sector. Industries include Agriculture, Construction, Development of Mobile Applications, Digital Advertising and Online Marketing, Fitness and Well-being, Food Processing and Distribution, Social Networking Applications, Software as a Service, and Unemployment and Welfare Services. The case mix provides diverse examples characterized by various maturity levels in terms of adoption of digital technologies and level of sophistication in their application. Two cases of digital social ventures are also included in the mix.

Bandera and Passerini's chapter, "What Do My Customers Really Want? Pivoting Digital Technology and Business Models in Emergency Response Management," presents the case of a digital startup developing applications for emergency and disaster management and its successful struggle to reconfigure its business model. As the title suggests, this case offers a notable example of leveraging business model innovation to face downstream challenges in digital value creation regarding the distribution and consumption of digital services.

In "The Dark Side of a Student Online Startup," Michael Dominik presents the case of an unsuccessful academic spin-off created to launch a new social network providing peer-to-peer academic support. The case shows how a key factor in explaining this failure was the company's limited success in building a robust and sizable user community enabling the distribution and consumption of user-generated content. The chapter also addresses the issue of the moral hazard that DE poses to vulnerable entrepreneurial categories, such as student entrepreneurs. The author argues that while digital technologies facilitate, accelerate, and democratize the creation of new ventures, such easing puts less experienced and mature entrepreneurs at a higher risk of failing and bearing high psychological and material costs.

A success story in building an adequate digital infrastructure connecting disabled jobseekers and companies willing to hire them is offered in the chapter by Ada Scupola entitled "E-BRO APS: Opportunities and Challenges for Digital Social Entrepreneurs." This case presents the creation and launch of E-BRO, a digital social venture based on a matchmaking platform that helps government employment centers to find jobs for applicants with a disability through a program funded by the Danish government. This case provides a unique mix of digital and social entrepreneurship and highlights the criticalities and challenges of interfacing digital startups with the public systems.

The case by John DiMarco in Chapter 4 shows through the author's direct experience as a designer and entrepreneur how digital technology helps aspiring startups accelerate the transformation of ideas into physical products and finally into viable ventures. While the product presented in this case, a fitness bar to improve stretching practice, is not digital, this case shows how inventors can exploit different digital enablers in each of the steps to build their new business, from ideation to prototyping, to intellectual property acquisition, to the starting of small-batch manufacturing and commercialization via an online channel. As contemplated by the digital value creation framework of Figure 0.1, the case also shows how the entrepreneur successfully designed a series of digital add-ons to create digital value enhancing the value proposition associated with the physical product.

Three cases, respectively by Ascúa, Minetti, and Borello (Chapter 5), Parente, Feola, and Celenta (Chapter 6), and Sörensson and Bogren (Chapter 7), show how DE is making its steady advance in agriculture, an industry often unjustly considered as traditional and digitally backward. Ascúa and colleagues present the case of a successful Argentinian venture Agroads that created a thriving digital marketplace connecting farmers and producers of agricultural supplies. The case shows how the company was able to grow considerably thanks to the forced digitalization imposed by the COVID lockdowns and leaves students with an open question on how the company could expand internationally and innovate its business model by leveraging digital technology once again.

Sörensson and Bogren identify a problem common to millions of independent small farmers: how can they establish an online presence, create online channels for direct marketing and sale of their products, and identify differentiation opportunities through additional revenue channels via agrotourism, educational initiatives, or food processing? In terms of the digital creation framework of Figure 0.1, the case shows how creating appropriate digital content and the need to implement an effective digital marketing strategy are the key critical challenges for digitally illiterate entrepreneurs operating in mature industries.

These cases show how these barriers can be successfully overcome and that agro-entrepreneurs can be innovative to transform these constraints and points of weakness into digital innovation, as discussed in the chapter by Parente and colleagues. The chapter presents the story of an Italian agricultural small business that successfully entered the food processing industry by valorizing a local tradition and transforming a local produce commodity, dry figs, into a gourmet specialty. In their attempt to attain complete control of the value chain to achieve the outstanding quality their customers demand, the entrepreneurs developed and patented an innovative oven based on Internet of Things (IoT) technologies to speed up and optimize the drying process. The case also shows how entrepreneurs can deal with the digital skill gaps by relying on collaboration with local universities.

In Chapter 8, Gamba, Minola, and Kalchschmidt explore several key advantages of business model redesign enabled by digital innovation in the case of an Italian construction company specializing in wooden buildings. In the middle of the COVID economic crisis, the company shifted from the traditional B2B model typical of this industry to a B2C approach by leveraging the Smart Home digital paradigm and its associated technologies driven by IoT and the pursuit of energy efficiency. The case also shows how digitalization can enable the servitization of the business model and highlights the importance of open innovation strategies to access the skills and capabilities needed to exploit digital entrepreneurial opportunities.

The case of Dodo Pizza by Dmitry Katalevsky in Chapter 9 tells the story of a successful Russian startup that managed to become one of the leading fast-food chains in the country. The case shows how digitalization changes the traditional fast-food industry by increasing transparency and promoting higher standards of service quality, helps small businesses identify additional sources of competitive advantage, and promotes innovation by enhancing customer experience. The case offers one more instance of how digital technology is changing the way entrepreneurs in traditional industries think and act and provides further examples of how the creation of digital value enhances the company's value proposition.

The case by Elia, Margherita, Del Vecchio, Secundo, and Izzo in Chapter 10 focuses on one of the significant business breakthroughs enabled by digital technologies, i.e., analytics-driven digital marketing. The authors present the success story of Buzzoole, an Italian digital startup specializing in influencer marketing. The case introduces readers to this novel and critical marketing technique and the technologies that support identifying appropriate influencers and managing influencer-based campaigns. The case also provides readers with a tool, the Digital Entrepreneurship Canvas, that students can use to describe the strategy of a digital venture based on seven main pillars (purpose, platforms, processes, people, performance, product) and their connection with a company's ability to create a positive social and environmental impact (planet).

Chapter 11 by Tschoppe, Tänzler, and Drews tells the story of Marketing Beats, another brilliant digital marketing startup that this time takes place in Germany. This case has an inner focus on how digital gazelles can manage their rapid growth without losing their proverbial agility (Burchardt and Maisch, 2019; Dove, 2001; Holbeche, 2018). A peculiar aspect of the strategy of a digital company is the process of optimization and redesign of its IT infrastructure as it becomes rapidly fragmented and inadequate to support the fast growth. The case shows that the consequences of neglecting the necessary realignment of strategy and IT produces many dysfunctions including loss of customer information, redundant data, lack of adequate project planning, and an inefficient level of documentation effort. Students are asked to develop solution proposals to help the company reconfigure its loosely integrated digital tool ecosystem while considering the impact of such a redesign on its processes and structure.

The case by Richomme-Huet and De Saint Julien in Chapter 12 can be positioned upstream in the digital value creation chain since the authors face the fundamental and often overlooked question of the appropriate form of digital content that will maximize its fruition by the target customers. In the case of Lenali, a Malian social network app, this form is digital audio. The Lenali case shows how the choice of integrating audio into a social media app was vital to determine the company's success in the local market, where many users are illiterate. Beyond these specific circumstances, the case introduces students to one of the next frontiers of digital transformation determined by the fast-growing digital speech and natural language processing applications market (Iandoli, 2023). Lenali was founded as a not-for-profit, so it offers another remarkable instance of a digital social venture with the bonus of analyzing social entrepreneurship in a developing economy.

Implications for Digital Entrepreneurs

It is common to hear questions such as: what is new with DE? Isn't starting or running a small business fundamentally the same thing regardless of whether a company goes digital somehow? If entrepreneurship in the digital age is changing, what are the most crucial elements of novelty?

The growing literature on the topic offers abundant evidence to answer these questions (Elia et al., 2020; Kraus et al., 2018; Nambisan, 2017; Sahut et al., 2021; Steininger, 2019; Zaheer et al., 2019). The cases presented in this book help to put research findings on DE in the context of entrepreneurs' daily life and challenges. Three elements of novelty stand out and identify concrete challenges that entrepreneurs must address:

1. The fallacy of the entrepreneurial hero
2. The emergence of cyber-entrepreneurs
3. The necessity of complementing the creation of core business value with digital value

We have already elaborated on the last point. Entrepreneurs, no matter the business they are in, must contemplate values to augment their value proposition by leveraging digital technologies. The cases presented in the book offer many examples of how this objective can be concretely achieved, ranging from the simplest ones, such as the creation of digital content and the establishment of an online presence, to the more sophisticated attempts involving developing new products incorporating state of the art but increasingly available and affordable digital technologies.

The fallacy of the entrepreneurial hero is the persistent but outdated belief that entrepreneurial action and outcomes result from individual effort and talent. While these are still crucial, their impact can be enhanced by the collaboration and sharing enabled and magnified by digital technologies. An increasing amount of entrepreneurship is made possible via the affiliation to digital platforms offering to small business the digital infrastructure they would not be able to afford on their own and access to new markets and customers (Acs et al., 2021). Of course, these advantages come with costs, including membership or transaction fees and, more importantly, the inclusion into marketplaces where competition is just one click away.

Another collective dimension of the life of a digital entrepreneur is the participation in a community of interests and wider ecosystems (Sussan and Acs, 2017) where everything is shared, from knowledge specific to the business to customer feedback and funding as it happens on crowdfunding sites.

Another element of novelty is the increased flexibility of digital business models. The Marlegno case in Chapter 8 by Gamba et al. provides a fitting example of a traditional B2B construction company transforming into a B2C service company able to leverage digital design to increase its ability to interact with customers while offering them added value services and unprecedented levels of customization via intelligent home technologies.

With the second point on the list, the emergence of cyber-entrepreneurs, we do not refer to digital security issues. As Amber Case put it (Case, 2010), technology, any technology, by enhancing or augmenting human ability, transforms us into cyborgs. The undertaking of an entrepreneurial project is increasingly made more accessible and faster thanks to the availability of new digital tools that assist entrepreneurs virtually in any step of new venture creation (see DiMarco and Dominik cases in this volume). For instance, many tools can help entrepreneurs transform their ideas into prototypes, such as 3D printing, app-making suites, or digital imaging tools. 3D printing can be used for small batch production as well. Many user-friendly, low-cost tools exist to create websites and implement e-commerce solutions, such as Shopify or Etsy. Platforms such as Amazon or Google offer entrepreneurs many digital solutions to promote their products, monitor web traffic, and access various types of analytics. These digital tools and services, whose list and accessibility keep growing every day, help cyber-entrepreneurs accelerate the process of new venture creation by limiting the number of resources needed in the early steps and increasing the learning rate thanks to information from the early market or community feedback.

The implications for entrepreneurs are then straightforward:

- Since digital social networks and communities facilitate DE, entrepreneurs need to identify what communities and ecosystems they must be part of and take active roles in them to exploit the advantages they offer in terms of knowledge spillovers, collaboration opportunities.
- Entrepreneurs must become digitally agile and savvy to adopt and use digital tools, helping them to increase speed and reduce risk in the idea to product to venture life cycle.
- Entrepreneurs must consider alternative business models and experiment with diverse alternatives.
- New products and services must be designed by identifying sources of digital value creation that can help entrepreneurs to augment the value proposition of their core business.

Pedagogical Notes

This book presents a rich compilation of real-world cases on digitalization, including relatively new startups to much more long-standing established organizations. The editors intend to share organizations' first-hand insights and experiences and make digitalization more understandable and tangible. Given that emerging technologies are now confronting every economic and societal sector, the digital economy is a highly volatile, uncertain, complex, and ambiguous setting that holds substantial challenges and opportunities for established organizations.

Through the cases presented, students, researchers, practitioners, and faculty will be able to investigate and analyze best practices and lessons learned from organizations that have succeeded (or not) in overcoming the challenges and seizing the digital economy's opportunities and those that possibly failed. This book illustrates how 12 companies have leveraged their capabilities to create innovations, develop digital business models, and transform themselves. These cases represent various industries (e.g., automotive, insurance, consulting, and public services) and countries (eight countries and three continents), reflecting the many dimensions of digitalization. As all case descriptions follow a uniform format, they are easily accessible within this book and provide insightful examples for practitioners and interesting cases for researchers, teachers, and students.

Each of the cases presented is no longer than 12 pages in length with the following structure:

- Abstract
- Case learning objectives
- Introduction/opening story
- Business and industry overview
- Problem statement
- Student challenges (e.g., discussion questions, assignments, etc.)

Each case is accompanied by detailed teaching notes provided separately only to instructors including:

- Case summary
- Teaching objectives
- Teaching strategy and assignment questions (differentiated for graduate and undergraduate courses)
- Videos and visuals related to the cases
- Detailed suggestions and instructions to teach the case, guide students to get started on assignments and problems, and to facilitate class/group discussions

This book could be used as a textbook for a class on digital entrepreneurship. The value creation framework provides a possible infrastructure for the syllabus. Each class could be dedicated to the analysis or solution of a case followed by in-class and home assignments with a focus on a particular step of digital value creation and specific technology enablers. Some time and additional readings in each class could be allocated for more theoretical reflections, as illustrated in the teaching notes or as decided by the instructor. Alternatively, the book would make an excellent companion textbook for classes in entrepreneurship and innovation designed on a case-based learning approach and inductive pedagogy to theory building (Dubois and Gadde, 2002; Eisenhardt and Graebner, 2007; Myers, 2013).

In any of the above, the use of case studies will help instructors to make classes more engaging by providing students with real-world examples, challenges they must actively solve, and opportunities for self or group-driven learning procured via additional research and collaborative assignments and discussions.

Audience

This book's primary audience is academic, specifically instructors teaching undergraduate and graduate classes in business, including innovation management, management of technology, entrepreneurship and new venture creation, marketing, and strategy. This book will also be of significant use in multidisciplinary programs combining entrepreneurship with digital technology, such as Information Technology and Computer Science, Computer and Software Engineering, and Digital Media and Communication.

As a secondary audience, we believe the book will be used for professional development and training initiatives for corporate entrepreneurship (large companies initiatives aimed at growing awareness and innovation opportunities/mindset in the digital space) or in training initiatives for entrepreneurs and small business owners or aspiring entrepreneurs such as accelerator programs and boot camps.

REFERENCES

Acs, Z. J., Song, A. K., Szerb, L., Audretsch, D. B., and Komlósi, É. (2021). The evolution of the global digital platform economy: 1971–2021. *ERN: Networks* (Topic).

Burchardt, C. and Maisch, B. (2019). Digitalization needs a cultural change: Examples of applying Agility and Open Innovation to drive the digital transformation. *Procedia CIRP*, 84, 112–117.

Case, A. (2010). We are all Cyborgs now. *TED Talk*. https://www.ted.com/talks/amber _case_we_are_all_cyborgs_now/transcript?language=en.

Chesbrough, H. (2020). To recover faster from Covid-19, open up: Managerial implications from an open innovation perspective. *Industrial Marketing Management*, 88, 410–413.

Dove, R. (2002). *Response Ability: The Language, Structure, and Culture of the Agile Enterprise*. New York: Wiley.

Dubois, A. and Gadde, L. (2002). Systematic combining: An abductive approach to case research. *Journal of Business Research*, 55, 553–560.

Eisenhardt, K. M. and Graebner, M. E. (2007). Theory building from cases: Opportunities and challenges. *Academy of Management Journal*, 50(1), 25–32.

Elia, G., Margherita, A., and Passiante, G. (2020). Digital entrepreneurship ecosystem: How digital technologies and collective intelligence are reshaping the entrepreneurial process. *Technological Forecasting and Social Change*, 150, 119791.

Holbeche, L. (2018). *The Agile Organization: How to Build an Engaged, Innovative and Resilient Business*. London: Kogan Page.

Iandoli, L. (2023). *When Solutions Are in Search of Problems: New Venture Creation in the Booming Market of Digital Speech Recognition*. SAGE Business Cases Originals. London: Sage.

Kolk, M., Eagar, R., Boulton, C., and Mira, C. (2018). How hyper-collaboration accelerates ecosystem innovation. *Strategy & Leadership*, 46(1), 23–29.

Kraus, S., Palmer, C., Kailer, N., Kallinger, F. L., and Spitzer, J. (2018). Digital entrepreneurship: A research agenda on new business models for the twenty-first century. *International Journal of Entrepreneurial Behavior & Research*, 25(2), 353–375.

Lyytinen, K. J., Yoo, Y., and Boland, R. J. (2016). Digital product innovation within four classes of innovation networks. *Information Systems Journal*, 26, 47–75.

Marion, T. J. and Fixson, S. K. (2020). The transformation of the innovation process: How digital tools are changing work, collaboration, and organizations in new product development. *Journal of Product Innovation Management*, 38(1), 192–215.

Millman, C., Wong, W.-C., Li, Z., and Matlay, H. (2009). Educating students for e-entrepreneurship in the UK, the USA and China. *Industry and Higher Education*, 23(3), 243–252.

Myers, M. D. (2013). *Qualitative Research in Business and Management*. London: Sage.

Nambisan, S. (2017). Digital entrepreneurship: Toward a digital technology perspective of entrepreneurship. *Entrepreneurship Theory and Practice*, 41(6), 1029–1055.

Nylen, D. and Holmstrom, J. (2015). Digital innovation strategy: A framework for diagnosing and improving digital product and service innovation. *Business Horizons*, 58, 57–67.

Sahut, J. M., Iandoli, L., and Teulon, F. (2021). The age of digital entrepreneurship. *Small Business Economics*, 56(3), 1159–1169.

Steiber, A., Alänge, S., Ghosh, S., and Goncalves, D. (2021). Digital transformation of industrial firms: an innovation diffusion perspective. *European Journal of Innovation Management*, 24(3), 799–819.

Steininger, D. M. (2019). Linking information systems and entrepreneurship: A review and agenda for IT-associated and digital entrepreneurship research. *Information Systems Journal*, 29(2), 363–407.

Sussan, F. and Acs, Z. J. (2017). The digital entrepreneurial eco-system. *Small Business Economics*, 49(1), 55–73.

Tapscott, D. (2015). *The Digital Economy: Rethinking Promise and Peril in the Age of Networked Intelligence*. New York: McGraw-Hill Education.

Zaheer, H., Breyer, Y., and Dumay, J. (2019). Digital entrepreneurship: An interdisciplinary structured literature review and research agenda. *Technological Forecasting and Social Change*, 148, 119735.

1. What do my customers really want? Pivoting digital technology and business models in emergency response management

Cesar Bandera and Katia Passerini

LEARNING OBJECTIVES

- Students learn differences between a product-based business model and a digital service-based business model, and the challenges unique to each.
- Students learn how a digital entrepreneur can pivot from a product to a service.
- Students learn the perils of misreading the market when developing digital services.

INTRODUCTION

Trial by Fire: Revisiting Emergency Response in the Aftermath of Haiti's Earthquake

"I really appreciate you coming all the way down from New Jersey to meet with us. But this morning we escalated to crisis mode, so we're going to have to postpone our kickoff to later in the year – sorry," apologized a visibly distraught Captain Ralph O'Conley to Steve (names changed for anonymity) at the entrance to the new Emergency Operations Center (EOC) at the Centers for Disease Control (CDC) in Atlanta (Figure 1.1). Captain O'Conley had recently awarded Steve's company JETTEI in Newark, New Jersey, a 24-month million-dollar contract to develop a video broadcasting system and install it at the EOC. Captain O'Conley's plan was to use this system to push healthcare videos to the cell phones of civilians (Figure 1.2) and responders trapped in public health emergencies, and on that day – September 29, 2010 – Captain O'Conley and Steve were going to officially begin the project.

"Don't worry about us. But now that I'm here, is there anything we can do to help?" asked Steve, concerned about the severity of whatever the emergency was that had "all-hands-on-deck" at the EOC, and unsure of what use he could be to the CDC before his flight back to Newark that evening.

Captain O'Conley had already turned his back to Steve and was returning to the EOC, when he stopped. "Well … now that you mention it, how soon can your company deliver the system?" Steve replies, "We can push the developers and get it to you a few months sooner – perhaps in nine months instead of twelve." Captain O'Conley turns to Steve, and with dread asks; "Can you get something up and running in Haiti today?"

"This is a joke," thought Steve, "accelerating the project schedule from 24 months to twelve hours, and adding international reach to what is supposed to be a regional broadcasting system." But seeing the commotion at the EOC, Steve knew the request was serious. News channels had been reporting all week that Haiti, recovering from its worst earthquake ever, was now being hit with a cholera epidemic. Steve wondered what had happened today that was not being reported in the news, and which had the CDC staff so concerned.

Seeing the confusion in Steve's face, Captain O'Conley explained the context of his request. Cholera victims die from dehydration, so the first round of treatment is intravenous saline solution. But that morning, CDC responders in Haiti discovered that well-meaning volunteers were inadvertently applying intravenous glucose solution to cholera patients (saline and glucose bags look similar), essentially killing them at the rate of one accidental death every 30 minutes. CDC posted on its website instructions on how to properly rehydrate cholera patients, with pictures of which bags to use and which to avoid, but with the Haitian infrastructure still down from the earthquake, few volunteers had access to any internet. "We need your system to push a video with visual instructions on rehydration to the cell phones of volunteers in Haiti. No text – just pictures and audio. Can you do it?"

Without waiting for a reply from Steve, Captain O'Conley took him to a small conference room next to the EOC. "You can work from here." Captain O'Conley quickly returned to a frantic EOC, leaving Steve alone in the conference room. "I guess that means yes," he thought. It was 10am EST.

Steve powered up his laptop and got on a speakerphone with JETTEI developers in Newark. They had a low-power prototype (which was largely responsible for the company getting a patent and the CDC contract) – perhaps it could be patched to do this one job. At the same time, it occurred to Steve that he probably knew less about cholera than the volunteers he had just been tasked to train. As if responding to a telepathic plea, Emergency Risk Communication Branch Chief Neil Hunter entered the conference room. "Ralph says you are going to need my help." Neil proceeded to outline the script for a video on caring for cholera patients, and showed Steve where CDC archived images he could use as visuals (Figures 1.3 and 1.4). By 1pm EST, a 45-second video was ready; it displayed the solution to use, the solution to avoid, and a voice-over meant that the volunteer did not have to read any text.

At 2pm, JETTEI was ready for a test broadcast to Haiti. To avoid confusing volunteers, Captain O'Conley instructed the video to first be pushed to the cell phones of some CDC responders in Haiti who were aware of the experiment. At 2:05, the responders respond. "We received the audio, but no visual." "OK – at least something got through, but we have to compensate for lack of carrier interoperability," Steve and the developers agree. Back to the drawing board – but at least not back to square one. Thirty minutes later, another test broadcast, with the same results, followed by more frantic debugging. At 3pm, another test broadcast. This one worked – the CDC responders received the entire video. Immediately, the video began circulation throughout Haiti, distributed through direct broadcasts from Newark and by the responders and volunteers forwarding the video amongst themselves via picture messaging. The incorrect rehydration of cholera patients quickly ended. But the thought that ten people might still be alive had he been quicker weighed heavily on Steve.

The Pivot

In December 2012, Steve and senior JETTEI staff flew to Atlanta to conduct a two-day training session of the video broadcasting system and officially "hand the keys" of the system over to the EOC. By then, CDC had used the system to broadcast public health videos in many incidents in addition to the cholera epidemic, including the chikungunya epidemic in the Dominican Republic, Hurricane Sandy in New Jersey, several flu and winter storm seasons across the US, and a federal anthrax preparedness campaign. During this time, JETTEI iteratively refined the system, making it easier to use and even added the ability to convert a PowerPoint file with voiceover and animations into an instant mobile broadcast. CDC and the company had the kind of good relationship that forms when two are in the trenches together.

At the end of the training session, Steve turned to Captain O'Conley and, as all tech developers tell their first clients, assured that the company was there to help CDC with any problems they encounter in the use of their new system.

"Oh – we don't plan on using the system," replied Captain O'Conley. Steve was sure he didn't hear that correctly. Captain O'Conley continued, "Don't get me wrong – it's a great system, and it has allowed us to do things we could not have accomplished otherwise. But the EOC is already saturated with technologies."

"But you paid JETTEI to build this for you!" replied Steve. "We've been working together every step of the way. Now you are going to abandon it?"

"Heavens no – we will still need to push videos. But we want you to use the system for us."

As soon as Captain O'Conley said those words, Steve looked back at the last two years. How could he have been so blind! In all these deployments, CDC had never actually used the system; instead, CDC would tell JETTEI what kind of broadcasts it wanted, and the company would make it happen. Even though the contract was to provide a product, the relationship had been one of a service provider.

"You do realize that it will be cheaper for you to use the system yourself, instead of calling us every time you need a video broadcast," said Steve unsure if he was happy or sad. "That does not matter – our goal is to have the fastest response time possible," replied Captain O'Conley. Recalling their initial conversation two years ago, Steve asked, "Now that I'm here, is there anything we can do to help?"

Figure 1.1   Emergency Operations Center at the Centers for Disease Control (Atlanta, GA)

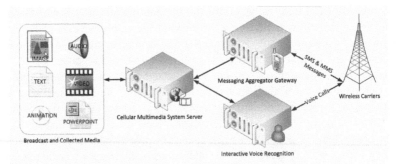

Note: The system broadcasts media to civilians and responders via two interfaces with wireless carriers – one for text and picture messaging, and the other for voice calls. The system also receives media from these people, improving the client's situation awareness.

Figure 1.2   JETTEI system architecture

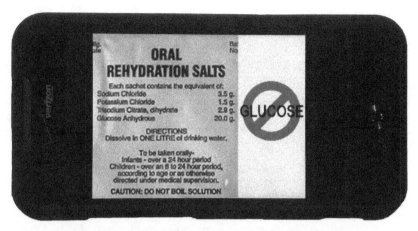

Figure 1.3   Screen shot of JETTEI broadcast to Haiti

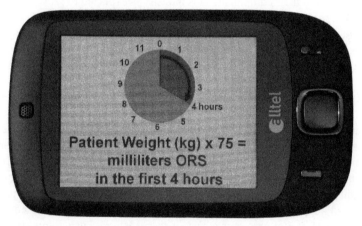

Figure 1.4   Screen shot of JETTEI broadcast to Haiti

BUSINESS AND INDUSTRY OVERVIEW

JETTEI is a wireless Value Added Service Provider (VASP), i.e., a company that adds value to the wireless network of its users. Most wireless value added services are person-to-person messaging services like WhatsApp. JETTEI is an example of an application-to-person (A2P) VASP, whereby the sender of the message is a machine, not a person. Other examples of A2P value added services are the text message (SMS) notifications you might receive from an airline about the status of your flight, or from your pharmacy about the status of your prescription. The paying customer of the A2P VASP is the organization on whose behalf the A2P VASP sends the message (e.g., the airline or the pharmacy); the recipients are users of the service, but not payers (Bandera, 2017).

The largest wireless A2P value added service is A2P SMS, generating $17.9 billion in 2020 (Mobilesquared, 2021) and growing at a healthy compound annual growth rate (CAGR) of 13.7 percent (IMARC Group, 2021). The main value proposition of JETTEI over A2P SMS is that short videos are more informative than brief texts. SMS is sufficient for simple notifications, but often ineffective when trying to explain something more complicated such as safety protocols (Bandera, 2016).

JETTEI plans to focus on the $124 billion global emergency response industry, which includes government agencies and NGOs. Emergency management systems provide digital and physical response in case of disasters caused by earthquakes, hurricanes, epidemics, explosions, floods, terrorist attacks, and other devastating events, supporting the deployment of first responders and their equipment. This industry is expected to grow at a CAGR of 6.7 percent, driven primarily by the information technology (IT) and telecommunications vertical segment, which includes mass notification systems (Markets&Markets, 2021). The outlook looks good for wireless A2P value added services in the emergency response industry.

PROBLEM STATEMENT

Because digital products and services are inherently virtual, the digital entrepreneur has fewer constraints and more options than the entrepreneur deploying products and services that require physical assets. The digital entrepreneur can choose from a broader array of business models, including business models that only work with digital products and services, that did not exist prior to the broad adoption of requisite technology (e.g., geolocation-enabled smartphones). The digital entrepreneur can also implement business models more quickly because they do not involve physical construction or supply chain. Indeed, the digital entrepreneur has to move quickly because the competitive digital landscape is moving quickly as well. Moreover, the more innovative the business model, the less precedent it has and thus the greater uncertainty (or less pre-existing empirical evidence) that it will work. However, more options and greater time pressure lead to more opportunities for mistakes. We discuss these below.

Accounting for Market Trends: From Digital Product Designers to Digital Service Providers

In terms of the evolution of IT, 2012 is several lifetimes ago. Since then, watching videos on cell phones has become the norm. So why is this case relevant? For several reasons. First, large-scale emergency incidents disrupt the region's electrical and communication infrastructure. What works reliably on a typical day will likely not work when the electricity that charges our cell phones and powers cellular towers goes out. The most basic technology in emergency management remains text-based communication, because it places the least demand on the wireless delivery and digital transportation system and is therefore resilient to disruptions in infrastructure (Gomez and Passerini, 2010). However, non-text content such as medical imagery required equally reliable multimedia communications, but which had yet to be deployed (hence Steve's value proposition).

Second, this case shows that Steve was not ready to conceive (or reconceive) a new business model, one that has emerged in the last ten years to the point that few organizations purchase software to maintain (in house or through maintenance contract). In most cases, organizations purchase a monthly or annual license to use software online, i.e., the software as a service (SaaS) business model (Gagnon et al., 2011). Had he reflected on this evolution, Steve would have anticipated the request from the CDC. In fact, SaaS is also becoming the preferred (and often the only) strategy of many software vendors as it guarantees a stream of revenue well beyond typical maintenance contracts. In principle, JETTEI could convert the product it built – and the turnkey service that CDC wanted – into an SaaS model. But what would be the up-front costs for JETTEI to develop the client-facing side of an SaaS offering, and for CDC to learn to use such an offering?

The scenario in this case underscores a critical element of digital entrepreneurship: your salesperson/customer care person is also your developer, and your developer needs to understand markets and shifts in the competitive landscape.

Steve seemed to have missed both but was able to quickly jump back into action because of his willingness to help and listen to dynamic and evolving needs. What is unaccounted for in this scenario is the preparation for and the understanding of future evolutions. For how long will the CDC have to rely on a single vendor as a bottleneck? Could the CDC consider sourcing the distribution of information to those who can do so at the local level? Can it be sourced from the crowds who might be distributing emergency alerts to each other?

Options in Project Management

There are lessons to be learned about crashing the schedule and being ready to do so. Typically, a project manager can crash a schedule by putting more people on the same tasks (if task can be broken down and assigned to more resources), or by fast-tracking tasks originally scheduled in a start-to-finish relationship, executing them instead in parallel (start-to-start) or at least accelerated for a few days when possible (Hall, 2012). In Steve's scenario, everything had to be deployed in parallel, with repeated deployment without testing. The release was the testing and when it failed, it had to be restarted.

Crashing a schedule/project is not always possible in knowledge tasks. In contrast, crashing a schedule/project is easier with physical and manual tasks that are repetitive and do not require significant background knowledge. This was not what happened in this scenario, where the significant resources were the developers in the main office in Newark, all who had to drop their other projects and focus exclusively on the Haitian emergency, creating significant backlogs in other areas. What if there were other emergencies at the same time? How does an entrepreneur deal with having redundant human resources in times of emergency when it is already hard enough for an entrepreneur to retain the resources s/he has?

Pilotitis

A pilot project is an exercise intended to quickly generate information that helps the entrepreneur evolve a prototype into a commercial product. Technology entrepreneurs are fans of pilot projects for several reasons. First, pilot projects inform the entrepreneur how their innovation performs in the real world, and how potential future customers use their innovation. The engagement of potential customers is a cornerstone of the lean startup methodology of entrepreneurship (Ries, 2011). Second, pilot projects build relationships with potential future customers. Third, because pilot projects are usually free to participants, entrepreneurs can use them to recruit potential customers.

An entrepreneur must be careful when interpreting the results of a pilot project. Misinterpreting the results of a pilot project risks strategic errors and jeopardizes the commercialization of the innovation. The most frequent error entrepreneurs make during pilot projects is forgetting that a potential customer participating in a pilot project and a paying customer will likely have different opinions, just as the opinions of a participant in a focus group should not be taken as the opinions of a paying customer (Constable, 2014).

Entrepreneurs completing successful pilot projects sometimes fool themselves into thinking that, because the pilot went well, their product is ready, and they forget that this maturation phase is still pending. The public health literature has gone so far as to coin the term "pilotitis" to represent the fact that, while the number of pilot projects is increasing, few mature into commercial deployment (Bhatia et al., 2020; Kuipers et al., 2008). Did Steve confuse having a good business relationship with having a product that customers want?

STUDENT CHALLENGES

Discussion Questions

1. Describe and contrast product-based business models from service-based business models. What are their advantages and disadvantages from the point of view of the user and of the provider? Why are service-based models becoming dominant in the software industry?
2. What changes should Steve introduce to the JETTEI business model to pivot from a product-based to a service-based business model? How could he implement this change quickly and cost-effectively?
3. Before changing the JETTEI business model, should Steve confirm that a pivot is necessary? Would more pilots help this decision?

Assignments

1. Steve may have to pivot JETTEI from a product-based business model to an SaaS business model. Draft a business model canvas (Osterwalder and Pigneur, 2010) for his new business model. Note that the payer and the consumer of emergency public health communications are not the same (Osterwalder and Pigneur, 2010).
2. Assuming the JETTEI pivot to an SaaS business model is successful, what new markets might Steve consider pursuing? Can he leverage the CDC pilot?

REFERENCES

Bandera, C. (2016). Design and management of public health outreach using interoperable mobile multimedia: An analysis of a national winter weather preparedness campaign. *BMC Public Health*, 16(1), 1–15. doi:10.1186/s12889-016-3104-z.

Bandera, C. (2017). Value-added service providers for mobile education: Empirical challenges and analytics. *Electronic Commerce Research*, 17(2), 317–333. doi:10.1007/s10660-016-9235-6.

Bhatia, A., Matthan, R., Khanna, T., and Balsari, S. (2020). Regulatory sandboxes: A cure for mHealth Pilotitis? *Journal of Medical Internet Research*, 22(9), e21276. doi:10.2196/21276.

Constable, G. (2014). *Talking to Humans*. N.p.: Giff Constable.

Gagnon, S., Nabelsi, V., Passerini, K., and Cakici, K. (2011). The next Web apps architecture: Challenges for SaaS vendors. *IT Professional*, 13(5), 44–50. https://doi .org/10.1109/MITP.2011.90.

Gomez, E. A. and Passerini, K. (2010). Information and communication technologies (ICT) options for local and global communities in health-related crisis management. *The Journal of Community Informatics*, 6(2), Article 2. https://doi.org/10.15353/joci .v6i2.2551.

Google (n.d.). *Rehydration of Cholera Patients – Google drive video*. Google Drive. Retrieved March 20, 2022, from https://drive.google.com/file/d/ 1ESJxHb0w0Rgh2wnplfv-Dv1-I3Iz4LRi/view (One of the cholera patient rehydration videos sent by the protagonist to Haiti).

Hall, N. G. (2012). Project management: Recent developments and research opportunities. *Journal of Systems Science and Systems Engineering*, 21(2), 129–143. https:// doi.org/10.1007/s11518-012-5190-5.

IMARC Group (2021). *Mobile Value-Added Services (MVAS) Market: Global Industry Trends, Share, Size, Growth, Opportunity and Forecast 2021–2026* (5401459). https://www.researchandmarkets.com/reports/5401459/mobile-value-added -services-mvas-market-global.

Kuipers, P., Humphreys, J. S., Wakerman, J., Wells, R., Jones, J., and Entwistle, P. (2008). Collaborative review of pilot projects to inform policy: A methodological remedy for pilotitis? *Australia and New Zealand Health Policy*, 5(1), 1–4.

Markets&Markets (2021). *Incident and Emergency Management Market Size, Share and Global Market Forecast to 2026* (September). https://www.marketsandmarkets .com/Market-Reports/incident-emergency-management-market-1280.html.

Mobilesquared (2021). *Safeguarding Revenue from A2P Messaging*. Interop Technologies.

Osterwalder, A. (2010). *Users vs Customers*. https://www.strategyzer.com/blog/users -vs-customers.

Osterwalder, A. and Pigneur, Y. (2010). *Business Model Generation: A Handbook for Visionaries, Game Changers, and Challengers*. Hoboken, NJ: John Wiley & Sons.

Ries, E. (2011). *The Lean Startup: How Today's Entrepreneurs Use Continuous Innovation to Create Radically Successful Businesses*. New York: Random House.

Squawk Box (2017). How this ship designer is disrupting the $7B greeting card market: LovePop CEO. *CNBC*, August 8. https://www.cnbc.com/video/2017/08/08/how-this -ship-designer-is-disrupting-the-7b-greeting-card-market-lovepop-ceo.html.

Notes

Centers for Disease Control and Prevention (n.d.). Details – public health image library(phil). Centers for Disease Control and Prevention. Retrieved March 25, 2022, from https://phil.cdc.gov/Details.aspx?pid=23320.

Appendices

One of the cholera patient rehydration videos sent to Haiti can be watched here: Cholera.mp4. Google Docs (n.d.). Retrieved March 25, 2022, from https://bit.ly/ cholera_rehydration.

2.   The dark side of a student online startup

Michael Dominik

LEARNING OBJECTIVES

- Students will learn how online digital startups can be easily founded by modestly informed or prepared student entrepreneurs but flounder when faced with challenging circumstances. Are student founders sufficiently prepared to make decisions and sacrifices necessary to succeed?
- Students will understand how failures of entrepreneurial ventures can result both in learning valuable lessons as well as in multi-form losses and unintended adverse consequences that impact others. Are student founders prepared for the negative consequences associated with a failed entrepreneurial venture?
- Students will be more advised, informed, and prepared for the potential dark side of entrepreneurship. Are student founders expressly aware of the strains and stresses of entrepreneurship?
- Students will learn about common mistakes or critical aspects that are often overlooked by entrepreneurs trying to monetize app development such as lack of adequate testing, cybersecurity aspects, and legal issues that are particularly relevant in the digital domain.

INTRODUCTION

It was well past midnight in his dorm room and twenty-year-old John was stuck and frustrated with writing an academic paper. While he was confident in his abilities to solve accounting homework problems, writing a paper was not his strength. Even at that hour, he reached out to another dorm mate struggling with accounting problems, and they agreed to help one another overcome their respective weaknesses. The year was 2016, and John was a second-year undergraduate student of finance at an American university with nearly 20,000 students. He thought to himself, there should be a quick and easy way for students to connect and help each other at any hour and at any place. His approach in responding to that thought showed his entrepreneurial mindset, even though he had never taken a course in entrepreneurship. He didn't know it at the time, but he was practicing opportunity recognition.[1] As one who was comfortable with the combination of hustle and hard work, John was a highly persistent young man, and he didn't give up easily. This quality was another trait associated with entrepreneurs and would both serve him well and with implications during the next four years.

Within weeks John had a vision that reflected the attractive world of digital entrepreneurship from a young adult's viewpoint: a software app where students could sell their intellectual talents to help or otherwise aid student peers who were struggling with schoolwork. And while John had not completed any courses in entrepreneurship, he speculated there must be some way he could make money from brokering that exchange whereby students can offer their tutoring and assistance services to other students without the intermediary of their own school's tutoring services department, which limited the time and place for students to help each other.

This lived problem experience, his assumption about others at his university, and his recognition of a problem revealing a possible opportunity became the spark for John's entrepreneurial action. Before the end of the semester, John had conceived and moved forward to create what would become his first company, an online, app-based Education Technology startup called Students United or "Stunited." He had never created a company before, but he believed that getting started on a software application company should be easy, even though he didn't have any technical skills necessary to do the software programming. His university had support systems in place to assist student entrepreneurs, and John would leverage their encouragement and assistance to quickly build his company, while his fierce independence limited the use of mentors, a practice that continued for years. John was well-spoken, smart, and quick-thinking, and he was good at selling his ideas and his vision.

While this was happening to John in the years 2016–2017, digital technologies had matured to the point such that taking the leap to create an entrepreneurial initiative requiring the development of a mobile software application did not require many resources or much experience. This ease of entry was also appealing to others whom he asked to assist him, some of whom anticipated financial windfalls that might be attractive; after all, weren't there entrepreneurs becoming wealthy millionaires with software apps? Within the year, John's idea for a mobile software app would win him first place and $4,000 at his university's student new venture competition along with free assistance for legal and marketing work. His startup was on the move, and even though John was only twenty-one years old, and had limited practical business experience, he was a real entrepreneur, and his university's ecosystem was growing along with its desire to draw out and assist budding student entrepreneurs. John's target market were fellow students, and as he traveled to other universities nearby, his promotional and in-person selling skills drew other students to his vision, even while there was no proven sustainable business model for Stunited.

This case explores the dark side of entrepreneurship education where digital entrepreneurship like the creation of John's company is easily enabled in an academic environment. Because of the ready availability of digital technologies such as rapid prototyping and application development tools, inexperienced entrepreneurs can more easily launch their ideas into digital initiatives. But just because this can be done, how should student entrepreneurs develop open eyes to the potential downsides to their venture? What are the benefits and risks of entrepreneurs who spend their time, their money, and, in some cases, other people's money on solutions that are more likely than not to end in business and financial failure in the hands of a young digital entrepreneur?

BUSINESS AND INDUSTRY OVERVIEW

Stunited can be generally classified as an educational technology (EdTech) company. Even though the solution was not specifically targeted for use in the classroom, it provided a function that supported learning in the university setting. The EdTech industry grew rapidly as the emergence of the internet promoted the notion that university education would almost entirely migrate to online delivery; however, such predictions have not yet come true. Even so, EdTech and its learning management systems such as Blackboard and Canvas have substantially changed the way students and faculty collaborate and share information, as compared to the use of printed course packs and trips to the library. Stunited was founded under the philosophy of using digital means – a mobile software application – to foster students helping other students and leap beyond the physical constraints of proximity or a prior relationship. John felt that he was creating something that empowered and united students to respond to the expectations, demands and stress of a university education – by selling their knowledge and skills to other students seeking that knowledge or skill.

After recognizing the opportunity in late 2016, within six months, with the help of some fellow university students with skills in mobile app programming, Stunited screen shots and simple functionality were developed, thus assisting John to win his university's annual startup venture competition.[2] By summer 2017, after John spent several thousand dollars of his own money to pay programmers to fully enable the app, Stunited was ready for launch, and hosted on Amazon Web Services with the first app release launched on the Apple Store (and eventually on Google Play in 2019).

While piloting and promoting the Stunited software app, John developed multiple and evolving themes and value propositions. One of Stunited's early value propositions was "Peer to peer tutoring."[3] This pivoted to "academic bartering" (Figure 2.1) where Stunited was positioned as a social academic marketplace for students to barter their skills and assignments with one another.

Figure 2.1   Stunited's evolving value proposition

The appeal of "give help, get help, make money" suggested a multi-faceted value proposition to students using the Stunited app. This later evolved to the financially appealing theme, "Education as a currency" (Figure 2.2), which targeted an appeal to students to earn money from their knowledge.

Figure 2.2   Stunited's focused appeal

A More Direct Message for Users to Leverage Education for Money

The Stunited business model was simple: students who needed tutoring or other academic help could swap or share skills, knowledge, or information in exchange for money. By providing the platform for this exchange, Stunited as a service bartering marketplace would receive up to 10 percent commission on each paid transaction. Stunited sought to be the number one app for students to exchange their academic assignments and skills with one another. The student Success Center at John's university was approached to explore how they could help John by examining Stunited as a possible adjunct for student peer tutoring, but the Center was turned off by the notion of a financial exchange associated with the assisting relationship, and no formal endorsement was created. This experience also helped John form his business model, when he realized that selling directly to universities represented a fractured and complex customer set that he would be unable to easily access.

While the first release of the Stunited app had only modest functionality, it improved substantially over time. Its eventual features allowed students to create a user profile that identified their university, academic major, year of graduation, and their academic strengths and needs, such as computer science, mathematics, natural sciences. Students could also prepare an offering proposal (Figure 2.3), such as offering to provide help solving engineering homework problems, and with that post a fixed rate of money to provide that service.

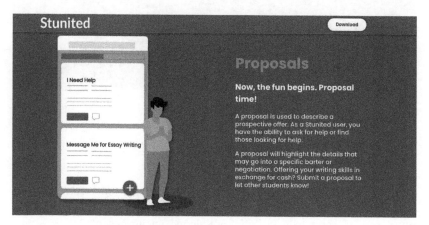

Figure 2.3   Stunited proposal model

The Stunited App Matching Buyers and Sellers to Barter Needs with Knowledge

Also, inspired by the success of the Tinder app, the Stunited app included a "cardstack" of student profiles that identified their strengths and needs. Stunited was created and viable, and the app showed that peer to peer student assistance could be created.

In late 2017, and starting his final year of undergraduate studies, John began to leverage his strengths as a salesperson and focused his efforts on getting students to download and use the app, to test and prove the first element of his hypothesized business model, that students would download the app.

John was a natural speaker and an outgoing communicator, and to promote awareness of Stunited and drive downloads for the app without spending a lot of money, he hosted many marketing and promotion events (Figure 2.4) where students hyped over the joy of the freedom that Stunited represented.

Figure 2.4   Stunited promotional event

A Low-Cost Marketing Approach to Raise Awareness and Drive App Downloads

At his own and other nearby universities, John successfully recruited more than fifty unpaid student "ambassadors" (Figure 2.5), giving them T-shirts and other swag to promote the visibility of Stunited among students.

Figure 2.5   *Stunited brand ambassadors*

Leveraging Unpaid Student Volunteers to Promote Stunited on College Campuses: Obscure Faces

John's fellow students from many universities seemed to enjoy being part of something that was fun, cool, and appealing. During his final undergraduate schoolyear, John juggled his class schedule, even missing classes to visit more than twenty universities in the northeast United States. By early 2018, there were more than 3,000 downloads of the app, but still with little barter or exchange activity. It was disappointing, but John kept moving forward in the same direction – promotion of the app and encouraging downloads – while also recognizing that he had yet to prove the viability of the Stunited business model, which required students to conduct transactions on the app. This aspect of his business model proved more difficult.

After finishing his undergraduate university degree in 2018, John's entrepreneurial mindset, optimism and persistence was still strong, and he remained confident about Stunited. He deferred an opportunity to take a well-paying professional job in the finance industry and continued to focus his time and efforts on Stunited, limiting his expenses by living at his parents' home and doing other part-time jobs to provide some modest income. Continuing to incur all software programming and marketing costs with his own money, John finally filled a critical resource gap in his business model when he brought in another business partner with a software development company who could reliably manage the software product development process.

Shifting product development to the software experts allowed John to continue to focus on his strengths of Stunited marketing and promotion, expanding and maturing Stunited's marketing plan (Figure 2.6). He leveraged social media, including a Stunited channel on YouTube,[4] featuring interviews with students to promote why Stunited could bring value and resolve weaknesses in their academic work and advice on what can be bartered on the Stunited app.[5]

Note: Adding influencers and search engine optimization to Stunited promotion.

Figure 2.6   The maturing Stunited marketing plan

John's student-entrepreneurship center relationship with his undergraduate university was mutually beneficial but also underrealized. As Stunited gained traction in downloads of its app, it was recognized as a top 200 for EdTech downloads, and the university promoted this accomplishment. Stunited was frequently listed in university briefings and presentations as one of its successfully launched startups, but John never formally reached back for assistance. During the COVID pandemic, John voluntarily served as a guest to speak to entrepreneurship classes at his alma mater. However, some at the university's entrepreneurship center saw John as so fiercely independent and confident that he did not easily receive advice and counsel and saw him as not highly coachable.

The year 2019 was slow for Stunited, with the same basic first release of the app, and very limited funds to market and promote. But John held firm in his optimism in Stunited, and he convinced an early-stage and local software development firm to work on improving the app while spending little of his limited personal funds. By summer 2020, the Stunited app version 2 was ready for release[6] to as much fanfare and promotion as could be afforded. The COVID-19 pandemic had come in March 2020, and with his deep optimism, John expected the pandemic to create positive impact for Stunited, because students were entirely remote and might be even more reliant to help one another. Promoting Stunited virtually was the plan, and John used all the tools at his disposal, including Facebook, Instagram, Twitter and LinkedIn. There were downloads and signups from students in nearly 200 secondary schools and universities, but still few actual exchanges from which Stunited could generate its revenue. The cost to gain each new user download was only a few dollars, but this cost was still consuming nearly all Stunited's modest funding.

As Stunited began to build download traction, John recognized that the firm needed more money than he himself could personally provide. John spent time competing in student startup competitions, gaining recognition and making contacts. John envisioned a Stunited exit strategy to be acquired by a large EdTech or lifestyle company with a student target market. John was a skilled communicator, a natural salesperson, but like many young entrepreneurs, he faced youth bias when talking to investors. He visited Silicon Valley and an incubator there, but the terms suggested would have required John to move there, and he was not yet ready for that. John made contacts in the New York City angel venture scene, pitching to angel investors and on podcasts that promoted startup firms.

Some wanted to take over his idea and relegate John to a secondary role, while most were simply not interested in the EdTech space or turned off by the business model. By mid-2020, John finally contacted angel investors who were willing to make a modest investment through a non-equity agreement, using a simple agreement for future equity (SAFE) model. Four angel investors put up $75,000 as part of a SAFE agreement and John could finally pay for further marketing to promote Stunited on search engines to build downloads and growth in users (Figure 2.7).

Traction:

As of: Oct. 6th, 2020

Monthly Active Users:	733
Weekly Active Users:	283
Daily Active Users:	78
First Opens	1,600
Screen Views	42,221

Note: Growth in select measures did not yield comparable Stunited revenue growth.

Figure 2.7   *Stunited late 2020 user metrics*

Traction:

_____

As of: Feb. 10th, 2021

Monthly Active Users:	2,930
Weekly Active Users:	1,674
Daily Active Users:	160
First Opens	8,615
Screen Views	189,866

Note: Growth in select measures did not yield comparable Stunited revenue growth.

Figure 2.8   Stunited early 2021 user metrics

By early 2021, Stunited had realized growth in active users and screen views (Figure 2.8) but was still struggling to gain traction in transactions – where Stunited would make its profit – beyond initial downloads and screen views. However, as Stunited attracted more users, it also attracted incognito threat actors who sought to maliciously social engineer the app, which posed a new and unanticipated menace to the firm. This small threat actor population caused major problems for Stunited. These users were not really students but used Stunited to create small-scale Stunited proposals for modest amounts of money, but then used the subsequent exchange on Stunited as the basis for which to demand several thousands of dollars from the paying students with threats to expose them to their university for potential academic integrity violations. John tried to assuage the students who were being threatened but they were significantly upset and no longer interested in using Stunited.

John struggled with how to handle these threat actors. He deleted their accounts. He communicated to them their violations of Stunited acceptable use policies. He prepared a video on how to know if others are credible on the app.[7] He investigated other legal options but found there was little taste in law enforcement for such veiled threats. John had very limited resources for legal help, having put nearly all the Stunited expenses into product development and marketing. He began to doubt the ongoing viability of Stunited yet persisted for several more months without significant exchange traction. John was running out of emotional energy to keep Stunited moving forward, which by this time required a full seed round of capital investment to take it to the next level.

The numbers for Stunited weren't viable, the revenue from commissions on student exchanges weren't sufficient to attract investors, and the potential legal exposure manifest by the threat actors was intimidating. John recognized that the business model for Stunited was not feasible or viable. Finally, in mid-2021, John concluded that Stunited could no longer continue to operate. He began to shut down the app site and inform his angel investors that their investment in Stunited was worthless. There were many lessons he had learned, but these had come at the cost of John's time, his surrender of other business and job opportunities, and the loss of his and his investors' money.

PROBLEM STATEMENT

The problems in this case center around the risks and adverse impacts of the Stunited experience, for both John and his emotional and financial supporters.

Entrepreneurs need to be confident and optimistic, and John reveled in being positive and persistent about the future of Stunited. But his personal ethics also recognized that when communicating to users, ambassadors, and investors, he might be conveying an overstated sense of confidence and possibility about the prospects for Stunited. Because he started Stunited from his dorm room four years earlier, John could look back and recognize his own illusion of expertise and naive confidence in his entrepreneurial abilities, which was in some form fostered by the university atmosphere and ecosystem that only lightly touched on personal, professional and financial risk factors. Despite having given thousands of hours of his time to Stunited, John never drew any payment or compensation for its nearly five years of existence. As a result, by the time John reached the deepest levels of personal and financial commitment to his venture, he found it difficult to anticipate the loss of jobs and money if the business failed, not until the very end.

John was a creative student and subsequent entrepreneur, but he never envisioned that Stunited could cause unintentional harm to students who were users of the app. This caused him emotional anguish and fear. When Stunited was going to cease operations, John felt anxiety and fear to tell his investors that Stunited was going to fold. He worried that potential future colleagues, partners, and investors might not trust him again with investing money in a new venture, and how this would affect his reputation and relationships with his early angel investors, who believed in him and trusted him, while also recognizing the risks of investing with a startup.

There were also adverse personal impacts on his life and personal well-being. While he was always supported by friends and family, John publicly stated that there were times he was mentally drained, stressed, and depressed while trying to promote Stunited and achieve his vision.

Despite the setback, John's entrepreneurial spirit was not broken. In fact, before the overwhelming difficulties at Stunited had become apparent, he had already created a new consumer-facing startup with another member of his immediate family that was gaining significant traction on social media, and within its first year had already gained more than one million followers on TikTok. This distracted some of John's attention from Stunited, but he believed he had already given his entire focus of time and effort to Stunited for several years, and whether Stunited succeeded or not would not be entirely within his control. But this parallel startup had nothing to do with Stunited, and was in a different industry with an entirely different business model. The collaborators, users and investors associated with Stunited would not be saved by the new startup's possible success. John felt conflicted about the failure of Stunited that was happening at nearly the same time another digital startup was succeeding.

STUDENT CHALLENGES

Discussion Questions

1. What should be a twenty-one-year-old student's realistic expectations for success of an online startup?
2. What are the types and magnitude of risks that a student entrepreneur might face when considering a digital entrepreneurial venture?
3. What should investors – whether angels, venture capitalists, institutions, or family and friends – expect when considering an investment in a student-led startup?
4. What might have been the nature of a productive relationship between Stunited and John's undergraduate university both before and after he graduated?
5. How should John have anticipated and dealt with the threat actors who were threatening Stunited users?
6. How should John have explained the shutdown of Stunited and the loss of $75,000 to his investors?

NOTES

1. See https://www.dropbox.com/s/5n7414q6vrwhyza/yt5s.com-Stunited App Overview_Founder%27s Story.mp4?dl=0.
2. See https://www.dropbox.com/s/rvqdnlkg5vdg05c/yt5s.com-John Rondi - Entrepreneur Competition_1A.mp4?dl=0.
3. See https://www.dropbox.com/s/952y09lx11skj0j/yt5s.com-Stunited App Promo Video.mp4?dl=0.
4. See https://www.youtube.com/channel/UCvXkrUaAmt4sYrnPvSiJ73A.
5. See https://www.dropbox.com/s/skgrwtd0dkpp93e/Stunited_What can you barter.mp4?dl=0.
6. https://www.dropbox.com/s/6978elq611216dh/yt5s.com-Stunited V2 launch-%28480p%29 %281%29.mp4?dl=0.
7. https://www.dropbox.com/s/bt53cp5znyysv7f/Stunited_How do you know. mp4?dl=0.

REFERENCES

Bandera, C., Santos, S. C., and Liguori, E. W. (2021). The dark side of entrepreneurship education: A Delphi study on dangers and unintended consequences. *Entrepreneurship Education and Pedagogy*, 4(4), 609–636.

Pittz, T. G. and Liguori, E. (2020). *The Entrepreneur's Guide to Risk and Decisions: Building Successful Early-Stage Ventures*. Bingley: Emerald Publishing.

Santos, S. C. and Liguori, E. (2019). Entrepreneurial self-efficacy and intentions: Outcome expectations as a mediator and subjective norms as a moderator. *International Journal of Entrepreneurial Behavior & Research*, 26(3), 400–415.

3.   E-BRO APS: opportunities and challenges for digital social entrepreneurs

Ada Scupola

LEARNING OBJECTIVES

- Develop an understanding of the characteristics and specificities of digital entrepreneurship in the context of social innovation and social enterprises.
- Gain knowledge about the motivation to and the process of establishing a digital social venture, in particular through partnerships with government.
- Develop an understanding of the barriers to digital social entrepreneurship in the early stages of the venture.

INTRODUCTION: LEVERAGING DIGITAL NETWORKS TO CREATE FLEXIBLE AND INCLUSIVE JOB OPPORTUNITIES

Simon, a middle-aged healthy man living in Copenhagen, Denmark, suddenly suffers a stroke. After several medical treatments and consultations with several doctors and other specialists at the hospital and rehabilitation centers, Simon is diagnosed as not being able to continue his full-time job as a bank manager, although he may be able to work a few hours per week in a less demanding job. Simon is too young to go on permanent retirement. However, even though Simon receives help from the authorities and especially the municipal job center, it is not easy for Simon to get a job with his health conditions: the process of finding a job is complex, takes too long, and involves several actors.

Vulnerable citizens must easily find their way to work: the idea for a new company based on this aim had been smoldering for many years before one former job-center employee, Jacob, ventured out to start a business. It had become apparent to Jacob that vulnerable citizens, the job center, external actors, and employers could all benefit from thinking about and working harder to build networks.

BUSINESS AND INDUSTRY OVERVIEW

It must be easier for vulnerable citizens to cooperate with the profession-als who are helping them to find a job: This is the philosophy behind the company E-BRO APS (translates into English as "E-Bridge-Limited Liability Company") which has developed a new digital platform to support flexi-job applicants at job centers. "There is too long a wait for vulnerable citizens to find a job, and there are too many systems, departments, and people they have to go through," concludes Jacob after meeting people on the edge of the labor market at his job at Jobcenter Brøndby for several years (E-BRO, 2019).

A flexi-jobber is an employee with reduced working capacity, who is in need of physical and/or mental job accommodations. Impaired working capacity means that the flexi-jobber needs to work fewer hours than a full-time employee or requires a longer amount of time to solve the task.

Jacob first trained as a designer, and then obtained a bachelor's degree in education sciences. He is in charge of flexi-jobs at the Jobcenter Brøndby and has a genuine interest in getting disabled citizens into work as quickly as pos-sible. The overall scenario is that the government establishes the employment laws that each municipality has to implement. Then, there are the citizens who have the right to go to the job center to get help to find a job. Although job centers do not have a tradition of working directly with potential employers, they actively collaborate with recruitment agencies, who are called "Other Actors" in the job-center-related bureaucratic jargon. Jobcenter Brøndby works with six recruitment agencies, who in turn collaborate with companies to find jobs for candidates. "Other Actors" are intermediary companies that operate in the local area; they help disabled citizens to find flexi-job opportunities while adhering to Jobcenter Brøndby's values and contract. It is optional for citizens who apply to the job center to engage with the authorized recruiting agencies. If the "Other Actors" do not deliver the results specified in the contract with the Jobcenter, then the contract is terminated, and they are substituted with dif-ferent recruitment companies. The Jobcenter posts the available jobs while the recruiting agencies find the right match by reaching out to potential employers.

Jacob and his manager recognize that the flexi-job process and network operate in an inefficient way. It typically takes a candidate up to several weeks to be allocated to a recruitment agency and up to several months (and sometimes years) to get a flexi-job. The Reform of the Disability Pension and Flexi-Job Scheme of 2012 brought about new changes to flexi-job regulations, and therefore Jacob and his manager, with whom he has a good working rela-tionship, had several conversations to discuss how to handle the consequences of the reform for their day-to-day job and for the lives of applicants. Their objective was to leverage the changes in regulations to get even more disabled citizens into work and to do it faster.

Jacob does not remember exactly who had the idea first. It involved a lot of discussion, reflection, and brainstorming, mostly between Jacob and his manager, but also with several employees at the Jobcenter.

The result was that Jacob started talking to one of his friends, an IT expert, and together they conceptualized an IT application that could solve the afore-mentioned problems facing applicants. The design of JobIntra, an innovative IT platform, started in 2012 and E-BRO APS was founded by Jacob and his co-founder, Rune, in the same year. In 2013, JobIntra was finally up and running.

JobIntra makes it possible to work with disabled citizens seeking a flexi-job by enabling them to navigate their applications across several municipal departments and "external actors" (E-BRO, 2019). Jacob's thorough knowl-edge of how the job center works as well as the needs of the job applicants served as a significant advantage in this process. In 2013, Jobcenter Brøndby convened all the recruitment agencies for a meeting. The process of imple-menting and using JobIntra was well on its way, and E-BRO was starting to take its first steps (Figure 3.1). Simply having all the recruitment agencies in the same place at the same time was an innovative practice both for the job center and the recruitment agencies. In fact, the "Other Actors" collaborating with the Jobcenter had never met each other before, either virtually or face to face.

Figure 3.1   *JobIntra website screenshot: "Create results for your job centers with JOBiNTRA: easily, efficiently and safely."*

E-BRO's direct customers are the job centers in different municipalities and the recruitment agencies that collaborate with these job centers. The company's indirect customers are the disabled people looking for a flexi-job. Before JobIntra, the process of finding a flexi-job at Jobcenter Brøndby was a linear process for disabled citizens (Figure 3.2). It started with the citizen contacting the job center and/or sending an application for a flexi-job; the job center then sent the application to just one "Other Actor" at a time. The "Other Actor" tried to find a job for the applicant, and if they did not succeed within an established period of time (usually a few months), they got back to the job center and the job center assigned the application to another recruitment agency, and so on, until a job was eventually found. It took at least six to twelve months, and even sometimes up to two years (Figure 3.2), to find a candidate a flexi-job.

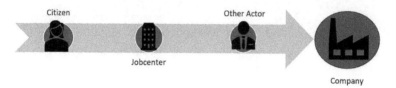

Figure 3.2   *Jobcenter Brøndby process*

JobIntra creates a flexi-job marketplace within which all the recruitment agencies compete and at the same time collaborate with the Jobcenter to find job opportunities for a given applicant. Further, the recruitment agencies and the hiring companies can directly communicate both with the flexi-job applicant and among themselves without going through the Jobcenter, thus speeding up the process substantially. JobIntra has thus increased both collaboration and competition among the different actors involved in finding a flexi-job (Figure 3.3).

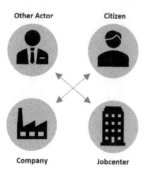

Figure 3.3   *JobIntra collaborative and competitive job finding process*

E-BRO APS's Concept and Business Model

*Figure 3.4   JobIntra website screenshot: "SOFTWARE FOR THE
                 SOCIAL AREA."*

The E-BRO business model is based on a simple idea: creating revenue by increasing both competition and collaboration between the different actors involved in finding a job for a disabled citizen (Figure 3.4). The principle that forms the basis of E-BRO's business model is that of "no win, no fee." E-BRO charges its clients for JobIntra installation costs as well as a six-month fee for each citizen added into the system by the Jobcenter. However, this fee is only paid to E-BRO if the citizen is hired within six months. The same payment principle applies to recruitment agencies.

E-BRO's business model is consistent with its philosophy of being a socially responsible company, its ultimate objective being to put disabled citizens into work as fast as possible before making a profit. The benefits, in fact, expand to the whole network. For instance, E-BRO had estimated that the break-even point for job centers adopting JobIntra in relation to the current costs of flexi-jobs contracts with recruitment agencies could be achieved by allocating only two flexi-jobs per semester. This is because, by adopting JobIntra, job centers can both save expenses in relation to Other Actors and eventually decrease the number of employees allocated to the task.

Brøndby Municipality was the first to adopt and implement JobIntra, and preliminary evidence shows that E-BRO's business model (1) helps more vulnerable people to get a job, and therefore a higher income; (2) secures employment more quickly; and (3) decreases Brøndby Municipality's public expenditure on disabled people. By increasing the intensity of competition between the Other Actors, JobIntra has increased the number of flexi-jobs available at a given point in time at Jobcenter Brøndby and contributed towards making Brøndby Municipality one of the Danish municipalities with the lowest unemployment rates among those offering flexi-jobs.

The Regulative Context: The Reform of the Disability Pension and Flexi-job Scheme

In 2012, the Reform of the Disability Pension and Flexi-Job Scheme was introduced by the Danish government under Prime Minister Helle Thorning Smith, and came into force on January 1, 2013. According to the Danish Agency of Labour Market and Recruitment the "two-focused reform seeks to increase employment by restricting the access to disability pension and instead providing either assistance to enter education through rehabilitation teams in the municipality, while ensuring that individuals with a lasting and significantly reduced working capacity enter the flexi-job scheme" (Ministry of Employment, 2019). The main objective of this reform of the disability pension is to get as many disabled people as possible into the labor market, preferably in non-subsidized employment. In addition, the reform shifts the focus towards investing resources to provide citizens the necessary assistance to obtain an education and/or secure employment rather than receiving a per-manent disability subsidy.

The target demographic of the Reform of the Disability Pension and Flexi-Job Scheme are citizens "with a complex set of problems, for whom social-, employment- and health-related challenges create barriers to entering the labour market, and where the lack of an interdisciplinary approach means that they are at risk of ending up on a permanent disability pension" (Ministry of Employment, 2022). To achieve this objective, the reform:

> includes the establishment of rehabilitation teams in each of the Danish municipal-ities. These teams are multidisciplinary by design, and include representatives from the employment sector, the health sector (municipal and regional), the social affairs sector, and the educational sector. The rehabilitation team will make a determination about whether a citizen should be assigned to an interdisciplinary rehabilitation program, flexi-job contract, disability pension, or another initiative. (Ministry of Employment, 2022)

The reform views flexi-jobs as a temporary solution. This means that the municipality must re-evaluate whether the person employed in the flexi-job is still qualified after 4.5 years. Under the flexi-job scheme, the municipality pays a subsidy that compensates for the reduced working capacity. The job center makes hiring decisions based on the recommendation from the rehabil-itation team. The reform was positively received: a 2019 evaluation report of the reform carried out by the Ministry of Employment states that "The munic-ipalities are working in line with the reform and its goals. The organizational framework which underpins the reform is thus in place, and all municipalities have set up rehabilitation teams" (Ministry of Employment, 2019).

Brøndby Municipality and Jobcenter Brøndby

Brøndby Municipality is part of the Capital Region of Denmark, and has approximately 35,541 inhabitants distributed over an area of 20.85 square km. The municipality consists of the three neighborhoods of Brøndbyøster, Brøndbyvester, and Brøndby Strand. Brøndby Municipality is located next to Køge Bay and is surrounded by the neighboring municipalities of Vallensbæk, Albertslund, Glostrup, Rødovre, and Hvidovre. In Brøndby, there are 6,000 owner-occupied dwellings, mainly detached houses and 10,000 public dwellings, which are primarily apartment buildings. Approximately 12 per cent of the municipality's areas are green areas. From a socio-economic point of view, Brøndby Municipality faces massive challenges: the lowest education level in Denmark, highest number of immigrants, and a high unemployment level. In Denmark, there are 94 job centers; citizens are assigned to the job center located in the municipality where they live. The most important task of job centers is to help citizens to find jobs when they become unemployed. The centers operate under national and local political frameworks and can undertake some of their own initiatives as allowed by these frameworks. Job centers are public, municipal organizations whose purpose is to implement the employment rules set by the government. Centers can cooperate with private individuals and companies, but there are limits to this because of the clear boundaries to what private and public actors can do, especially when it comes to using data about citizens. In the last few years, Jobcenter Brøndby has made a targeted effort to get the municipality's approximately 350 flexi-jobbers into employment. Jobcenter Brøndby has four employees, and has collaborated with a number of recruitment agencies to find flexi-jobs for disabled applicants (Brøndby Municipality, 2019).

PROBLEM STATEMENT: THE CHALLENGES

In 2018, Jacob resigned from the Jobcenter to fully focus on the digital venture, E-BRO APS, and establish it in the market. Jacob, however, found it difficult to establish contact with the different job centers because "the public sector is not open to innovative ideas." As of January 2019, only five job centers had adopted JobIntra in Denmark.

Jacob faced numerous barriers. For instance, a critical obstacle for the Jobcenter Brøndby was the integration of JobIntra into the existing IT systems. These systems were created by another IT provider and designed in a way that made it hard to change and modify them for adoption of the new platform.

Other types of barriers were related to the slow rate of adoption of JobIntra by other job centers in Denmark. Time is of course critical from a cash-flow perspective, because E-BRO would not achieve financial self-sufficiency without an adequately high volume of users and contracts.

In this respect, the municipal administrative system is a significant barrier because of its slow decision-making process. Many people are involved at different levels and in different departments at the job centers and in the municipality, and consensus must be achieved when it comes to adopting new solutions. These decision committees might include job center employees, job center leaders, the administration, and the municipal board.

According to Jacob, a key issue is that the organizations in the public sector, including job centers, very rarely challenge themselves or are challenged to improve by threats or opportunities in the external environment. Critical questions such as How do we innovate?, How do we adapt to changing conditions?, How can we reorganize internally to profit from the adoption of better technology? are typically not asked in the public sector.

Finally, Jacob feels that E-BRO is somewhat "stuck in the middle." The company provides an IT solution, which is a social innovation, developed for the purpose of benefiting a group of socially disadvantaged people; however, some official bodies do not see E-BRO as a social economic company but just as another service provider. For this reason, while E-BRO has applied for different grants funded by public money, the company has not been able, so far, to secure any funding through this method. Therefore, Jacob feels at a dead end, locked in a system whose inertia can kill the company or be a serious obstacle for its growth.

Other potential barriers are of a more contingent nature. The success of E-BRO and JobIntra strongly depends on whether, in the geographical area surrounding the Jobcenter adopting JobIntra, there are recruitment agencies willing to work with flexi-jobs as well as companies and other organizations with the need and will to employee flexi-jobbers. Fortunately, Brøndby Municipality is located in the Greater Copenhagen area, where there are many partners to work with.

CONCLUSIONS

E-BRO is a digital entrepreneurship venture operating within the field of social entrepreneurship (see appendix for definitions). E-BRO's main product, JobIntra, is a digital social innovation that has revolutionized the flexi-job process at the municipality level (Brøndby) in two ways. First JobIntra has increased collaboration among the different parties involved in finding a flexi-job, and thus has increased competition between the various recruitment agencies, with great benefit to citizens, the municipality, and the society as a whole.

The first and most important impact of JobIntra has been an increase in flexi-job employment in Brøndby municipality and a reduction in the amount of time required to find a job. This has improved the quality of life for flexi-jobbers in terms of work identity, higher income, and larger personal networks.

At the community level, by getting *more* disabled people in employment *faster*, JobIntra has had a socio-economic impact on both Brøndby Municipality and the Danish society at large by providing an effective service to disadvantaged social groups while reducing public expenditure.

Finally, at the organizational level, the use of the platform has had a positive impact on job satisfaction both for the Other Actors and for Jobcenter Brøndby employees. For example, at Jobcenter Brøndby, employees have freed up time that they can allocate on the most difficult cases or other activities. The recruitment agencies have shifted their focus from competing for job centers to competing for flexi-jobs. The Other Actors are so enthusiastic about and satisfied with JobIntra that they recommend it to other job centers.

Despite these positive aspects, E-BRO is struggling to grow. The most critical barriers to growth are all related to the challenges in getting public systems to innovate and collaborate with external partners. This is even more the case when collaboration requires integration of different technological platforms. Digitalization requires fast decision-making processes and agile organizational structures that are able to adapt and change quickly. Another major determinant of the slow diffusion of digital technology in the public system is the lack of interest or motivation of public organizations in adopting innovation.

Additionally, it turned out to be difficult to get policy makers involved to favor the adoption of JobIntra by other municipalities. Such involvement could strongly benefit disabled citizens entitled to flexi-jobs, the municipalities, the recruitment companies, and society as a whole. Last but not least, the fact that some official bodies recognize E-BRO as a social venture while others do not is a sign that the status of companies like E-BRO – in serving the public welfare system, but adopting technology and mindset that are more common in the for-profit world – is not clearly recognized in Danish society.

It took extensive effort on the part of Jacob and Rune to navigate the bureaucracy and innovation inertia of the public eco-system. For instance, it took three years to launch JobIntra at Jobcenter Brøndby. Such long reaction times are not compatible with the pace at which digital companies operate and evolve. E-BRO must identify alternative pathways for its growth that are fully under its control while still remaining loyal to its original mission and values.

STUDENT CHALLENGES: QUESTIONS FOR DISCUSSION

1. Based on the E-BRO case, can you identify the critical challenges that a digital social entrepreneurship venture faces? How do these differ from a company operating in full for-profit markets?
2. How should the company diversify its business to be less dependent on public finance (for instance, what would happen if the budget allocated to the policy is cut by the government or the reform is altered)?
3. What can the company do to promote JobIntra adoption by other job centers and employment agencies?

REFERENCES AND FURTHER READING

Brøndby Municipality (2019). http://www.Brøndby.dk/borger/jobogledighed.aspx (accessed April 29, 2019).

Danish Agency for Labour Market and Recruitment (2022). Reform of the Disability Pension and Flexi-job Scheme (2012). https://www.star.dk/en/recent-labour-market-policy-reforms/reform-of-the-disability-pension-and-flexi-job-scheme-2012/ (accessed January 11, 2022).

Dees, G. J. (2001). The meaning of "social entrepreneurship". The Center for Advancement of Social Entrepreneurship (CASE), Duke University. https://centers.fuqua.duke.edu/case/knowledge_items/the-meaning-of-social-entrepreneurship/ (accessed November 20, 2021).

E-BRO (2019). https://www.jobintra.dk/om-E-BRO/ (accessed April 23, 2019).

E-BRO (2022). https://www.E-BRO.dk (accessed January 13, 2022).

Ministry of Employment (2019). http://www.bm.dk (accessed May 2, 2019).

Ministry of Employment (2022). http://www.bm.dk (accessed January 13, 2022).

Mulgan, G., Tucker, S., Ali, R., and Sanders, B. (2007). Social innovation: what it is, why it matters and how it can be accelerated. The Young Foundation.

OECD (2000). OECD LEED Forum on Social Innovations. https://www.oecd.org/fr/cfe/leed/forum-social-innovations (accessed November 20, 2021).

TEPSIE (2012). *Doing Social Innovation: A Guide for Practitioners*. A deliverable of the project: 'The theoretical, empirical and policy foundations for building social innovation in Europe' (TEPSIE), European Commission – 7th Framework Programme. Brussels: European Commission, DG Research.

APPENDIX: DEFINITIONS OF SOCIAL INNOVATION AND SOCIAL ENTREPRENEURSHIP

A good starting point for the analysis of the case is the definitions of social entrepreneurship and social innovation provided below. According to Dees (2001), social entrepreneurs are actors that take on the role of change agents in the social sector, by:

- Adopting a mission to create and sustain social value (not just private value);
- Recognizing and relentlessly pursuing new opportunities to serve that mission;
- Engaging in a process of continuous innovation, adaptation, and learning;
- Acting boldly without being limited by resources currently in hand; and
- Exhibiting a heightened sense of accountability to the constituencies served and for the outcomes created.

The OECD (2000) forum on social innovation states that:

> Social innovation refers to the design and implementation of new solutions that imply conceptual, process, product, or organizational change, which ultimately aim to improve the welfare and wellbeing of individuals and communities. Many initiatives undertaken by the social economy and by the civil society have proven to be innovative in dealing with socio-economic and environmental problems, while contributing to economic development. To fully tap the potential of social innovation, an enabling policy framework is needed to support public, non-profit and private actors to co-construct and implement socially innovative solutions and thereby contribute to address socio-economic issues, build stronger territorial resilience and better respond to future shocks.

4. The role of digital technologies in the development of the Shape Stretch body stretching bar: a case study in product innovation and management resources

John DiMarco

LEARNING OBJECTIVES

- Understand the role technologies play in accelerating product development and intellectual property procurement.
- Comprehend how technologies enabled the entrepreneurial and experiential learning experiences required to create a physical consumer product.
- Apply design thinking to entrepreneurial and business problems.
- Analyze cases to understand entrepreneurial process and previous executions.
- Create new ideas that require design thinking to address problems and market voids.

INTRODUCTION: INNOVATION AND STRETCHING

Product development is born out of innovation, which is the creation of new solutions to problems using better design. Innovation is delivered in two forms, incremental and radical, which are both needed to bring completely new technologies to society and to foster better solutions to consumer and industry problems. Radical innovation, according to Norman (2013), occurs less frequently and involves monumental shifts in the way we do things. Incremental innovation occurs over time, with systematic approaches to making existing solutions better for people. This is the typical path for most product designs, with the design iterated and tested, only to be modified after problem discoveries lead to new modifications. This cycle continues in a somewhat blind state, with decisions on new features and usage tossed around and tested – this process is known in the product development industry as hill climbing, and it is the method that Norman (2012, p. 281) calls "the secret to incremental innovation," the process of blindly climbing a hill to find the best and final direction, which is how the Shape Stretch body bar was created.

The Shape Stretch journey was seeped in making and modifying designs in order to enhance and fully embrace the user's experience with the product. This process took several years to complete in order to get a marketable version of a product, but was accelerated through the use of technologies that generated creative tasks such as product design iterations, intellectual property application, and a host of other entrepreneurial activities needed to bring a product to market.

Three keys to moving the Shape Stretch project forward included the process of:

1. Researching and ideating to create a product prototype
2. Developing ancillary product content
3. Securing intellectual property.

This case discusses how the use of digital technologies contributed to the process progression. The case describes instances where using digital technologies helped the innovator in product design and development, and the manager in patenting and market-ready product production.

Looking at the case through the lens of the innovator, the product developer assembled a team of subject matter experts in engineering, physical therapy, chiropractic, martial arts, and athletic training to begin a product development journey with the product manager to design and produce an original solution for stretching. The story of the Shape Stretch body stretching bar illustrates how digital technologies can help in both product innovation and product management.

As highlighted above, there were two roles in the Shape Stretch development that benefited greatly from digital technologies – that of the innovator and the manager. The product innovator, who works as a product developer, innovating and creating the product, needs to create prototypes and designs. The product manager works to develop the business aspects of the product such as the online presence, intellectual property, and product materials and branding elements.

Design Ideation Accelerated by Utilizing Technologies

The Shape Stretch body bar is a physical product that requires factory manufacturing and production. It is made of carbon steel and offers both a device and educational component. In this case, design thinking was critical to building a final product, which is an approach to solving problems. The innovator needed to undertake research to better understand how to create a novel solution that would attain both usability and patent procurement.

The product innovator first needed to understand existing solutions in the marketplace and those inventions protected by patent. The innovator performed competitive research on Amazon and Google to find existing similar products occupying the health and fitness space. This allowed visualization of other solutions, which provided a launch pad to create new iterations and a completely new design leading to prototyping. Using Google Patents, the innovator gained insights into existing inventions, which allowed clearer paths for developing a new device that could warrant patent application and eventual approval.

Prototyping

Design thinking can be characterized by using practice and innovation requiring interdisciplinary collaboration, successive ideation, and user testing (Curedale, 2013). Using a lean startup strategy, which uses a user and product centered approach to build and test a product with rapid iterations, the initial design for the Shape Stretch body stretching bar was "Frankenstein" prototyped – an agile process of experimenting with materials and form, similar to the approach of Dr. Frankenstein as he crafted his creature from parts of human and animal corpses. Less dramatic, in this creative case, PVC and copper tubes were assembled to make the desired form of a stretching bar. Once the form was iterated, the final physical proportions of the product needed to be translated into numerical measurements that could be replicated to produce a consistent product form, with each being exactly the same as the others.

Getting to the Frankenstein stage required a series of different technology tools. First, for two-dimensional creation, making a basic form for the product, vector drawing technology was utilized by the innovator to draw different product forms using the professional drawing application, Adobe Illustrator. Acceleration of design iterations was simplified by using Illustrator as it allowed digital experimentation in 2D of shapes and sizes of product components without establishing exact dimension or exclusive details. This use of technology allowed rapid creation of different product footprints that would be translated into a 2D drawing with exact specifications for computer aided production from raw materials into finished product (Figure 4.1).

To craft a more detailed product model for production, more drawings needed to be made using three-dimensional software that allowed both product modeling in three-dimensional space, but also two-dimensional measurements for use in a manufacturing environment.

To complete the product drawings, computer aided design software by Autodesk called AutoCAD was used to produce designs with the production numbers needed to manufacture the product using CNC (computer numerical controls). The CNC controls allow the factory to set up machinery to bend, connect, and separate materials into product parts. AutoCAD provides a modeling environment to create 2D and 3D product drawings to show orthographic views from the front, top, left, right, bottom, and rear. These computer drawings are used for both productions, but may also be used for marketing and intellectual property applications in the future.

Note: This image was originally created in Adobe Illustrator as a product mock-up and then professionally rendered by a draftsperson for a patent application submission. It was translated into product specifications.

Figure 4.1   2D design patent figure drawing showing form

With design specifications estimated, and a mechanical drawing in hand, it was time to create a manufactured prototype. By creating a manufactured prototype, also known as a product design sample, the factory and product innovator and manufacturing vendors interacted closely to ensure that the manufacturing process was feasible, and the equipment and staff were capable of the desired output. This stage also allowed the manufacturing company to clearly isolate any potential pitfalls, needed tweaks to the design, and final costing based on time and resources needed.

Product Management and the Role of Digital Technologies

Patent and trademark technology tools
The Shape Stretch product management process was aided by technology tools to acquire information to validate approaches to final product development.

Patent and trademark research was executed on the USPTO website, through database searches using keywords to seek out past inventions and marks that have been registered (Figure 4.2). The product manager was able to establish a list of past patents for references and use them for both application and competitive analysis. As well, after application was made to the USPTO, the online patent center provided the product manager, who was the applicant, to check the status of the patent through the Patent Application information Retrieval (PAIR) system. This process began after a year of development.

The product manager hired a draftsman who created drawings that were submitted to the United States Patent and Trademark office (USPTO). These drawings were created by hand, scanned and digitized for submission electronically to the USPTO. The drawings needed to follow USPTO guidelines depending on the application and claims based on information provided on the USPTO website.

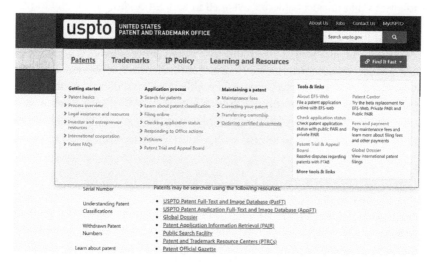

Figure 4.2   USPTO homepage providing educational information on patents and access to the PAIR system

Costing technology tools
Costing was a research task executed by the product manager that benefited greatly from database and internet technology. Developing a physical product requires finding a vendor with the appropriate manufacturing capabilities. Previously product managers relied on printed registers and word of mouth recommendations, now they can use online tools such as the Thomas Register, which offers a United States and Canada index of manufacturers categorized by specialty areas. Using the technology tools of the Thomas Register, the

ability to find factories, suppliers, and costing information was accelerated as each manufacturer and supplier can be searched by keywords targeting industry, product, location, and capabilities. This allows the product manager and developers to quickly assemble a list of potential vendors to establish product material lists and manufacturing costs.

Creating Brand Materials Using Technology

Creating educational and brand materials that complement the Shape Stretch body bar required technology tools for graphic design, publishing, and printing. The product manager utilized digital tools for digital design. By using Adobe Photoshop, demonstration images were retouched and clipped after shooting to create a poster that visually guides users through the various stretching exercises. This process was performed using digital imaging technology so that images could be swapped in and out of designs rapidly to test for user understanding. For brand design, Adobe Illustrator was used to create the logo type and brandmark for Shape Stretch, which eventually received a USPTO trademark (filed electronically). When performing logo design, different iterations need to be created in order to finalize a mark before submitting a finalized trademark application to the USPTO. In addition, demonstration videos were developed using TechSmith Camtasia and Adobe Premiere, and were uploaded to YouTube before being deployed on the e-commerce website, which was another phase on the path to commercialization.

E-Commerce Development

The Shopify application was used to develop the ecommerce website and online article blog for the product website ShapeStretch.com. The product website was needed, even before sales had begun, in order to establish the goods in commerce for the Shape Stretch trademark application. Using DIY (Do it Yourself) web technology, the Shopify website technology allowed the product manager to create an ecommerce website without writing code or having web design skills. The manager only needed to collect the images and write the website copy. The need for a traditional web designer and coder was replaced by digital technology tools for web output.

Trademark Clearance

The Shape Stretch trademark name was searched for clearance using the Trademark database search engine (TESS), then filed online using the USPTO trademark application system, and in 2021 the Shape Stretch tradename was issued a United States Trademark. The goal of the TESS research is to "clear" the mark from other marks, so as to identify uniqueness and therefore increase the chances the application for trademark will achieve USPTO registration (Figure 4.3).

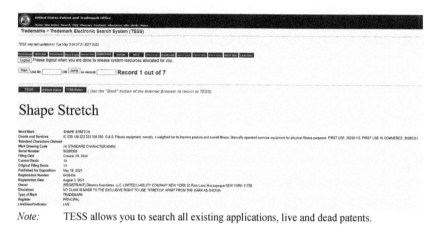

Note: TESS allows you to search all existing applications, live and dead patents.

Figure 4.3 *Shape Stretch record in the trademark electronic search system (TESS)*

Final Product Materials

After iterations of materials and designs, managing factory testing and output, and securing patent and trademark protection, the Shape Stretch product was market ready. The product consists of three components, the apparatus (bar), the educational materials (poster), and online tutorials (videos).

BUSINESS AND INDUSTRY OVERVIEW

The health and fitness industry consists of health clubs, equipment manufacturers, and service providers including freelance instructors, personal trainers, coaches, and physical therapists. The stretching product industry is a blend of target markets, with potential customers of Shape Stretch ranging from physical therapists using the product in practice, to a college or high school athlete looking to avoid injury, to an active person who needs increased flexibility, to older or recovering clients who need to stretch for better blood circulation and mobility. This breadth of product potential required business and industry research that crossed over into several areas requiring investigation of scientific literature, popular news articles, and feedback from professionals in various fields that rely on stretching. As well, customer data was needed, not just for

Shape Stretch, but for other products in the stretching space across medical, fitness, martial arts, athletic performance, flexibility, and recovery. This led to a scouring of competitor websites and reviews to build an understanding of trends, stakeholders, and where media attention in the product space has gone.

PROBLEM STATEMENT: SELF-STRETCHING, A PROBLEM FOR DESIGN

Understanding how to create a product that solves a problem is difficult. For Shape Stretch, as with other products, user problems were identified through initial user testing of prototypes. Once critical user needs were identified, product accessories and educational materials were finalized. Digital technologies were used to accelerate the research, production, and intellectual property processes.

Stretching can be difficult to perform and confusing to learn for many people across age, size, and range of motion (ROM) levels. This led to a product question (PQ) set aimed at developing core attributes of form and function for the product.

- **PQ1:** How can stretching be made easier for different users, so it can fit a daily routine?
- **PQ2:** How can device design make stretching easier for the user and increase range of motion?
- **PQ3:** What educational materials are needed to support users toward daily or weekly stretching activities?

STUDENT CHALLENGES

Now that you better understand how technology can be used in product innovation and product management in meeting milestones, you can practice the process.

Research Assignment 1: Research and Ideate a New Product Idea Invention

1. Identify an industry to develop a mock product that solves a common problem. Pick a category of products in that industry and narrow down to one product type. It should be a physical product that can be held and used to perform a human function. (Fitness for example is an industry, and stretching is the product category, and a body stretch bar is the product type.)

2. Research the chosen industry on Google and Amazon shopping sites to determine existing products, companies, and history of consumer usage (study user comments).
3. Create a research notes set that chronicles the product industry, category, and product type.

Problem Analysis Assignment 2: Define an Initial Problem Set with Three Product Questions (PQ)

1. From your research in assignment one, identify and define a product problem set of three questions that are addressed by existing product solutions.
2. Write a report that lists the product category and problems set based on research notes. Present your findings to your classmates.

IP Research Assignment 3: Discover Prior Art and Intellectual Property through the USPTO

1. Search the patent database to explore existing inventions in your category. (Use the Pair system or Google patents).
2. Create an infographic showing existing patented artwork (2–3 live and dead examples) in your product category.

Design Assignment 4: Ideate a Mock Product Design

1. Sketch or collage different forms to explore physical product possibilities using digital tools such as Sketch Up, Fusion, Illustrator, or Photoshop.
2. Create three to four iterations that highlight unique benefits based on the different designs.
3. Create a presentation board showing design iterations and proposed specifications (2–3 designs).

Naming Assignment 5: Create an Original Product Name Different than Existing Trademarks

1. Name a newly ideated product. First, use the TESS system to search to see if an existing similar trademark exists that matches your proposed name; if so, try different names.
2. Create a simple word mark or full logo design with the product name you decide on using DIY tools such as Canva or Adobe Spark.

3. Photograph your materials and present the product to your classmates for feedback and further iteration in a poster board, Google website, or Google Slide deck.

REFERENCES

Curedale, R. (2013). *Design Thinking Pocket Guide*. Los Angeles: Design Community College.
Norman, D. (2013). *The Design of Everyday Things* (2nd ed.). New York: Basic Books.

5. Agroads case: technological solutions for the agricultural sector

Rubén A. Ascúa, Andrea Minetti and José A. Borello

LEARNING OBJECTIVES

- Learn how digital technology is transforming agribusiness.
- Identify the most relevant technological vectors of Industry 4.0 that the company uses in its products.
- Understand how e-commerce is affecting internationalization opportunities for small businesses.

INTRODUCTION

Digital technologies – including digital platforms, sensors (Internet of Things), drones, big data, and artificial intelligence – play a significant role in agri-food chains at different levels. Some of these technologies can be applied directly to the agricultural production process, such as information platforms for decision making and precision agriculture machinery; others, such as big data, are employed by organizations that carry out research and development for agricultural applications (Sotomayor at al., 2021). In recent years, digital media and online platforms, in particular, are increasingly used by companies in the agricultural sector for sales and marketing applications.

Looking ahead, extraordinary growth is on the horizon. Digital innovations, for example, have accelerated the development of various services that provide up-to-date weather information, predict commodity price trends, and enable farmers to make online purchases. All of this in a sector that has typically been very conservative and slow to adopt technological innovations.

In business-to-business farmers' markets, online marketplaces empower buyers, give sellers access to new outlets and customers, make pricing more transparent, and simplify trading. This is the scenario in which Agroads was created, in an attempt to capture the business opportunities that the digital revolution was opening up in all sectors as well as in agriculture (Figure 5.1). Mr.

Rodriguez, CEO, and founder of Agroads, felt like a digital pioneer in the early 2000s when digital innovation was foreign to most operators in the industry. Fast forward 20 years and the pandemic changed everything. Forced by the roadblocks imposed by the COVID pandemic, many of Argentina's agribusinesses adopted videoconferencing, and were now more open to incorporating e-commerce into their sales operations. Agroads is now well-positioned to take advantage of its early vision that digital technology could change Argentine agriculture for the better, but new challenges now await (Agroads, 2020, 2022).

Figure 5.1   Agroads logo

For many years agricultural machinery manufacturers had developed a network of dealers and distributors throughout the country using traditional methods of communication. These kinds of networks are still the main channels to reach out to customers in different areas of the country, even though companies operating in the agricultural sector are now more open to new technological applications. This centralized model is being impacted by platforms such as Agroads as well as by over-the-top operators like Facebook, and Google, which allow manufacturers to directly reach out to producers and contractors in a very targeted and direct way. In addition, any friction in communication has been eliminated thanks to popular social media and chat applications such as WhatsApp (which is very popular in Argentina).

The key for organizations and professionals is to be able to see digital change not as a threat but as a great opportunity. The main challenge for Agroads is to ride this momentum and position itself as a valid alternative for sales and distribution beyond the market of innovators and early adopters. These challenges entail providing existing and new customers with an even more compelling value proposition to make clear the benefits of going digital. This is not an easy task in an industry that has been, until recent times, very reluctant to adopt digital technologies for cultural, industrial, and logistical reasons, including the difficulty of bringing high quality connections in remote areas in such a vast country as Argentina.

INDUSTRY OVERVIEW

Global agricultural production more than tripled between 1969 and 2015, due in part to Green Revolution technologies that improved productivity, and to the significant expansion of the use of land, water, and other natural resources for agricultural purposes to cope with increasing demand from a fast-rising world population. In the same period, food and agriculture underwent a marked process of industrialization and globalization. Food supply chains have lengthened dramatically as the physical distance between farm and table has increased, and consumption of processed and packaged foods has skyrocketed in all but the most isolated rural areas.

To meet demand in 2050, FAO, the United Nations Food and Agriculture Organization, estimates that agriculture will have to produce almost 50 percent more food, feed, and biofuels than in 2012. In sub-Saharan Africa and South Asia, agricultural production would have to double to meet growing demand, while in the rest of the world, growth is expected to be about one-third above current levels. This assessment considers recent UN projections that the world population will reach 9.7 billion by 2050 (FAO, 2017).

To address this challenge, agri-food systems must become more productive, profitable, transparent, sustainable, and resilient to external shocks, such as those caused by climate change. Smallholder farmers, who manage 80 percent of the world's cropland and 60 percent of food production, are particularly vulnerable to these shocks. They will have to adopt new agricultural production processes and, in turn, face limited access to information and agricultural assets, finance, and markets. In the wake of COVID-19, it is more urgent than ever to transform the functioning of current food systems. They must be more agile and resilient to unforeseen events (IADB, 2021). This leads to the conclusion that companies operating along the agri-food production chain will also experience these challenges. Considering the characteristics of today's more connected and digitally savvy farmer, a promising scenario for Agroads' business model can be expected.

The COVID-19 pandemic caused complications of all kinds, which have inevitably affected all productive sectors. Yet, in Argentina, the agricultural and agro-industrial sectors have been considered "essential" since March 2020 (the month in which COVID-related restrictions began in the country), that is, subject to few operational limitations. Despite these obstacles, some positive aspects should be mentioned. One of them is related to the rapid and effective adoption of new technologies. In this sense, one of the great beneficiaries has been e-commerce, considering that the pandemic accelerated electronic marketing. As a result, Agroads consolidated its leadership as the number one marketplace for agricultural products and services in Argentina, particularly in the Pampas region.[1]

The agricultural machinery sector was the main protagonist of e-commerce in 2020 with the purchase and sale of equipment. In addition, Agroads' users were able to purchase inputs, spare parts, and equipment through the platform. The increasing availability of data, combined with the emergence of data analytics tools such as AI, big data, and machine learning, is making it possible for digital consulting firms to provide farmers with more detailed insights and recommendations. In previous generations of services, general information on market prices, weather, nutrition, and best practices was disseminated to a wide network of farmers through more traditional methods of interaction (phone, events such as fairs in which face-to-face interactions took place, visits by state extensionists, etc.). Those methods are gradually being replaced or complemented by virtual tools.

The Beginnings of Agroads and its Recent Trajectory

In the beginning, Mr. Rodriguez did not work full time on the venture, and he was employed in the IT department of a company in the city of Rafaela, Argentina. His wife also worked part-time, until the workload in the company started to increase, which led them to focus 100 percent on their business. These were the early years of the commercial deployment of internet in the country (2002–5). Like mushrooms, a number of very small software firms were being created by young professionals in a number of cities in the Pampas (Albornoz, 2006).

The first programmer joined the business in 2006 and ended up spending 10 years with the company. Shortly thereafter, Mr. Rodriguez's wife began to assume full management responsibilities for the company. This three-person team ran the company for about five years. They worked from the living room of Mr. Rodriguez's parents' house until they finally moved into an office (Figure 5.2). That was a big change – Agroads was no longer a hobby, but was starting to look like a real business. The company continued to grow and increased its staff by adding sales and marketing people, as well as another programmer.

In 2005, there was very little competition and companies were starting to need digital solutions, and according to Mr. Rodriguez, now CEO of Agroads, this early mover advantage put them in a privileged competitive position that allowed the company to generate some profits even during frequent financial crises. In years when traditional supply channels were characterized by fierce competition, the digital marketplace created by Agroads became a beacon in the darkness, because it helped small farming businesses to reach the market directly and at a very low cost. Agroads' expansion was also possible because of the existence of a large unified market of machinery, inputs, and services around extensive agricultural activities in the Pampas.

Source: Agroads.

Figure 5.2   *One of the walls of the current Agroads offices*

One of Agroads' key differentiating factors is that the company is obsessed with making user experience as simple and as effective as possible. For example, from the very beginning, Agroads invested significantly in the design of a powerful search engine into its platform, so that its customers could find the products they were looking for as quickly as possible (Figures 5.3 and 5.4). Since then, Agroads has made usability and simplicity key factors in guiding further improvement of its platform. Agroads learned to focus on these key aspects and decided to outsource non-core activities. Initially, employees performed a range of functions, some of which were not part of their job description, such as coders and programmers. This lack of clarity in the design of job positions led to the creation of a small in-house core team. Many functions were outsourced to help in scaling the business while remaining lean and agile. For example, the company relies mostly on external professional help when it comes to marketing. By focusing on its core business and the platform, Agroads found a way to create a scalable business model without having heavy and costly overheads.

Note: The website can be accessed at www.agroads.com.ar.
Source: Agroads.

Figure 5.3 *Usability and simplicity in the design of desktop and mobile effective digital interfaces at Agroads*

Note: The website can be accessed at www.agroads.com.ar.
Source: Agroads.

Figure 5.4 *Usability and simplicity in the design of desktop and mobile effective digital interfaces at Agroads*

In terms of financing, Agroads has never accessed third-party financing; it has always financed itself with its own capital by reinvesting the proceeds coming from its sales. The platform is constantly being updated from the technological point of view, for instance through the addition of new functionalities to further improve user experience. However, Agroads' business model has remained relatively unchanged through the years.

Another factor that influenced the company's development was the introduction of mobile devices. Today, 80 percent of Agroads' online traffic originates from mobile devices. In 2019, Agroads added to its portfolio the product "Agroads Analytics." This tool enables farmers to make data-driven decisions, for example by providing information on the performance of ads on the Agroads platform. Thus, farmers can better manage their digital sales leading to more business opportunities. The tool provides an overview of the impact of publications made on Agroads with objective data (impressions, clicks, contacts, and ads), as well as by supporting the identification of the geographical origin of visits. Agroads Analytics makes it possible to visualize the impact of the products sold on the platform through the quantification of the clicks received by an ad and the transformation of such clicks into actual sales. This analytical engine also helps Agroads monitor the evolution in time of a client's business on the market in which it operates. Agroads uses these analytics to support its internal decision-making process. It also shares this information with its customers hoping they will adopt the same data-driven approach in making decisions for themselves.

This is a clear example of the application of an Industry 4.0 vector: business intelligence (BI). This technological enabler refers to the provision of data that allows all types of companies to make better decisions. The incorporation of new services and innovations to the platform is based on a process of quick and iterative validation of these novelties via agile methodologies. A rule of thumb is that each early idea must be tested within a week of its adoption. On more than one occasion, it would not be an exaggeration to say that Agroads was able to sell a product before it was fully developed.

As for the characteristics of the entrepreneurial team, perseverance, restless innovation, and genuine passion for what they do stand out. The company CEO and top management all excel in a fundamental entrepreneurial skill for the digital environment: the ability to listen to their customers and to identify a problem-driven approach to the development of new services.

The CEO of Agroads often mentions a key lesson learned over 15 years of work experience: the transformation from an operational entrepreneur to a strategic entrepreneur requires being part of broader technology and market ecosystems, building and managing talented teams, and learning how to create a digital strategy and execute it through proper planning.

Business Model

Since the beginning, the Agroads revenue model has been based on a "free-mium" business model; that is, a model based on the idea that clients can, initially, opt for a free entry-level offer. Once in contact with the client, the firm offers a premium version that is paid for, with the possibility of accessing other functionalities, a greater volume of transactions or the simple fact of not having to display advertisements.

Only the clients who need more functionalities generate revenues for the company. That is why Agroads' objective is to transfer as many free users as possible into paying customers via service customization. That was the first change the company recognized. Many clients only need an online commerce platform while others have more sophisticated needs (or can develop an appetite for more advanced services). Thus, Agroads began to design offers differentiated by type of customer.

Currently, it is one of the most important online platforms for agriculture in Argentina, made up of a community that exceeds 400,000 people connected to do business. Most of them have businesses in and around the large portion of the country dedicated to extensive agriculture and cattle raising (annual crops such as soybeans, wheat, maize, sorghum, etc.). This online platform generates a volume of information with high added value in a dynamic, volatile, and competitive business context. Agroads' platform is grounded on three pillars: community, infrastructure, and data. As far as the community pillar is concerned, the company implements various activities to strengthen relationships with its more loyal and returning users so that they will consider using additional functionalities. This community aims to democratize knowledge. To do this, Agroads puts agricultural producers in contact with technicians and consultants as well as with the best information, and the major agricultural companies. By simply registering on the platform, users can make online inquiries to the most outstanding specialists in different agricultural topics, access quality technical information, and interact with peers to share experiences and information. The infrastructure of the platform is state of the art: customers have numerous functionalities, such as CRM, payments, logistics, and so on.

On the data side, the firm offers two products. One of those tools, to which we already made a reference, is Agroads Analytics: a tool based on real data on the impact of posts that considers variables such as impressions, clicks, contacts, and ads. This makes it possible to identify the geographical origin of the visitors and evaluate the scope of the publications according to the category. The objective is to optimize business strategy and contribute to marketing decisions and business planning thanks to market knowledge. From this data, the platform allows access to different reports having an intelligent visualization of the performance of the products.

Theecondecondd tool the company is working on is an algorithm that allows farmers to predict what they need and offer them a "menu" of options that include the best offers based on their interests, such as commercial conditions, product characteristics, and geolocation. Agroads observed that clients often do not have time or do not have the training to interpret the data obtained, which is why over time this second product was created: # BeOne, an agency that provides services to companies that need to be in Agroads and at the same time on social networks. In other words, what the agency does is to leverage Agroads Analytics to generate hyper-segmented audiences and reach out to users with highly accurate marketing messages at the time they need them. Here the richness of the service offered by Agroads is evident. According to the General Director of the company, the objective is to support clients throughout each step of their buying or selling experience and simplify the process through the creation of different tools.

Agroads' revenues are generated in various ways. The most important revenue source are the 1,500 premium clients who monthly pay from $7,000 to $60,000 (Argentine pesos). Other revenues are generated via ads and data analysis tools on the platform. Through this mix the company was able to close the year 2021 with over $130 million in turnover (about 1.3 million US dollars at 2022 exchange rates).

In the future Agroads intends to offer payment solutions for the different needs of producers: agro cards and grain exchange. Logistics, on the other hand, is a complex issue. But the company is aware of this situation and is willing to build the foundations of a new, simpler business in the field, putting the end customer at the center. Agroads, these last 15 years, has been part of the digital transformation of the entire industry, but it is not alien to the reality that it is a constantly evolving market.

Through the data generated and the information analyzed, Agroads will have the challenge of improving user experience, in which all applications and functionalities for the producer are integrated. In this sense, community development will be a central theme in the company's strategy: providing trust, a sense of belonging, and being useful with the tools that are provided.

Currently, Agroads has a series of competitive advantages that allow it to be one of the leading agro marketplaces in Argentina:

- First to market: 15 years of experience and organic growth.
- Brand recognition: 120,000 brand searches per month from Google.
- Data volume: due to the monthly processing of 100 million interactions.
- Network effects: having more than 600,000 users and 1.6 million monthly visits (95 percent organic).

E-Commerce as a Tool for the Internationalization of Companies

The literature has basically dealt with the internationalization processes of production and service companies, while the internationalization of e-commerce companies has not been analyzed with similar interest by academia. In many existing accounts the internationalization process of a company normally begins with initially modest export operations, serving this experience as a platform for future international expansion (Lu and Beamish, 2001). Given that SMEs generally do not have sufficient resources to advance in more complex instances, it is the ideal means to begin internationalization (Dalli, 1995). Through exports and a progressive internationalization process, a company gains economies of scale and scope and diversifies its market destinations. The firm also gains new sources of income and may find new sources of ideas for product and process innovations (Golovko and Valentini, 2011). The Swedish school, through the so-called "Uppsala model," developed the business internationalization model (Johanson and Vahlne, 1977), which focuses on a gradual process in stages. In the context of this model, four stages of internationalization are identified: exports, installation of marketing offices abroad, internationalization of the value chain (imports of inputs), and investment for production in the main destination markets (Johanson and Wiedersheim-Paul, 1975).

In the case of e-commerce firms such as Agroads, some (or all) of these steps may be bypassed, for, in essence, these firms are born global. Yet, because of a number of barriers their actual reach may only be national or regional. Some of those barriers are language, transaction restrictions (currency, payment methods, legal limitations, etc.), and delivery and logistics. For example, although Agroads' platform has the potential to expand into neighboring countries where the same language is spoken (Spanish is also spoken in Uruguay, Paraguay, Chile, and Bolivia) other problems preclude its diffusion in its current format. In fact, Agroads' expansion in Brazil has required not only the use of a different language (Portuguese) but the development of a different platform.

Agroads began its entry into Brazil a few years ago. The Brazilian website currently has 600,000 users operating on its platform and close to two million visits. The growth of agriculture in Brazil and the COVID-19 pandemic have encouraged a greater use of this digital platform among farmers.

Thus, although Agroads' initial Argentinian platform was, in fact, born global, other factors limit the immediate global reach of the site. Paradoxically, the internationalization process is not checked by physical restrictions: physical borders have been crossed from the very beginning. An "analog geography" has, in fact, been superseded by a virtual network. Yet, several new restrictions and problems need to be solved. Perhaps surprisingly, local issues such as legal restrictions, transaction limitations, the nature of local supplies, and logistics problems pose barriers and limitations that require new solutions.

Industry 4.0 in SMEs in Emerging Markets

The level of diffusion of the new technologies involved in the so-called Industry 4.0 (I40) is still incipient in Latin America. The I40 has two dimensions. On the one hand, the top-down policies in which governments encourage the productive system to adopt the engines of this technological revolution. And, on the other, the business dimension promoted by large transnational companies and the network of smaller firms making up any value chain. The main motivations of SMEs for the incorporation of these new technologies are: the need to solve a number of business problems, the search for process efficiency, and the willingness to deliver higher quality products and services to customers. Digitization poses a qualitative leap for SMEs that forces them to rethink their operations. In that process, connections with customers and suppliers need to be revised while the skills of human resources have to be updated. The term I40 refers to a new model of organization of production processes and control of the value chain based on information and communication technologies. It is based on the possibility of configuring "intelligent" factories that will integrate the physical with the virtual, which implies the articulation of computer systems and manufacturing processes, the deployment of decentralized decisions and "self-organizing" optimization mechanisms (McKinsey, 2016; Basco et al., 2018).

The case of Agroads differs from what has been pointed out for "analog" SMEs as it operates in the ICT industry and by its very nature the company seeks to overcome the typical obstacles that SMEs must face in economies such as Argentina's. Some of these obstacles are: the lack of knowledge about these new technologies; the lack of infrastructure; limited connectivity; the shortage of qualified human resources; culture, organizational habits and resistance to change; the difficulties of access to financing; and the deficiencies of the education and training system; among others. The partition of the production process and virtual internationalization allow Agroads to operate efficiently and competitively (Motta et al., 2019).

Of the set of digital technologies that comprise the I40 and affect production processes, the following can be highlighted: Internet of Things (IoT), advanced and collaborative robotics; big data, data science or data mining; cloud computing, artificial intelligence and machine learning; additive or 3D printing; and virtual reality and augmented reality. The case of Agroads presents as one of its competitive advantages the combination of the following technological vectors of the I40: IoT + Big Data + Machine Learning + Cybersecurity + Virtual Reality + Cloud Computing. This combination enables its business model to integrate the information systems of suppliers, clients, and other users in the e-commerce platform.

STUDENT CHALLENGES

Discussion Questions

1. Why do you think agriculture is considered a traditional sector? Why would the introduction of digital technologies be particularly disruptive?
2. How can digital technology support the internationalization of the firm? Identify opportunities, obstacles, and barriers to adoption.
3. How would a similar situation unfold in the context of your country or region? Choose another example of a marketplace/industry and discuss the internationalization opportunities enabled by digital technologies that it offers.

Assignments

1. Summarize the factors that were key in the development of Agroads as a technological business.
2. Which of the Industry 4.0 vectors do you see applied in the case of Agroads? Do some additional research on these technological enablers and identify possible applications for small businesses and which obstacles may hinder adoption.
3. What alternative business models might the company consider adopting? Is business model-driven innovation an option for the company? Identify and sketch an alternative business model using the Business Model Canvas.

NOTES

1. Pampas, literally "plains," is a large natural region in Center-East Argentina. This region concentrates some of the major cities of the country and the most fertile land for agriculture. It is currently dedicated mostly to the extensive cultivation of soybeans, wheat, maize, sorghum, and other middle-latitude crops. Other activities are also carried out such as cattle raising, dairy, and others.

REFERENCES

Agroads (2020). 15th Anniversary Celebration. https://youtu.be/24dC8Os35PM.
Agroads (2022). Official Blog. https://blog.agroads.com.ar/.

Albornoz, I. (2006). "Software para el sector agropecuario." Universidad Nacional de General Sarmiento, LITTEC. https://www.academia.edu/19783502/Software_para_el_sector_agropecuario.

Basco, A., Beliz, G., Coatz, D., and Garnero, P. (2018, July). *Industria 4.0 Fabricando el futuro*. UIA, BID, INTAL.

Dalli, D. (1995). The organization of exporting activities: Relationships between internal and external arrangements. *Journal of Business Research*, 34(2), 107–115.

FAO (2017). *The Future of Food and Agriculture*. http://www.fao.org/3/i6881s/i6881s.pdf.

Golovko, E. and Valentini, G. (2011). Exploring the complementary between innovation and export for SMEs' growth. *Journal of International Business Studies*, 42, 362–380.

IADB (2021). *Overview of the Agribusiness Ecosystem for Small Farmers in Latin America and the Caribbean*. Inter-American Development Bank. https://publications.iadb.org/publications/spanish/document/Panorama-del-ecosistema-agrotecnologico-para-los-pequenos-agricultores-de-America-Latina-y-el-Caribe.pdf.

Johanson, J. and Vahlne, J. E. (1977). The internationalization process of the firm: A model of knowledge development and increasing foreign market commitments. *Journal of International Business Studies*, 8(1), 23–32.

Johanson, J. and Wiedersheim-Paul, F. (1975). The internationalization of the firm: Four Swedish cases. *Journal of Management Studies*, 12, 305–322.

Lu, J. and Beamish, P. (2001). The internationalization and performance of SMES. *Strategic Management Journal*, 22(6–7), 565–586.

McKinsey (2016, August). *Lo digital en la industria: From buzzword to value creation* (ed. Caylar, P.-L., Noterdaeme, O. and Naik, K.). McKinsey Digital.

Motta, J., Morero, H., and Ascúa, R. (2019). *La industria 4.0 en las mipymes manufactureras de Argentina*. United Nations publication LC/TS.2019/93. CEPAL.

Sotomayor, O., Ramírez, E. and Martínez, H. (coords.) (2021). *Digitalization and Technological Change in Agricultural and Agro-Industrial SMEs in Latin America*. Project documents (LC/TS.2021/65), Santiago, Economic Commission for Latin America and the Caribbean (ECLAC)/Food and Agriculture Organization of the United Nations (FAO).

6. Leveraging collaboration between academic research and SMEs to support digital transformation in the agri-food Italian industry: the case of Santomiele

Roberto Parente, Rosangela Feola and Ricky Celenta

LEARNING OBJECTIVES

- Understand opportunities provided by the Internet of Things (IoT) to innovate a traditional agricultural business, especially in food processing.
- Frame digital transformation as a strategy to transform a threat into an opportunity.
- Learn how digital technological innovation can help companies to restructure their value chain.
- Become familiar with the concept of entrepreneurial orientation and its impact on the propensity of an SME to innovate.
- Understand the importance of the collaboration between universities as a way to support the successful digitalization of SMEs.

INTRODUCTION

> Ours is a true art of quality craftsmanship and we distinguish ourselves by always focusing on a high-quality production cycle that combines history, tradition and the search for new flavours. (Antonio Longo, Speech at the United Nations on May 12, 2018, New York)

The tolling of the bell from a thirteenth- century church in the historic town of Prignano Cilento (Italy) surprised Antonio Longo and Corrado Del Verme on the balcony of their company building, as they enjoyed the view of the undulating landscape of southern Italy. They were proud that their work as entrepreneurs in the local farming industry had helped to preserve and valorize the landscape that they cherish. The goal that the two friends and partners set themselves 20 years before had been achieved only in part. Preserving the landscape and valorizing the area and its culture in a sustainable and financially viable way seemed to be an endless task. But the ambition for continuous improvement is in the entrepreneurial–DNA of Antonio and Corrado. The search for new solutions to improve their products, contribute to the promotion of their region, Cilento, and enhance the economy of their immediate community is an undeniably key component in Santomiele's strategy.

Cilento is an area with an agricultural vocation and a predominantly rural social character and economy. In the last few decades, almost all the young people have emigrated abroad or to the north of Italy in search of work in industry or in the public sector. Although nowadays the situation has improved, job opportunities remain few and the area still endures a high rate of emigration. As a consequence, the average age in Cilento is today about 55 years old and many villages in the mountains are being abandoned.

Against these negative trends, the Cilento region has become increasingly more popular at home and abroad as a tourist destination because of its natural beauty, slow lifestyle and, in particular, for the "Mediterranean diet."[1]

This popularity is partly due to the work of entrepreneurs like Antonio and Corrado, who have been able to valorize and export the "Cilento" brand all over the world through its excellent agricultural and natural food processing traditions.

Fig farming in Cilento has changed considerably as a result of the popularity Santomiele has generated. In recent years, the success of the product determined the arrival of new competitors which, along with the generational change, put Santomiele's supply systems under considerable stress. Antonio and Corrado had to face a supply crisis, a real threat to the company's business. The main risk for the company was that they might end up with not enough figs to process or with a supply of figs that does not meet Santomiele's high quality standards.

In response to these threats, Antonio and Corrado initiated a process of digital transformation of their business. With the support of the local university (Salerno), they developed a technological solution based on the Internet of Things, which allowed them to innovate a critical process in the processing of the figs. The solution developed to tackle a supply threat ended up allowing Santomiele to innovate a process and create a new product: a new type of drying oven. Antonio and Corrado have now numerous strategic opportunities in front of them, but they are unsure about which ones they should pursue.

One big dilemma is whether they should choose to change their supply chain by providing technology to their suppliers or to internalize some critical processes. Still another option could be to diversify their business by developing a new industrial product to sell to other companies.

Antonio and Corrado have not figured out a solution yet, but they are happy that one threat has given rise to several opportunities. Now they have to choose which direction to take. This is a crucial decision for the future of the company, but to grasp its true importance it is necessary to first discover the history of Santomiele.

COMPANY AND INDUSTRY OVERVIEW

The Santomiele Story: A Modern-Day Business Fairy Tale

The history of Santomiele began in 1930, when Antonio Longo (senior) returned from Argentina with the savings of years of work. He bought a six-hectare estate bordering a small plot of land he had inherited from his father in a rural locality called Santomiele, not far from the ruins of the ancient Greek town of Paestum in southern Italy.

With the help of some farmers, he planted about 3,000 fig and olive trees. Antonio's plan was to grow produce and sell it to food companies, who would process it to make products such as olive oil and dried figs, a sweet delicacy popular in Italy and now also in other countries. Thus, his business was far upstream in the food processing industry value chain and most of the added value ended up in the hands of food processing companies, with little margin left to farmers like Antonio.

Source: Courtesy of Santomiele.

Figure 6.1   *Fresh figs*

Source: Courtesy of Santomiele.

Figure 6.2   Dried figs

Fresh white Cilento figs (Figure 6.1) are dehydrated (Figure 6.2) by exposing figs to air and sun. This is a necessary step in the processing and storing of figs, which are easily perishable. Drying must commence within 24 hours of harvesting. The dehydration process increases the concentration of sugar in the fruit and transforms figs into a quite natural and healthy dessert.

Back in 1930 Antonio would have never dreamt that one day his dried figs would be served at the table of Queen Elizabeth II and sold in fancy gourmet stores around the world. The quality and quantity of the figs he grew rose steadily, reaching 5,000 kg (about 11,000 pounds) of annual dry product by the end of the 1950s. However, after Antonio's death in the 1970s, the company began a slow decline which eventually led to the cessation of the business.

In the mid-1990s, Mr. Longo's grandson, whose name was also Antonio, had recently graduated in geology at the Sapienza University of Rome, and returned to his native land determined to set up a business and a home there. He met his friend Corrado Del Verme, an employee at a local bank.

Antonio and Corrado understood that the only way they would achieve their professional and personal objectives was to create value for their community by enhancing Cilento's inland areas. These had great potential but, as their economy was still mostly based on low value-added supply chains and backward agricultural practices, they had been left out of the more prosperous developments taking place along the coast. The old estate was now almost completely abandoned, but Antonio wanted to start out from that old shed and those fig trees and build something beautiful. He knew that he could not make it alone; he needed the managerial skills and entrepreneurial intuition of his friend Corrado. One day, while visiting the old estate, the two friends made a promise to each other: they would resuscitate, innovate, and make a profitable business out of an ancient local tradition, the production of dried white figs.

In southern Italy, figs are grown mainly in the Campania and Calabria regions. Back in the day, fig farming had its share in the Italian agricultural production, reaching its maximum yield at the end of the 1950s with 60,000 tons of figs produced and exported worldwide. However, the dried figs had never been considered a specialty product and were sold in bulk on the market at very cheap prices. This left minuscule margins, which translated into little profit for farmers, partly because most of these establishments were small and lacked economies of scale.

The unattractiveness of the business coupled with the transformation of the Italian economy from an agricultural to an industrial one in the 1960s slowly brought fig cultivation to a halt in Cilento. By the end of the 1990s, production had collapsed, and dried figs survived only thanks to a very limited, family-based production that was mostly destined to be sold and consumed locally.

To make things worse, figs from Asia and Africa started invading the market and were being sold at a fraction of the local price thanks to the use of cheap labor and a poor-quality production process based on the use of unhealthy and possibly toxic chemicals as well as via the addition of sugar to cover the poor taste and aroma of the produce.

In just a few decades, Cilento almost completely lost a millennium-spanning agricultural tradition that had started in the sixth century BC when ancient Greek colonizers settled in the city states of Magna Graecia such as Paestum and Velia, whose ruins are today part of the Cilento national park.

Following the competition from foreign figs and the abandonment of Cilento's local fig production, it became extremely difficult to find Cilento figs on the market, and the few available were often poorly marketed as a low value commodity. This included generic packaging and the absence of proper communication to inform customers about the history of the product, its quality, and its connection with an ancient culture and tradition.

The Company Was Born in a "Garage"

Antonio and Corrado started the business with precise ideas about their mission: "to develop an eco-sustainable company that could revitalize local traditions and innovate fig cultivation and processing while generating value for the entire territory."

The goal of the two young entrepreneurs was to transform the fig from a bulk commodity to a specialty product that could be sold with high profit margins. Their fundamental belief was that excellence could be achieved by paying the highest attention to every detail. This meant starting from the raw material and internalizing every step of the production, from the harvesting of the right fruits to packaging and proper marketing.

In 1999, with these objectives in mind, Antonio and Corrado renovated the old farmhouse, along with the old shed which they like to call their "garage," on the Santomiele estate. They invested 2,500,000 Italian liras each (equivalent to €1,800 today) to fund the Santomiele company. On that occasion, the two friends set themselves a rule: for the first few years they would not sell to friends or relatives. The goal was to face the competition head-on: the market would be the final judge of their work.

The two entrepreneurs thoroughly researched the recipes and ancient techniques for the production and conservation of dried figs, which had survived only in the memory of some old farmers and local housewives. Corrado and Antonio's vision was to take the fig back to the ancient processing method, adhering to the rhythms of Mother Nature and without resorting to any chemical treatment.

As there were only a few fig trees left on the Santomiele estate, Antonio and Corrado decided to source the product from local farmers. They selected their farmers carefully among those who applied the practices of sustainable agriculture. To obtain this supply, Antonio and Corrado paid their suppliers for the product at a substantially higher price than the current market value.

The farmers harvested and dried the fig and provided Antonio and Corrado with the product ready for the processing phase. According to classic recipes, the dried figs were used to produce peeled figs, "capicollo" of figs and dried figs with almonds (Figures 6.3 and 6.4).

Note: Figs with almonds are considered the best.
Source: Courtesy of Santomiele.

Figure 6.3   Figs with almonds

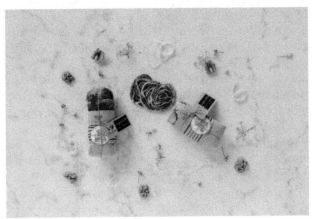

Note: A capicollo is a hand-made mixture of peeled figs mixed with walnuts, wild fennel, citrus peel and flavored with spiced rum.
Source: Courtesy of Santomiele.

Figure 6.4 *Capicollo of figs*

Antonio and Corrado were aware that to be able to make their products as natural as possible, they would have to innovate the manufacturing process. Many farmers did not hesitate to resort to an abundant use of chemical products to obtain homogeneous figs, but these techniques ended up depriving the fruits of their unique flavor and nutritional value.

Fig sterilization was the first and the most complex step of the production process that Antonio and Corrado performed in their garage. Figs dried in the open air had to be sterilized to kill bacteria and other organisms that could spoil the product and compromise its long-term preservation. Figs require a lot more heat and sunlight than other types of fruit during the drying process and attract insects as they are very sweet. The two entrepreneurs innovated the process by introducing a washing process to reduce the use of chemicals, a technique that had never been used until then. This was when Antonio and Corrado realized that the problem was too hard for them to solve on their own and that they needed help from skilled professionals with expertise in the chemistry and biology of food preservation.

They reached out to the Department of Food Engineering at the University of Salerno, and thanks to this collaboration they managed to find a viable solution for the organic sterilization of figs by washing them in water, lemon, and bicarbonate. The sterilization process took place in-house and was fully monitored, but the most critical issue was to convince fig producers not to use chemical products during the initial fig drying process. When Antonio and Corrado tried to explain the reasons behind the choice to use an organic approach, they encountered strong resistance from the farmers.

When Antonio and Corrado look back at their history, they believe that to make farmers understand the importance of using an organic approach to enhance product quality and with that the reputation of the whole territory was one of the hardest challenges for them.

Farmers would not understand at the beginning because they had been in the habit of serving a market that did not pay attention to quality. On the contrary, Antonio and Corrado's target was from the very beginning a market niche of consumers looking for superior gastronomic experience, and who can appreciate a product's superior quality and can afford to pay a premium price. The determination of the two young entrepreneurs and their ability to communicate their vision helped to convert even the most skeptical producers. Of course, the fact that Antonio and Corrado were willing to pay a higher price than their competitors to secure the best figs in Cilento helped. Finally, the company approach proved so successful that Santomiele ended each year with a profit, starting from the first year of business.

The market began to increasingly appreciate Santomiele figs, and more staff had to be hired until, in 2011, the garage of the ancient Santomiele estate had become too small for production activity. Antonio and Corrado then decided to relocate to new premises in Prignano Cilento, a strategic position from a logistical point of view as it was closer to the farmers who supplied the company.

The opening of new headquarters and the abandonment of a garage is a step that is often associated with successful Silicon Valley start-ups, which manage to open their offices in a New York skyscraper or create exclusive campuses near San Francisco. This is a bit like what happened to Corrado and Antonio, except they, loyal to their mission of contributing to the economic renaissance of their region, decided to renovate an ancient oil mill in the historic heart of Prignano (Figure 6.5).

The property is located next to the ancient Marquises' Palace of the Cardone family (seventeenth century), while the company entrance is opposite the thirteenth-century church of San Nicola di Bari. Prignano is an ancient village steeped in history and beauty, a special and highly evocative place where design, culture, and art come together to express the beauty of the territory in a culturally stratified language. This is where Antonio and Corrado moved the company's official headquarters and production laboratory.

Exploring the building is a sensory experience capable of restoring the soul. The large windows look onto the skilled local artisans who manually process the figs one by one using techniques following ancient traditions. Beauty fills the eyes, and one can enjoy a quote from Parmenides on the wall or vintage photos of an elderly peasant woman. According to Corrado and Antonio, it is precisely this attention to detail that is the secret of Santomiele's success,

Source: Courtesy of Santomiele.

Figure 6.5   The Santomiele headquarters

a success borne out by the appreciation of customers at home and abroad, including Queen Elizabeth II.

The growth of the company revenues through the years gives a quantitative measure of the success of this small business, which in 12 years managed to achieve a turnover of over €700,000 and reached over €1,100,000 in 2019 (Figure 6.6).

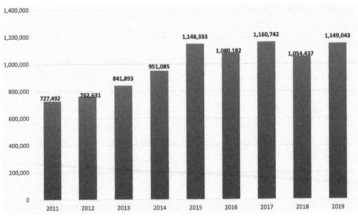

Source: Balance sheet data, re-elaborated by the authors.

Figure 6.6   Business turnover 2011–2019

Besides the attention to details, the second key element in the firm's success is the constant innovation of the ancient craft which, the authors believe, is the only way to achieve company objectives and revolutionize the fig growing sector. As Corrado likes to say, "We are always at year zero, we need to invest in research and innovation to improve our products."

Indeed, research and innovation have been fundamental to the company's growth strategy. When the Santomiele market began to grow, Antonio and Corrado realized that they could differentiate their offer and develop, or rather invent, another product: fig molasses. In collaboration with two university departments, Antonio and Corrado have made fig molasses through a process that excludes the use of machines. The combination of research and entre-preneurial spirit has led Santomiele to take the dried fig and create a product formerly considered of no value,[2] a new product registered as "La Melassa Santomiele" and sold on the company website for €250/liter ($300 per pound).

Santomiele Today: The Challenges of Digitalization

In 2020 the company counted over 50 local suppliers (mainly small, family-run businesses), 15 full time employees involved in the artisanal processing of figs and another 15 seasonal workers employed during the peak summer produc-tion phase.

The work done over the years in revolutionizing the fig growing sector and the value created for the local economy have made Antonio and Corrado "the men of fairy tales," capable of transforming the pumpkin into a carriage and Cinderella into a princess.

In 2018 Santomiele represented Europe on the UN day dedicated to small and medium-sized enterprises. What the UN particularly appreciated was Antonio and Corrado's ability to develop a sustainable business model capable of combining the enhancement of human heritage and local products, in line with the objectives of the 2030 agenda for the Sustainable Development Goals launched by the United Nations.

The story could have ended here with a "happy ending" but, as with many fairy tales, there were pitfalls and obstacles along the road. Even for Santomiele it was not yet time for "happily ever after." The last few years have seen notable changes in the Cilento fig growing sector. When Antonio and Corrado started their business, dried figs were considered a product of little value compared to other fruits. For instance, pine nuts sold for €6/kg and hazelnuts for €4/kg, while Italian figs sold for a maximum of €1.20/kg. Thanks to Antonio and Corrado, dried figs are now appreciated all over the world and sell at prices that may exceed €70/kg.

Santomiele's success has made the fig growing sector very attractive. In the wake of Santomiele's success, thousands of previously abandoned hectares in Cilento have been recovered, regenerated, and planted with fig trees. In its first 20 years of business, Santomiele generated over 1,000 new hectares of fig trees in its supply chain. A growing market and bright prospects for a product that is increasingly appreciated abroad have thus attracted other entrepreneurs seeking to carve out a market share.

Corrado and Antonio are not afraid of competition and have the same spirit of 20 years ago in seeing the market as the only true judge of their work. However, increased competition is creating challenges in ensuring supply. One problem lies in the obvious increases of price. Another challenge is that over the last few years, many of the 50 farms in the Santomiele supply chain have undergone generational change, with the result that almost all those farmers whom Antonio trained in eco-sustainable agriculture 20 years ago are no longer there. Unfortunately, in many cases the trust on which the collaboration between Santomiele and its suppliers had been based did not transfer to the younger generation.

Over the last two years, young farmers have increasingly failed to fulfill their contractual commitments to the firm. Under the typical contract, they must guarantee their supply to the company, but they frequently sell their figs to competitors for only a few euros more per kg, resulting in a serious problem for Santomiele's production.

Another critical issue concerns fig production. Given the growing market demand, some producers have been making massive use of chemical products to accelerate and increase fig production, going against the slower natural drying process and drastically impacting on quality. For Antonio and Corrado, this is unacceptable since Santomiele's brand is built on a philosophy and on values that are strongly opposed to this approach.

Ever since the beginning, Antonio and Corrado have led the company while relying on a local ecosystem of suppliers and collaborators and totally out-sourcing fig production and drying. The only land they cultivated themselves was the old farm in Santomiele. A possible solution to respond to the supply chain crisis might be to internalize the cultivation of figs. However, this solu-tion would be costly and impractical in the short term because it takes several years at best for a fig tree to become productive.

During the 2020 summer season, Corrado had an intuition that could solve most of their problems: internalizing the fig drying activity. The drying process is a critical step in the supply chain, and in the current business model it was the responsibility of the individual farmer-supplier. Corrado's idea would allow Santomiele to solve both the qualitative and the quantitative challenge in fig supply. If they bought the fresh figs, they could control the drying process and ensure no chemicals were used. At the same time, they would have a first mover advantage in purchasing the fresh figs before their competitors. For Corrado, the internalization of the drying process would offer a solution even in the short term and allow the firm to both implement the internalization of production and ensure autonomy in the long term.

However, internalizing the drying process was complex for reasons of space and time. It requires much more space than was then available to the company because the figs must dry in the sun for about 15 days. Besides, fresh figs are easily perishable, and the drying process must start as soon as they are harvested. Finally, figs are harvested in August and the classic drying methods would thus result in a seasonal bottleneck in the process and large quantities of the raw material could go to waste.

As an experienced manager, Corrado did what he had always done in the past: he studied the market to find out if there were suitable solutions for drying figs. He also analyzed other supply chains to see whether solutions developed for other types of fruit could be adopted for figs. Antonio and Corrado visited Tuscany and Emilia-Romagna, two regions in northern Italy renowned for the excellence of their agricultural practices and food processing methods, to study the operation of some machinery but without finding a solution. However, the two friends were not discouraged by their initial lack of success and came to the firm conviction that what did not exist could be invented.

They began to consider the specific features of the fig drying process and set about developing machinery capable of optimizing the process and maintaining a high level of product quality. The most critical issue that Corrado had identified in the solutions used in other supply chains was that the ovens were closed and powered by electricity. The fig, on the other hand, needs to be dried with heat and sunlight to maintain its taste and nutritional value. Furthermore, industrial ovens are expensive to run because of the surging costs of electricity.

Corrado's novel idea entailed developing an oven powered by solar energy and equipped with solar panels that stored energy to keep the oven temperature constant even during the night to enable a continuous 24-hour drying process. This solution made it possible to exploit a criticality of the fig and transform it into a strength: during the day the fig dried in the warm sunlight and the process continued through the night thanks to the electric energy generated by the solar panels.

Antonio and Corrado decided once again to innovate the fig growing market by turning to research and collaborating with the Department of Industrial Engineering at the University of Salerno. A month after the first contact with the team leader, the research group started to work on the problem.

The initial design of the solar oven aimed to simplify and speed up the fig drying process, but the prototype developed in the laboratories at the University of Salerno and at Santomiele headquarters exceeded all the expectations. It was a truly smart oven which allowed the drying process to be constantly monitored thanks to the Internet of Things technologies, which made it possible to collect data on various critical parameters, including the volume, weight and humidity of the fig, as well as environmental parameters inside the oven cells, such as temperature, humidity and airflow (see Box 6.1). The solar oven has also been patented.

BOX 6.1   THE FOCUS ON THE INTERNET OF THINGS

The expression "Internet of Things" was first formulated in 1999 by the British engineer Kevin Ashton, co-founder of the Auto-ID Center in Massachusetts. The Internet of Things (IoT) refers to the technological development whereby, over the internet, potentially every object of daily experience acquires its own identity in the digital world. The IoT is based on the idea of "smart" objects interconnected to exchange information owned, collected and/or processed.

The IoT is a paradigm that, potentially, knows no application boundaries: from cars that communicate with the road infrastructure to prevent accidents to home appliances that coordinate to optimize power management, and production plants that exchange data with manufactured goods for the management of their life cycle.

The technological revolution of the IoT can be accomplished across all areas. Companies in any sector use IoT solutions to collect a great deal of information on the functioning of devices and on the people who use them through the multiplication and evolution of connected devices.

The evolution of the IoT in terms of market and technologies is facilitated by its integration into the main innovative trends on the digital scene. In this sense, big data, artificial intelligence and blockchain represent increasingly important pieces of the IoT ecosystem because they can foster new business opportunities, new features and new services starting from IoT devices and their connected objects.

Identifying the optimal drying point required a long period of observation, experimentation and empirical data collection in close collaboration with the computer engineers of the university research group. By monitoring and analyzing the data, it was possible to observe that at certain times of day the temperature in the oven would exceed 70°C (158°F), which significantly compromised the drying process. This led to the development of a solution to cool the oven to keep the temperature constant. Through suitable adjustments and modifications of the initial prototype, the research group was eventually able to optimize the drying process.

For now, the figs are placed in the oven and then subsequently removed manually by the operator. What changes is the determination of the optimal drying point, as the technology supports the operator's decision-making process. The operator's experience is no longer a crucial feature, but it maintains an important role within the process in terms of supervision and quality control. This solution ensures greater consistency in the final quality of the products. In addition to increasing quality, the solar oven allows Santomiele to halve the drying process from 15 to 7 days.

The solar oven is a "smart" solution, which allows the company to innovate the fig transformation process (Figure 6.7). The digitalization of the transformation process generates large amounts of data on fig volume, temperature, hydration level, etc. This data is analyzed in the university laboratories by the research team and included in reports to company employees. By analyzing this information, Santomiele's experienced employees can enhance the production process to upgrade final product quality. Digitalization makes it possible to both improve the production process and offer the final consumer more information about the product, thus increasing the company's value proposition.

Source: Courtesy of Santomiele.

Figure 6.7   *The prototype of the solar oven*

Given the positive results achieved in drying figs, Antonio and Corrado also tested the oven with other types of fruit. The tests returned excellent results in terms of both time and product quality. As the fig drying process uses the oven for only two months a year, the oven was tested with other types of fruit to explore the possibility of introducing new products and diversifying the product mix.

PROBLEM STATEMENT: SANTOMIELE AND ITS CHALLENGE TO BUILD THE FUTURE

Admiring the landscape at the foot of the ancient Church of San Nicola, Antonio and Corrado still think about the theme of the meeting: how to make the most of this digital innovation?

The choice to differentiate the product mix could certainly be a smart decision for the firm, as it offers the opportunity both to repay the costs of the ovens and to enter new markets.

Corrado felt it was time for Santomiele to increase production even before the supply chain crisis. He has also had a dream for several years: to set up the Cilento Fig Consortium. In his view, the development of the district could create the conditions to relaunch the whole local economy in an even more important way. To achieve this goal, Santomiele could rent the solar oven to all farmers, so that even those with little experience could carry out the drying activity and thus supply a greater quantity of figs so that the Santomiele company could increase sale volumes. Leasing the oven to farmers would allow them to obtain better and standardized products, retain farmers and innovate the entire fig chain, generating value for the entire area. Furthermore, this approach would allow Antonio and Corrado to overcome the limitations of controlling the fig drying process by farmers, thus avoiding the mandatory internalization of the process.

Another viable path would be to produce the ovens and then sell them to other fruit-drying companies. These are mainly located in Spain, North Africa and South America, so the solar oven solution could also be very useful for reducing pollution and costs related to heating the ovens. The oven is a technological solution that preserves and enhances ancient drying traditions. Powered by solar energy and with no use of chemicals, the oven has zero impact on the environment. The characteristics of the smart oven would make it attractive for the large sector of dried fruit. Commercializing this solution, however, would require an industrial and commercial partner and perhaps a new joint venture.

The oven is now only a patented prototype, but Antonio and Corrado see opportunities in all possible alternative applications. However, they realize that they must make a timely decision because their sector is changing, the fig supply chain is attracting more and more entrepreneurs and it is becoming increasingly difficult to find quality raw materials.

Antonio and Corrado are thinking about strategic choices, following a digital technological innovation. The options mainly concern whether to pursue objectives related to the differentiation of products or the restructuring of the value chain.

The two partners are faced with two main variables to consider: the time and resources necessary to implement the various choices.

STUDENT CHALLENGES: DISCUSSION QUESTIONS

1. Summarize the business challenges and the key management character-istics that enabled digital innovation at Santomiele. Analyze traditional (non-digital) SMEs running traditional and/or artisanal businesses in your city/region. How could digital technologies be used to solve problems and/or improve their business?
2. Analyze the case and summarize the successful elements of the collabo-ration between the university and Santomiele. Analyzing your university (especially the technological transfer point) and the entrepreneurial eco-system in the area, what opportunities do you think there are for collabo-ration in the digital transformation of SMEs? What would be the benefits for SMEs? And the benefits of research?
3. The entrepreneurs identified three different options to exploit the devel-oped innovation (differentiating the offer; restructuring the value chain; enlarging business activity by selling the innovation). Antonio and Corrado have not yet decided what to do. Put yourself in their shoes and try to answer the following questions as a consultant:
    (a)   What are the benefits and risks of each option?
    (b)   How could each option be implemented?
    (c)   Have all possibilities been considered?

ACKNOWLEDGMENTS

We are extremely grateful to Antonio Longo and Corrado Del Verme for their time and hospitality. We also extend our thanks to the research team of Prof. Antonio Pietrosanto, and to PhD student Marco Carratù, for the time devoted to us and for helping us understand the development of the solar oven.

NOTES

1.   This diet is diffused in many countries surrounding the Mediterranean such as Greece, Spain, Italy, and North Africa. It is characterized by an abundance of vegetables, fruits, seeds, smaller proportion of carbs, and limited intake of meat and animal fat. The physiologist Ancel Keys and his wife studied the diet extensively and found evidence that it was associated with lower-than-average incidence in the population of certain diseases such as cardiovascular problems and diabetes, among others. Ancel Keys spent many years in Cilento studying local habits and medical records. A museum dedicated to his work and to the

Mediterranean diet was established in Acciaroli after UNESCO in 2010 recognized the diet as part of the immaterial human cultural heritage.
2. In Cilento, if a person is compared to a dry fig, it means they are of little use or value.

REFERENCES

InfoagropoliTV (2021, November 6). *La Lavorazione dei Fichi del Cilento.* YouTube. Retrieved April 6, 2022, from https://www.youtube.com/watch?v=0mjH3bPSe64 (Video-documentary on Santomiele).

Opificio Santomiele – Prignano cilento. (2018, February 28). YouTube. Retrieved April 6, 2022, from https://youtu.be/47QIlkbNdno (Interview with Antonio Longo).

Santomiele (n.d.). Retrieved April 6, 2022, from https://santomiele.it/ (Santomiele website).

7. Bringing the traditional farm into the digital era: entrepreneurship with digitalization and diversification

Anna Sörensson and Maria Bogren

LEARNING OBJECTIVES

- Students will learn how traditional industry can gain a competitive advantage through the adoption of digital technologies.
- Students will gain skills on how entrepreneurs can broaden their business through diversification with the help of digitalization.
- Students will develop and gain skills to create a plan to help the farm develop further in the digital marketing arena.
- Students will discuss and gain skills on how communication from a traditional industry can be developed through digital marketing.
- Students will learn how sustainability can be an asset for entrepreneurs within nature-based businesses.
- Students will learn how a farm may educate its customers.

INDUSTRY AND BUSINESS OVERVIEW

Nature-Based Businesses

Nature-based businesses are businesses within agriculture, forestry, landscape management, and other natural resource-based commercial activities in rural areas. Nature-based businesses include traditional businesses such as agriculture and forestry (Figure 7.1) and new emerging businesses based on nature's resources, such as tourism.

Figure 7.1   Traditional agriculture within the nature-based businesses

Entrepreneurs in these businesses are considered to have a good forecast for growth and development since there is a high demand for products and services such as locally produced food, renewable energy, nature experiences, and rural tourism (Pettersson and Arora-Jonsson 2009). In rural areas, these businesses provide significant income and are therefore of great importance where business development is concerned. Nature-based businesses are often seen as providing a way of living for entrepreneurs with a certain value and vision (Pettersson and Arora-Jonsson 2009). Politicians often see this industry as having the potential for growing and creating new businesses. Since this industry is of such importance, it is interesting to see how these entrepreneurs develop their business ideas using digitalization.

Over the years, nature-based businesses have struggled with, for example, the decline in milk prices and access to slaughterhouses. Today, another struggle for these businesses is how to get into the digital area. Many countries consider food production a vital industry, but it is surrounded by strict regulations and subsidy systems. Despite the availability of subsidies, European agriculture has suffered from political changes that have led to less support for entrepreneurs with nature-based businesses such as agricultural businesses, which has led to an added focus on tourism. These changes have resulted in a steady decline in agricultural businesses (Suess-Reyes and Fuetsch 2016). Previous research has shown that diversifying businesses into tourism, for example, is one way to create new business using existing resources such as buildings, labor, or equipment. Hansson et al. (2013) have shown the importance of, for instance, farm diversification into the tourism sector and how this may change the identity of farmers (Vik and McElwee 2011). Today's society is moving rapidly towards a more digitalized future. Today, digitalization is a must for companies to increase productivity and remain competitive in the market. Digitalization in business can improve interaction between companies and customers, which often results in increased cost efficiency.

For many entrepreneurs running nature-based businesses, the primary motivation is the lifestyle they can offer and how they can be run as family concerns. Starting a business is often triggered by personal lifestyle goals combined with the goal of living in a certain rural area, which often opposes pure economic driving forces (Andersson Cederholm 2015). Entrepreneurs with nature-based businesses are often driven by the desire to choose their lifestyle. Nature-based businesses are also often family enterprises due to family tradition (Anthias and Mehta 2003), and many farms have been passed from one generation to the next. Andersson Cederholm (2015) argues that family interests, personal lifestyle, leisure, and commercial interests are all important dimensions when discussing nature-based businesses with entrepreneurs, who might not be driven by purely economic factors. Previous research has also shown the importance of tradition and heritage among entrepreneurs in nature-based businesses (Figure 7.2). These reasons are important for understanding what motivates

Figure 7.2   *Traditional farming and its lifestyle, often with the cattle on summer pasture*

entrepreneurs regarding nature-based businesses (Getz and Carlsen 2000; Hildenbrand and Hennon 2005; Andersson Cederholm 2015). It is important to realize that different types of entrepreneurs exist within this industry, and they have different goals for their businesses (Sörensson and Dalborg 2017). It is essential for entrepreneurs to understand how the digital market affects them in today's world. It can be anything from reaching existing customers to finding new customer segments, building brands, and creating an awareness of the lifestyle as a nature-based entrepreneur.

The Jamtland farm is a family business run by Anna Jacobson and Stefan Johnson. In addition to themselves, they have one full-time employee on the farm and two employees who work as needed. Their four children also help with farming on special occasions, such as during harvest. Anna and Stefan grew up on farms in the same small village. When they were young, Anna's family farm had cattle and horses. Stefan's family farm was not run as a farm during that time, but it had been run as a farm by his grandparents at an earlier time. Anna and Stefan started their working life in very different professions; Anna worked for the municipality, and Stefan worked as a carpenter. Many studies discuss how farmers often are combiners or hybrid entrepreneurs, meaning they have other work besides working on a farm. While this was the case for Anna and Stefan when they had jobs outside their farm, as the farm grew and the children came into focus, the farm became their primary work and income.

Farmers' motivation for diversifying is complex and includes many considerations other than economic reasons. The motivation underlying farmers' decision making is possibly context-dependent and therefore embedded in and dependent on their business situation (Hansson et al. 2013). Many farms are run like family businesses; therefore, the family's situation may play a more important role when decisions are made to expand the farm. When Anna and Stefan had children, it became more important for them to work in their home village and not have to commute. From that day, the farm developed from a small farm to one of the largest cattle farms in the region. The two owners started their business on Stefan's farm and later included the barn on Anna's homestead. After that, they purchased other farms and have additional pasture for the animals during the summer.

Today, the Jamtland farm consists of several farms, with the two original ones in the same village as their main base. Their business has several parts: cultivation of barley and wheat, cows that produce milk, and cattle, pigs and lambs for meat production (Figure 7.3). The milk from the cows is their main income, and it is sold to the local dairy company. During the moose-hunting season, they also hunt and sell moose meat and further processed products from the meat such as sausages and lambskin from the lambs. The animals are sent away for slaughter, and then the meat is returned to the farm and sold to private consumers. The farm covers around 1,100 hectares, which also contains forest that they occasionally sell to a Swedish timber company. They grow food for the animals (Figure 7.4), except protein supplements for the cows. The protein supplement is integral for the milk, but at the same time, it represents a significant cost for the Jamtland farm.

The legal structure of the farm is two individual limited companies. Stefan's company focuses on the cows, both in terms of milk and meat, while Anna's company covers sheep breeding. This structure exists because larger farms are subject to a permit requirement, and in 2000, the maximum limit for a company was 200 animal units. Because the Jamtland farm had more than 200 animal units, it was divided into two companies. Today, the maximum limit is 400 animal units, but the Jamtland farm has continued with two limited companies.

Figure 7.3   Barley is one of the products from the fields

The company has been making a living from milk production since 1993 and is stable in the market, as they deliver milk to a large milk buyer. Their location in the region is relatively central, which means it is not as costly to transport the milk as it would be if they were more remotely located. Because they are relatively central and have been in the industry for a long time, they have an advantage, and they are within the degree of maturity in the product life cycle.

Figure 7.4   *Wheat is another crop that grows on the farm*

Technological and Digital Development Over the Years

When Anna and Stefan started their business at the farm in 1993, they had a large mobile phone, which was expensive to buy and use but gave them the flexibility to be reached in the barn and fields. They also had an answering machine and a fax machine. At that time, they used the computer as a typewriter and for bookkeeping. The approach to the computer then was a fear that something might go wrong or that a data virus could infect it.

The Jamtland farm was very early with digitalization in the barn. They were one of the first in the region to digitalize when they installed milk robots in 2003. The cows walk by themselves into the barn to the robots when they need to be milked, and the computer program monitors the animals. It is possible to see the amount of milk and measure the salinity to see if there is any udder inflammation. In 2021, the Jamtland farm invested in the next generation of new and modern milk robots. The computer program is now even more advanced. Via a computer placed in the barn or via a mobile phone application, the owners can see when the cows burst, are pregnant or need extra energy. Other measurements are how much fat, protein, bacteria, and white blood cells the milk contains. They can also follow the status of all the cows, for example, which of them has "milk permission" for the moment, allowing them to be milked. If the farmers need to do something with a specific cow, they program the computer to lock that cow in a special box and not release her until they have done what is needed. Both Anna and Stefan are constantly connected to the milk robots' computer program and use their mobile phones extensively for monitoring and controlling the cows. Their barn is one of the most modern and technologically advanced in the region.

Another digital investment for the production was the modern John Deere tractor they bought in 2018. This tractor has many settings for driving. With its GPS puck, it is possible to program a running track with precision. This can be used, for example, when spreading fertilizer or sowing. A considerable advantage is that they can fertilize more where needed and less where not needed, which reduces the risk of eutrophication.

Anna and Stefan reflect on the bookkeeping program they have used for more than 25 years and the contact with authorities that has developed over the years. Now, the bookkeeping program systematizes everything clearly, and they can digitally send all that is needed directly to the tax authorities. All their contacts with authorities regarding applications and decisions of different grants for farmers are handled digitally. Anna and Stefan prefer the smooth handling of things with authorities digitally and whenever it suits them instead of being dependent on office hours. They state that they would not be able to run the farm today without the internet, either the operation or the administration.

Inside the operation, they have been up to date for a long time with digital solutions, but they could improve their relationships with customers. The Jamtland farm does not have a webpage, but in 2018 they started to sell directly to customers via the "REKO-ring." REKO-ring means fair consumption, and the business idea is to connect producers and consumers within a given area to sell and buy local food, using Facebook as a communicative platform. The REKO-ring is both a concept and a digital tool and was presented in Sweden in 2016. It is a non-profit organization. Anna posts information on the REKO-ring Facebook page about what the farm sells. Then she takes and confirms orders from customers there. She thinks it is an excellent direct sales method: "It is simple and easy; I know what to bring because the customers book in advance. It is focused in time, and the customers pay via Swish" (a Swedish pay solution via mobile phone).

About the time they started to sell their products via the REKO-ring, Anna also developed a Facebook page for the farm. Anna got some help from their children to get started, but she has managed the page independently since then. The main goal of their Facebook page is to provide information about the farm and their products and to use it for contact with customers. Anna and Stefan also see their Facebook page as a valuable tool to inform their neighbors, for example, when they fertilize the fields or if animals are escaping. In addition, they have an educational ambition to write about what happens on a farm since many young people today do not have any connection to farming. Anna thinks it is convenient to communicate with customers via Messenger, SMS, or email, while Stefan still prefers to speak with customers and other contacts directly on the phone.

Some milestones in the business were when they built a new modern barn on their farm with space for more animals and installed solar panels that supply the barn with electricity. Another milestone for the barn was in 2021 when they bought a new state-of-the-art milk robot plant to replace the older one. Another crucial milestone in their business was a few years ago, when they ended the collaboration with the large slaughterhouse and the use of the large meat producer as a sales channel, to instead turn to a smaller slaughterhouse and sell the meat from beef, lamb, pig and moose to an increasing extent directly to the customer (Figure 7.5). However, the milk is still sold via intermediaries. A few years ago, they also developed the business by raising sheep and selling lamb and skins from the slaughtered animals directly to consumers (Figures 7.6–7.8). This led to some new customers for the farm and a need to better communicate directly with their customers. Selling via REKO-ring was one way of doing this. During the time they have operated the farm, they have constantly developed the operation and management with new technology and have diversified their business with new products.

Figure 7.5   *Pigs at the farm*

PROBLEM STATEMENT

Anna and Stefan at the Jamtland farm have taken advantage of the opportunities digitalization can provide today when it comes to the production and administration of the farm. However, there remains development to be done at the farm. They can develop their direct sales to new consumer segments, take care of their new business ideas and develop them, work more with how they can facilitate relationship-building digitally, pursue their educational ambitions towards customers, and use their sustainability concern more in their marketing

Today, the farm sells products to different customer segments. The largest customer is the intermediator for milk production, which is a stable customer. Presently, they sell lamb (Figure 7.6), beef, and moose meat directly to consumers, which means the customer has more options and can be more easily attracted to purchase. Anna tells us that meat prices are high, and the demand for locally produced meat is positive when the product is trendy in today's society (Figure 7.7). The meat is sold both to restaurants and private customers via direct sales. Both segments value food that is locally produced. The customers are willing to pay a higher price to gain a better product of higher quality. They are also aware of the social and environmental dimensions and that the products are produced in the region and contribute to work opportunities and shorter transportation. The customer base for the farm's direct meat sales can be increased. Which customer segments should the farm target? Could they be more specific in the segmentation of the private customer group?

The farm also distributes products for direct sale. Most of these sales take place via the REKO-ring and directly from the farm, which works well. However, can this distribution be developed more? Here, they need to make strategic choices: Are they providing the right meat products? Should they have a website with ordering features, like a webshop? Is the Facebook page or the REKO-ring the best choice for direct sales? What should the website and Facebook page be used for? At the moment, customers who visit the farm to buy meat make their purchases in a building with many freezers. Anna has a dream of a more welcoming farm shop. Maybe this is something to plan for in the development of the farm. Overall, how can the farm's transfer to more direct sales be facilitated by increased use of digital media for orders/confirmations and more extensive marketing of the farm?

Anna and Stefan have a lot of ideas and visions to expand and increase sales and turnover. Diversification of the farm can give them income from different customer segments. Anna speaks warmly about the possibility for customers to visit the farm, for example, by staying in a guest house. The Jamtland farm has several empty buildings on the property that can be used for various purposes in the future, including a restaurant, farm shop, and bed and breakfast (B&B). These ventures would depart from the previous products and expand their traditional products. Farms in the region have had events such as when the cows are released from the barns in the spring. Anna has even thought that such an experience could take place online and on the farm. Their ideas about people visiting and staying at the farm can shape new business ideas that need to be developed in a more detailed way. A marketing mix (price, place, product, and promotion) should be discussed for each idea. Which consumer segments does the farm want to reach for the farm shop, restaurant, and bed and breakfast, and how should they reach them? It is crucial to launch innovations correctly in time. Being too early or late on the market can result in the loss of customer relationships because a competitor is already providing what consumers ask for.

The Jamtland farm has stable relationships with its customers, which for the most part consist of regular customers and acquaintances. They have great opportunities to develop their network of contacts and nurture their current customer relationships with the help of marketing and becoming more active on social media. This is a crucial issue for them: How can they facilitate relationship-building digitally with both existing and future customers? Nurturing the company's customer relationships can also improve the company's ability to succeed with innovations and realize new ideas. Their knowledge about marketing and social media is limited, and Anna and Stefan realize that more marketing efforts are required. They only have a Facebook page at this time, but they would like to have a proper homepage. The farm also needs a logotype that visualizes its different business areas. Anna handles the Facebook page since Stefan has no interest in that. She gets some help and ideas from their children, but the staff working in the barn are not involved in handling the Facebook page. Anna understands that they need to improve in updating and being active on their Facebook page, but she does not have enough time. How can they develop their relationship marketing in social media? Which social media channels should they use, and for what? What kind of values could the logotype and homepage communicate? What kind of functions should the homepage have?

Another ambition Anna and Stefan have is educational since many young people today do not know much about farming and animals. In this respect, they could welcome school classes at the farm. Anna is interested in teaching their existing customers and society about farm life and their animals. She feels that there is a lack of knowledge regarding how food is produced in today's society, and she thinks they have an educational responsibility. This educational ambition could be done both through study visits like inviting schools to the farm and through information in digital channels. How could the farm work with its educational ambition through digital channels and study visits for different segments?

The Jamtland farm is environmentally conscious, and so are its consumers. Consumers today ask for locally produced food and food that has not been transported a long way. While the farm is not certified according to any label, Anna and Stefan try to be aware of sustainability in all they do. Anna says they try to maintain an active environmental mindset. For example, regarding the slaughter of moose on the farm, they reduce the environmental impact in the form of transport. Customers are asking for ecological products, but the farm has not had time to investigate if this is a good investment. The farm owners are aware that sustainability from different perspectives affects customers, and perhaps sustainability is something they should be more focused on in their digital marketing strategy. How can they show the farm's sustainability efforts on social media? What should they consider if they apply for sustainability certification for the farm?

Overall, the Jamtland farm has expanded and used digital technology to facilitate Anna and Stefan's work. Now, they can take the next step in using digitalization to develop relationships with different customer segments based on the farm's diversified business.

Figure 7.6   *Sheep at the farm*

Figure 7.7   Meat products that are sold from the farm

Figure 7.8   Sheepskin that the farm sells directly to customers

STUDENT CHALLENGES

- How would you advise the company to leverage digital communication to grow its business?
- What digital market strategy should they embrace concerning existing and new business ideas?
- How would you create a plan to help the company develop further in the digital marketing arena?
- How can this farm leverage digitalization to grow its businesses in a sustainable way?
- How can the farm use sustainability in its digital marketing strategy?
- What other ideas do you have for the company in terms of identifying entrepreneurial opportunities associated with digitalization?
- How would you recommend the farm work with its educational ambition towards teaching different customer segments and through different channels?

REFERENCES AND ADDITIONAL READING

Andersson Cederholm, E. (2015). Lifestyle enterprising: The 'ambiguity work' of Swedish horse-farmers. *Community, Work & Family*, 18(3), 317–333.

Anthias, F. and Mehta, N. (2003). The intersection between gender, the family and self-employment: The family as a resource. *International Review of Sociology/Revue internationale de sociologie*, 13(1), 105–116.

Bell, J. and Loane, S. (2010). 'New-wave' global firms: Web 2.0 and SME internationalisation. *Journal of Marketing Management*, 26(3–4), 213–229.

Bouncken, R. B., Fredrich, V., and Kraus, S. (2020). Configurations of firm-level value capture in coopetition. *Long Range Planning*, 53(1), 101869.

Brouthers, K. D., Geisser, K. D., and Rothlauf, F. (2016). Explaining the internationalization of ibusiness firms. *Journal of International Business Studies*, 47(5), 513–534.

Ferreira, J. J., Fernandes, C. I., and Kraus, S. (2019). Entrepreneurship research: Mapping intellectual structures and research trends. *Review of Managerial Science*, 13(1), 181–205.

Fossen, F. M. and Sorgner, A. (2021). Digitalization of work and entry into entrepreneurship. *Journal of Business Research*, 125, 548–563.

Getz, D. and Carlsen, J. (2000). Characteristics and goals of family and owner-operated businesses in the rural tourism and hospitality sectors. *Tourism Management*, 21(6), 547–560.

Hänninen, M., Smedlund, A., and Mitronen, L. (2018). Digitalization in retailing: Multi-sided platforms as drivers of industry transformation. *Baltic Journal of Management*, 13(2), 152–168.

Hansson, H., Ferguson, R., Olofsson, C., and Rantamäki-Lahtinen, L. (2013). Farmers' motives for diversifying their farm business: The influence of family. *Journal of Rural Studies*, 32, 240–250.

Hennon, C. B. and Hildenbrand, B. (2005). Modernising to remain traditional: Farm families maintaining a valued lifestyle. *Journal of Comparative Family Studies*, 36(3), 505–520.

Hildenbrand, B. and Hennon, C. B. (2005). Above all, farming means family farming: Context for introducing the articles in this special issue. *Journal of Comparative Family Studies*, 36(3), 357–366.

Hull, C. E. K., Hung, Y. T. C., Hair, N., Perotti, V., and DeMartino, R. (2007). Taking advantage of digital opportunities: A typology of digital entrepreneurship. *International Journal of Networking and Virtual Organisations*, 4(3), 290–303.

Kraus, S., Palmer, C., Kailer, N., Kallinger, F. L., and Spitzer, J. (2019). Digital entrepreneurship: A research agenda on new business models for the twenty-first century. *International Journal of Entrepreneurial Behavior & Research*, 25(2), 353–375.

Kraus, S., Roig-Tierno, N., and Bouncken, R. B. (2019). Digital innovation and venturing: An introduction into the digitalization of entrepreneurship. *Review of Managerial Science*, 13, 519–528.

Laudien, S.M., Bouncken, R., and Pesch, R. (2018). Understanding the acceptance of digitalization-based business models: A qualitative-empirical analysis. *Academy of Management Global Proceedings*.

Lundberg, C. and Furunes, T. (2021). 20 years of the *Scandinavian Journal of Hospitality and Tourism*: Looking to the past and forward. *Scandinavian Journal of Hospitality and Tourism*, 21, 1–13.

Matt, C., Hess, T., and Benlian, A. (2015). Digital transformation strategies. *Business & Information Systems Engineering*, 57, 339–343.

Mithas, S., Tafti, A., and Mitchell, W. (2013). How a firm's competitive environment and digital strategic posture influence digital business strategy. *MIS Quarterly*, 37(2), 511–536.

Nambisan, S. (2017). Digital entrepreneurship: Toward a digital technology perspective of entrepreneurship. *Entrepreneurship Theory and Practice*, 41(6), 1029–1055.

Niemand, T., Rigtering, C., Kallmünzer, A., Kraus, S., and Matijas, S. (2017). Entrepreneurial orientation and digitalization in the financial service industry: A contingency approach. *Proceedings of the 25th European Conference on Information Systems (ECIS), Guimarães, Portugal, June 5–10, 2017* (pp. 1081–1096).

Parida, V., Sjödin, D., and Reim, W. (2019). Digitalisering som möjliggörare av avancerade tjänsteaffärsmodeller i småföretag i Norrland. In K. Wennberg (ed.), *Entreprenörskap för en levande landsbygd: 15 texter om landsbygdsutveckling och entreprenörskap i Norrland* (pp. 117–130). Familjen Kamprads stiftelse.

Pettersson, K. and Arora-Jonsson, S. (2009). *Den Osynliga Entreprenören: Genus och Företagande i De Gröna Näringarna*. Stockholm: LRF's Jämställdhetsakademi.

Postma, A., Cavagnaro, E., and Spruyt, E. (2017). Sustainable tourism 2040. *Journal of Tourism Futures*, 3(1), 13–22.

Richter, C., Kraus, S., Brem, A., Durst, S., and Giselbrecht, C. (2017). Digital entrepreneurship: Innovative business models for the sharing economy. *Creativity and Innovation Management*, 26(3), 300–310.

Schumpeter, J. A. (1934). *The Theory of Economic Development*. Oxford: Oxford University Press.

Sörensson, A. and Dalborg, C. (2017). Female entrepreneurs in nature-based businesses: Working conditions, well-being, and everyday life situation. *Society, Health & Vulnerability*, 8(1), 1306905.

Suess-Reyes, J. and Fuetsch, E. (2016). The future of family farming: A literature review on innovative, sustainable and succession-oriented strategies. *Journal of Rural Studies*, 47, 117–140.

Vadana, I. I., Torkkeli, L., Kuivalainen, O., and Saarenketo, S. (2020). Digitalization of companies in international entrepreneurship and marketing. *International Marketing Review*, 37(3), 471–492.

Vik, J. and McElwee, G. (2011). Diversification and the entrepreneurial motivations of farmers in Norway. *Journal of Small Business Management*, 49(3), 390–410.

Wentrup, R. (2016). The online–offline balance: Internationalization for Swedish online service providers. *Journal of International Entrepreneurship*, 14(4), 562–594.

8. Escaping the "tortoise shell paradox": digitalization and servitization in the green building construction industry – the case of Marlegno

Davide Gamba, Tommaso Minola and Matteo Kalchschmidt

LEARNING OBJECTIVES

- Comprehend how digitalization could be a source of entrepreneurial opportunities and competitive advantage.
- Understand servitization and servitized business model enabled by digital transformation.
- Introduce open innovation strategies that cope with new skills and capabilities needed to exploit digital entrepreneurial opportunities.

INTRODUCTION

> The company's slogan is its payoff: sustainable innovation. Whatever we do, Marlegno brings state-of-art digital technology inside timber buildings with the utmost respect to the environment. This approach gives value to our customers through comfort and energy performance. (Angelo Luigi Marchetti)

> We would like to be a laboratory of excellence able to bring the best of our sector to customers. When we develop a new building, we want it to represent the most updated technology application offered in terms of structure, systems, design, and services. (Angelo Luigi Marchetti)

The CEO's words clarify the warp that makes up the Marlegno company's identity, where past and future collide uniquely. On the one hand, wood represents the past. Wood is a raw material that was formerly thought to be a poor expression of building architecture and that today serves as a distinctive signal for environmentally aware customers. On the other hand, digitalization symbolizes the future through which smart homes are connected to people and objects rather than separate entities from their internal and external environments. It is from the successful management of this trade-off that Marlegno was born.

Marlegno started its business in 2000 as B2B subcontractor of prebuilt timber roofs for local construction companies. These were excellent times for the Italian construction industry, which was surging thanks to the recent introduction of the Euro currency. While on the other side of the world the bankruptcy of Lehman Brothers led to the climax of the subprime mortgage crisis, in 2008, Marlegno reached a turnover of 8 M€ and had about 20 employees. Unfortunately, Marlegno's customers – usually small and heavily indebted – became insolvent within a couple of years. As a result, in 2010, the company shifted to a B2C target selling directly to final customers. This disruptive business model change allowed Marlegno to survive this financial tsunami maintaining unchanged turnover over the next three years. At the same time, the percentage of B2C customers in the firm's portfolio constantly increased. Despite everything, however, surviving was not enough for the Marchetti family. "We lived in a comfort zone where we felt good, almost satisfied just to be alive and not because we have grown up from this experience!" the CEO stated.

As the three Marchetti brothers discussed the abovementioned situation, opposing arguments emerged. Marlegno could constantly have a year-by-year higher percentage of B2C customers that would help its portfolio differentiation if the current strategy had been pursued as-is. In this first scenario, incremental innovations would be the source of processes optimization to develop employees' skills and capabilities effectively. Furthermore, financial exposure could be controlled through this approach. At the same time, however, it would also endanger the company to the "tortoise shell paradox." Angelo Luigi Marchetti coined this term to describe Marlegno's business stalemate: choices that allowed it to survive after the 2008 financial crisis became a burden that hindered business development. "Small companies as Marlegno usually focused only on their own business, protecting themselves from what happens outside their box, reducing costs and investments to survive. Nevertheless, this is a tortoise shell that limits growth," he said. Alternatively, Marlegno could change its approach to business investing in R&D to become more competitive and differentiate itself from competitors. R&D investments represent a challenging path that may lead to a shift from being a follower of market trends to being a leader able to shape the green building sector and enter new market niches. Emerging technological trends are based on innovation through the digitalization of the building lifecycle stages. Thus, it could be expected that this scenario would have potentially disruptive consequences for the entire business according to the innovation model adopted and the outcomes reached.

In 2015, the decision to break the business deadlock could not be postponed further. Hence, the Marchetti family had to choose how to let Marlegno grow.

BUSINESS AND INDUSTRY OVERVIEW

It seemed natural for us to develop the professional activity of designer, construction manager and then builder, started in the 60s by our father. Following his footsteps, we focused on wood. In Italy, the green building sector is still a niche market. Following the models of countries such as Austria and Germany, all the practical, aesthetic, and environmental advantages that wood entails are beginning to be appreciated by final customers. (Siro Marchetti)

Marlegno is an Italian family-owned company based in Bergamo and founded in 2000 by the Marchetti family. The company operates in the green building sector (NACE rev. 2's code 16.1),[1] designing and manufacturing customized timber houses, buildings, and structures. Revenues steadily increased through the years, reaching €14.1 million in 2019. Marlegno has been managed since its origins by the Marchetti brothers. Angelo Luigi, the company's CEO, and Siro. Their sister Anna – who had been a partner since its foundation – joined the company in 2018 as HR manager. Interestingly, the workforce's schooling rate is exceptionally high due to the operations department's use of a qualified workforce for budgeting, architectural and engineering design, project management, logistics, purchasing, and direction of the building sites. The company plays an active role in the local entrepreneurial community, which is interpreted as an opportunity for benchmarking and learning. In particular, the CEO is a member of the board of directors of the local industrial entrepreneurs' association (i.e., Confindustria Bergamo) and the Lombardy Energy Cleantech Cluster. In addition, he is President of Assolegno (the association of primary wood processing and construction industries) and co-founder and president of EDINNOVA. The latter is a network for the construction industry's innovation management and knowledge transfer among professionals.

Marlegno has an engineering-to-order production strategy, a typical feature of the construction industry's firms. Marlegno buildings differ from the competition in the high degree of quality and customization pursued thanks to the numerous interactions with the customer. Every building project starts from drafting about three hundred requirements' specifications. Currently, each project is managed by a project manager who is the point of contact between Marlegno and the final customer and is responsible for the correct order implementation.

Since its establishment, Marlegno has operated in the building construction industry. It works in the branch of manufacturing and trade concerned with the construction, maintenance, and restoration of residential, public, industrial, and commercial buildings. Knowing the economic and technological scenarios that characterized the building construction industry is essential to understanding the Marchetti family's dilemma.

Building Construction and Real Estate Industries' Economic Trends during the 2008 Financial Crises

In Italy and other countries globally, the building construction industry is closely linked to real estate. After decades in which relatively easy access to credit destined for the purchase of houses by households allowed the building construction industry's constant development, starting from 2008, a first setback occurred. The latter was due to the crisis in the subprime mortgage market, which made credit institutions very cautious in granting loans in conditions of rising interest rates. All this was reflected in the building construction industry. In fact, during 2009, the credit crunch continued, and categories of potential buyers (e.g., immigrants, singles, and temporary workers) could no longer access credit. Consequently, the buildings' prices and transactions dropped. The latter recorded a reduction of about 15 percent compared to the previous year. It was the first significant signal, the prelude to the negative trend that occurred during 2010 and 2011: the country's unemployment increased exponentially, while business and consumer confidence decreased along with the willingness to buy a house. The year 2012 was the "annus horribilis" of the Italian real estate and building construction markets. A significant contraction in prices was recorded (Figure 8.1), and sales volumes began to plummet (−25.8 percent compared to 2011). In addition, the tax burden that affected second homes determined an increase in the real estate offer. The minimum peak of transactions was reached in 2013, but prices were still falling. Inside the credit market, there were the first signs of a recovery in demand for loans from households, which seemed to be regaining confidence despite the not brilliant trends in the consumption and labor market. In 2014, mortgages restarted thanks to the European Central Bank's injection of liquidity into the financial markets through so-called Quantitative Easing. Transactions increased, while prices had not yet taken off. Last, real estate demand continued to grow slowly during 2015. All this still did not transfer to prices, which continued to decrease less than before and then headed towards stability. This scenario imposed a radical rethinking of the Italian building construction industry through new approaches based on sustainable and circular business models, renovation of the existing real estate assets, and new technologies.

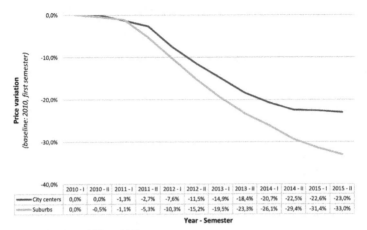

	2010 - I	2010 - II	2011 - I	2011 - II	2012 - I	2012 - II	2013 - I	2013 - II	2014 - I	2014 - II	2015 - I	2015 - II
City centers	0,0%	0,0%	-1,3%	-2,7%	-7,6%	-11,5%	-14,9%	-18,4%	-20,7%	-22,5%	-22,6%	-23,0%
Suburbs	0,0%	-0,5%	-1,1%	-5,3%	-10,3%	-15,2%	-19,5%	-23,3%	-26,1%	-29,4%	-31,4%	-33,0%

Year - Semester

Source: Monitor Immobiliare, 2021.

Figure 8.1   *Real estate price trends in Italy during 2010–2015*

Building Construction Industry's Technological Trends

In 2015 the building construction industry was influenced by digitalization as a driver of the green building concept. By definition, a green building reduces or eliminates adverse impacts on climate and the natural environment through its design, construction, or operations while also having the potential to create positive effects.

Digitalization's first viable option to reach these sustainable goals is represented by process innovation, namely the introduction of a new or considerably improved manufacturing or delivery method, including significant changes in techniques, equipment, or software. As the CEO said: "Our goal is to create increasingly eco-sustainable elements increasingly considering the costs of any lifecycle phase." In that sense, existing business processes and workforce efficiency can hugely benefit from digitalization.

Digitalization also favors the servitization of the producer's business model, especially for the building lifecycle's use stage. Servitization refers to the transition in an enterprise's business model from products (i.e., buildings) to a combination of products and services, the so-called product-service systems (hereafter PSS). Servitization generates higher use-value, value-based pricing, and capabilities to support co-creation. Servitization is not a recent trend in the industry. What has changed over the last years is the sense of urgency perceived by managers caused by customers' pressure and competition within manufacturers' commoditized markets. This situation encourages proactive action to capitalize on technological advancements such as digitalization

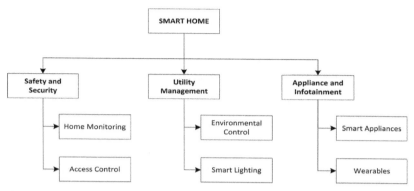

Figure 8.2   Smart home segments

to capture customer relationship value and expand the market potential. In that sense, there are two categories of building services from the end user's perspective: primary services and smart home services. Primary services are represented by energy (i.e., electricity and gas), water (i.e., supply, drainage and adequate plumbing), escalators and elevators, security and alarm systems, fire detectors and safety systems. Such services are designed and integrated into the early building design and construction stages following strict standards and building codes. Primary service can benefit from the digitalization of the product (e.g., alarm system control through digital devices). On the other hand, the so-called smart home services generate more and more interest among building construction industry entrepreneurs. The term smart home has many connotations (Figure 8.2). For example, the smart home in the healthcare industry is employed as a residential space that improves illness prevention by monitoring residents' health, habits, and life patterns. In the energy business, technological advancements and research in smart homes are centered on the efficiency of energy facilities, including demand-oriented energy production and utilization. In our context, it refers to house components with various internet and mobile applications related to the Internet of Things (IoT) and Artificial Intelligence (AI). IoT and AI allow the analysis of data collected by sensors and translate them into information and services, performing monitoring and predictive activities. For example, sensors are capable of detecting the state of health of the building, diagnosing consumption and anomalies in real-time, adapting the internal comfort in relation to the people present, adjusting ventilation, humidity, and temperature, and so on.

Both potential scenarios (i.e., process innovation and servitization) would impact Marlegno's organizational structure. New re-engineered processes and servitized business models need critical resources and capabilities to succeed in such significant changes as data processing and interpretation skills.

Escaping the "Tortoise Shell Paradox"

> Innovation is a mindset, a mental approach that must lead you not to sit down after reaching a goal. It leads you to question your certainties. (Angelo Luigi Marchetti)

After a series of all-night meetings and analyses, the Marchetti family decided to change the firm's approach to their business, starting to invest in R&D about 3 percent of its yearly turnover. Marlegno began collaborating with external research centers and organizations, such as universities and start-ups, adopting an open innovation[2] approach. These collaborations led to the realization that both process and servitized business model innovation capabilities were not present in Marlegno. At the same time, the company introduced new professional figures, while the existing ones were upskilled. Digitalization represented a driver towards the green building concept. In addition, it is an integrated part of the new corporate culture set up, at the root of that integration concept of information, data, processes, and the entire business organization.

Process innovation

Thanks to the participation in the four-year level-up project, a research and development initiative funded by the international research group Horizon 2020, Marlegno has begun to digitize its production processes in partnership with SCM Group. This challenge's technological and digital heart is the "Oikos x" machining center. "Oikos x" has an innovative six-axis machining head unit capable of processing elements up to 18 meters long and 1.25 meters wide with millimeter precision. Thanks to the Maestro beam&wall program, which is wholly integrated with the most popular CAD systems on the market, a digital twin of the processes can be created, which benefits productivity and cost. Vibration sensors installed on "Oikos x" allow to check and measure machine operations to detect real-time problems, leading to predictive maintenance. Alessandro Greppi, Marlegno's innovation manager, pointed out that all the company's machinery will benefit from implementing SCM's IoT Maestro connect platform. The latter will allow for data collection about performances and the status of the various technologies, creating a digital register. The project allowed a shift from unstructured operations and maintenance activities to a fully digitized system. This innovation impacted the production time and the operating costs of the process.

Servitization of the business model

Marlegno decided to start to servitize its model by developing a set of services, both in the pre and aftersales phases. These services aim to address customers' needs through a long-term-oriented relationship that seeks to optimize the total cost for the customer. As stated by the CEO, the company stopped selling "just cubic meters of wood," adding sales based on the value transferred to the final customers. The B2C services provided are listed in Table 8.1.

Table 8.1   *List of Marlegno's offered B2C services*

Phase	Service	Digital technologies used
Presales	Cost budgeting	CPQ
	Architectural design	BIM and VR
	Building practices management	-
	Dialogue with banking and insurance institutions (not brokerage)	-
Aftersales	Ordinary maintenance	IoT
	Predictive maintenance	AI

Digitalization represented a key factor for the delivery of these services. For example, architectural design is based on a BIM platform.[3] At the same time, cost budgeting was performed by developing a CPQ system[4] that simplifies generating an offer for customers, who can receive a cost estimation of the desired building directly through the step-by-step tool accessible through Marlegno's website. The most innovative project started by the company is founded on the cognitive building concept, which enables an even more advanced scenario compared to smart building. In this case, homes can self-learn and regulate themselves proactively from data collected through sensors installed within the structural package of the timber frame walls. In that sense, a building is transformed into an actor able to auto-regulate, enhance people's comfort, and send information about its health status to Marlegno's customer care department. In such a way, maintenance will be performed just if needed. Customers can monitor the building's performance through a smartphone app. This project was possible thanks to the partnership that Marlegno developed with IoTty, a local start-up specialized in IoT systems development. "The goal is to create houses capable of self-organizing and assisting those who live there, in the name of energy efficiency and structural protection," the CEO said. Last, Marlegno started using virtual reality (VR) in presales services. VR allows the customer to see and "be immersed" in the house from the design phase. As well as machinery for advanced prefabrication, this innovation reduced errors and production times.

Organizational structure change

Marlegno started to pay great attention to the innovation of its organizational structure and to the new products developed and the servitized business model introduced. Anna Marchetti began as the first HR manager, emphasizing the enhancement of employees' hard and soft skills. Digital training (e.g., data interpretation and use of software tools) crossed all company's departments, with a particular focus on the operations department following the introduction of the new technologies. As mentioned by Marlegno's innovation manager: "I believe that our job has always been in constant change. In recent years, there has been a great interest in digitalization and improving both production and managerial processes. The reasons are the greater search for efficiency given the increase in globalization and competitiveness between companies." In general, resources reskilling and upskilling have used both the training provided by consultancy companies for staff training and the opportunities offered by the network created by Marlegno's CEO. The HR department guided Marlegno in introducing the first non-family manager – who comes from a multinational IT company – and launched the first objectives-based incentive plan for its employees. In addition to the HR department, the marketing function was introduced (Figure 8.3), representing an unconventional choice in a traditional industry such as building construction. This department, made up of four internal people and several external agencies, was created to actively contribute to the company's growth by continuously improving the relationship with Marlegno's customers and prospects, especially B2C ones. Prospects were appropriately clustered into communities to strengthen corporate brand recognition. Each potential or current customer was profiled and reached through marketing campaigns to create long-term relationships and allow Marlegno to respond immediately to requests. Simona Lovati, Marlegno's CMO, mentions how marketing activity has educational and cultural implications, both internally and externally. For example, Marlegno curates "Percorsi sostenibili," a series of webinars 15 minutes long during which experts, suppliers, and customers of the green building sector are interviewed to deal with specific issues. Topics treated are not focused exclusively on the products but also include all the services offered by Marlegno. The goal is to reinforce the community's identity to address the webinar, intercept new potential members, and collect needs in a bottom-up logic. The attention to the data and its interpretation to transform it into practical actions is very high. As stated by the CMO:

> Initially, the social networks' reports highlighted a predominantly male audience. Our posts had a high technical imbalance, with a tone of voice that needed to be completely redesigned. Brand awareness does not only involve technicalities but also emotions. The customer chooses Marlegno for its unique selling proposition.

We have therefore rethought communication to balance the messages conveyed and optimize investments by creating value and above all a constructive and transparent relationship with our followers.

Figure 8.3   *Marlegno's organization chart*

Epilogue: A New Thin and Elastic Shell

The advances mentioned above are just an overview of the initiatives implemented by Marlegno. In conclusion, it is valuable to note that significant product innovations were introduced. One example is Tavego – a range of eco-sustainable structural floors and load-bearing walls assembled without glues and made by certified wood. Another example is AdESA, which is a dry prefabricated system designed according to the building's morphology to extend its useful life. It consists of insulated timber panels connected to the structure, with the triple function of an energy coat, an anti-seismic shell, and a layer for architectural restyling. Both innovations' development benefited from the partnerships between Marlegno and local universities, confirming how open innovation represents a weapon that SMEs can use to utilize skills and resources from outside. Talking about what has happened since 2015, Marlegno's CEO stated that "Through innovation and digitalization, we were able to escape the tortoise shell [paradox] making it thinner and more elastic." These few words are empirically proved in the long list of prizes that Marlegno received for its entrepreneurial initiatives, including a first prestigious "Prize of the Prize" for innovation in 2016 and a second in 2019. The three strategic milestones that the company has experienced are summarized in Table 8.2.

Table 8.2   *Marlegno's lifecycle strategic milestones*

Year	Milestone	Outcome
2000	Building construction industry's good times	Marlegno was founded
2010	Customers' insolvency	The business model shifted from B2B to B2C
2015	Business stalemate (aka, "tortoise shell paradox")	Investment in R&D

STUDENT CHALLENGES

1. How would you describe the SME strategy before the financial crisis? What were the drivers that led the SME to innovate its business model? Can this business model innovation be replicated in other industries?
2. How does digitalization influence process innovation in a traditional industry SME? What were the factors that played a fundamental role in the innovation process?
3. How does the servitization of the business model gain from digitalization? What could be the main challenges SMEs face in adopting such a business model?
4. How does digitalization shape the company's organizational transformation and corporate culture? Is employees' reskilling and upskilling a consequence of technologies adopted, or, vice versa, a propaedeutic to innovation?
5. What do you think the company should do in the future to stay ahead and maintain an edge in the digitalization of its business?

ACKNOWLEDGMENTS

We are highly grateful to the Marchetti family and Marlegno's employees for the time they dedicated to interviews performed in February 2021. They provided input and suggestions for writing this case directly from their experience.

NOTES

1. Notwithstanding that the construction industry is classified in NACE rev. 2's section F (codes from 41 to 43), Marlegno chose to formally classify its activities within section C devoted to manufacturing activities: code 16.1 is related to sawmilling and planing of wood. For more information about NACE rev. 2, see: https://nacev2.com/en.
2. For more information about the open innovation approach, see: https://en.wikipedia.org/wiki/Open_innovation.
3. For more information about BIM, see: https://en.wikipedia.org/wiki/Building_information_modeling.
4. For more information about CPQ, see: https://en.wikipedia.org/wiki/Configure,_price_and_quote.

REFERENCES AND FURTHER READING

Fondazione Symbola and Unioncamere (2015). *Rapporto Green Italy 2015*. See paragraph *3.3 Edilizia*, pp. 132–144. https://www.unioncamere.gov.it/P55A3043C310S144/i-dati-di-greenitaly-2015-di-fondazione-symbola-e-unioncamere.htm.

Tronvoll, B., Kowalkowski, C., and Sörhammar, D. (2021). Transforming small and medium-sized enterprises (SMEs) to digitally enabled landscapes. In C. L. Pedersen, A. Lindgreen, T. Ritter, and T. Ringberg (eds.), *Big Data in Small Business: Data-Driven Growth in Small and Medium-Sized Enterprises* (pp. 209–225). Cheltenham, UK and Northampton, MA, USA: Edward Elgar Publishing.

WEBSITES AND WEBPAGES

Level-Up (n.d.). *Demonstrators: Marlegno*. Retrieved April 1, 2022, from http://www .levelup-project.eu/technology_demonstrators/marlegno.
Marlegno S.r.l. (n.d.). *Company website*. Retrieved April 1, 2022, from https://www .marlegno.it.
Monitor Immobiliare (2021, March 15). *Tecnocasa: la domanda immobiliare si sposta dal centro*. Retrieved April 1, 2022, from https://www.monitorimmobiliare.it/ tecnocasa-la-domanda-immobiliare-si-sposta-dal-centro_20213151240.
Redazione Economia (2015, June 5). *Marlegno e la domotica di IoTty: così la casa in legno diventa intelligente*. BergamoNews. https://www.bergamonews.it/2019/06/ 05/marlegno-la-domotica-iotty-cosi-la-casa-legno-diventa-intelligente/310890.

FURTHER RESOURCES

Marlegno | Innovazione Sostenibile (2021, May 4). *Level-Up Project: la digitalizzazi-one dei processi produttivi* [Video]. YouTube. https://www.youtube.com/watch?v= NUQGFgCV8iE.
SCM Woodworking Technology (2021, July 30). *MARLEGNO I Build the future with CNC machining centers for wood construction*. YouTube [Video]. https://www .youtube.com/watch?v=6VhzzXwxInM.

9. The case of Dodo Pizza: how a Russian pizza making startup transformed itself into a thriving digital company

Dmitry Katalevsky

LEARNING OBJECTIVES

- Understand how digitalization is changing the traditional fast-food industry by increasing transparency and promoting higher standards of service quality.
- Consider various sources of competitive advantage for a growing fast-food chain in a digital economy.
- Analyze how digital technology is changing the way entrepreneurs in traditional industries think and act.
- Demonstrate how digital technology can be used to promote innovation and enhance customer experience.

INTRODUCTION: THE START OF A PROMISING BUSINESS JOURNEY

> Dodo Pizza is where technology meets pizza delivery. Through combining expertise in building software, restaurant operations and franchising, we strive to elevate pizza experience on a global scale. (Company's address to its Franchise Partners)

The first Dodo Pizza store was opened in 2011 in the small Russian city of Syktyvkar, 1,300 km from Moscow, with a population of less than 250,000. It will take more than 17 hours to commute from Moscow to Syktyvkar by car – a rather tiring trip. In 2012, a year after Dodo Pizza was opened, Syktyvkar was ranked 129 out of 165 for the quality of city life. A center of Russia's wood manufacturing, the small city of Syktyvkar definitely was not a friendly place to start a new pizza making business. But Fyodor Ovchinnikov, a 30-year old entrepreneur with a first unsuccessful startup, was not a guy who would give up easily.

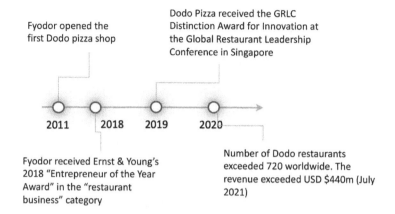

Fyodor opened the first Dodo pizza shop

Dodo Pizza received the GRLC Distinction Award for Innovation at the Global Restaurant Leadership Conference in Singapore

2011 2018 2019 2020

Fyodor received Ernst & Young's 2018 "Entrepreneur of the Year Award" in the "restaurant business" category

Number of Dodo restaurants exceeded 720 worldwide. The revenue exceeded USD $440m (July 2021)

Figure 9.1   *Dodo Company's timeline: in 10 years from one pizza store to an international chain*

Fyodor founded his first business in 2002 when he was 21, right after finishing his studies at the History Department of Syktyvkar State University where he majored in archeology. His parents tried to persuade him not to pursue business in the harsh Russian environment. However, Fyodor was dreaming of opening a modern book-store in Syktyvkar. He didn't have any starting capital, so he applied for a business loan to the biggest Russian bank, Sberbank. His application was declined, and he had to try again. With great difficulties, he managed to file another loan application for RUB 400,000 (equivalent to USD 15,000). This time, he was successful, and this sum of money was enough to launch a small 40 square meter bookstore in one of Syktyvkar's supermarkets. The next several years proved to be turbulent for Fyodor. Although he had had a successful start and managed to expand his business up to eight stores at the peak, the sales didn't grow fast enough to cover the costs, and eventually his business collapsed. In 2011, he went bankrupt and lost control of his business. That was a painful experience.

Nevertheless, in 2011 Fyodor decided to start a second business and to reinvent the world of making pizza (Figure 9.1). At that time, Papa John's, one of the leaders of the global market, had more than USD 1 billion of annual revenue. In Russia, Papa John's already had seventeen pizzerias. Although the Russian market had no nationwide pizza chains at that time, the timing could not be worse. The country was suffering from the global economic downturn of 2008–2009 that had a severe impact on the Russian economy.

Despite the doubts voiced by his family and friends, Fyodor was determined to reinvent the global pizza market. Soon, he opened the first pizza shop in Syktyvkar. At that time, there were about twenty pizzerias in Syktyvkar, a city of less than 250,000 people. Many people thought he was insane opening one more pizza shop. Initially, it was located in a cellar to save on rental payments, and was operating as a delivery only facility. Later, Fyodor managed to add more space and a dine-in area. Despite being the CEO and founder, Fyodor usually worked from the kitchen, rather than his office (which didn't exist at that time). Prior to opening his own business, he learnt how to make pizza working for one and a half months at McDonald's, Papa John's and Sbarro pizza chains in Saint Petersburg in 2010. In those days, working in the evenings, he carefully took notes of the equipment, made useful observations, and memorized best practices of managing a fast-food chain. Now, he trains his employees based on the lessons he learnt making pizza, mopping the floor, cleaning the kitchen, and working as a cashier himself (Figure 9.2).

The dodo bird was chosen as the company logo. The dodo was a flightless bird that was endemic to the island of Mauritius, east of Madagascar in the Indian Ocean. By the end of the seventeenth century, the bird was extinct as a result of hunting by European colonists who treated it as an easy source of fresh meat.[1] The word "dodo" is easy to pronounce and memorize. The idea behind using the dodo bird for a logo was the idea of trust and transparency of the company to its customers (having no natural predators, the bird trusted the people who hunted it).

Fyodor's creative mind was stretching far beyond the way traditional pizza making businesses are operated. From day one, he started to innovate and experiment with various business models.

Source: @D.Katalevsky.

Figure 9.2 *The Dodo Pizza Restaurant in Odintsovo, Moscow region*

COMPANY AND INDUSTRY OVERVIEW

Innovations in the Operating Model

The mission of the company is to bring joy to its customers "with delicious pizza, a culture of trust, openness, and a desire to exceed expectations": "We create moments of joy through delicious food and sincere service."[2]

That was easy to say but hard to deliver as service quality was not usually the advantage of many pizza delivery businesses back in 2011. One of the key features of the Dodo Pizza that quickly gained recognition with clients was the company's promise to deliver pizza within one hour. Should the courier be even one minute late, the company would provide the customer with their pizza free of charge. For a small Russian town it was a very unusual promise that generated a lot of interest from the customers. The company trusted the clients and if the client insisted that the delivery was late, the company never argued and always provided pizza for free. Initially, some employees thought that this could hurt the company financially as people might start cheating to get a free lunch. However, the clients appreciated this and the number of orders increased.

Another important distinctive feature is the unique openness of the company. Unlike many of his rivals, Fyodor from the very beginning tried to be fully transparent. In some sense, he revolutionized the tradition of pizza making in Russia by providing open access to the full process of pizza making through web-cameras installed in the kitchen of the pizza shop. In the beginning, not all the company's employees supported this idea. Indeed, nobody likes to be watched. However, eventually the idea was accepted. Today, every Dodo Pizza kitchen worldwide is equipped with a camera streaming video directly to dodopizza.ru. Having placed an order, the customer can get access to the video stream and watch live how their pizza is being cooked. Back in 2011–2012, interested clients were frequently invited for a physical kitchen tour. This helped the young and ambitious pizza making company to win the customers' trust. The culture of openness is deeply rooted in the philosophy of Dodo Pizza, as described in Box 9.1.

BOX 9.1   DODO PIZZA'S PHILOSOPHY

Our philosophy. We think that openness will make the world better. To open up means to trust, believe in people and their good intentions.

Our need. We are not afraid of criticism. We are not phobic or paranoid. We are happy to share.

Our communication style. We don't conceal fails and share financial details. It endears people to trust us.

Our quality control. Anyone can come to the kitchen and check if we observe our standards.

Our driver of improvement. Transparency brings us hints, insights, and inspirations. Openness is crucial.

Source: https://brandbook.dodopizza.info/en/#!brand/values.

Full transparency is not just words. For instance, the company follows the principle of salary transparency enabling everyone to view the salaries of each employee. The same principle is applied to the pizzerias. Profitability indicators of each of the 730+ pizzerias are used as the basis for weekly and yearly performance ratings. Operating a wide franchise network, Dodo Pizza carefully rates each pizza shop based on strict quality criteria (inspections are frequently arranged; inspectors are selected from customers; mystery shopping is practiced frequently). Ratings are available to all partners (franchisees) of Dodo Pizza. If the rating is low, the franchisee can lose a pizza franchise.

Another key element of the company philosophy is continuous service improvement. In order to fulfill this, the company frequently practices "Director Days" when top-managers of Dodo Pizza together with the founder perform routine "blue collar" activities: i.e., they work as pizza makers, cashiers, cleaners, and engage in delivery to get new insights on how to improve the service. This helps to make decisions that are "not high in the sky." All top managers hired by the company start from pizza making and kitchen internships.

> Why do we need it? [asks Fyodor discussing the Director Day in his blog on July 28, 2014]. Easy! We need it in order not to lose ties with production, to communicate with our clients and employees, to check personally, how it is working in practice what we decided sitting in the office. We do it to motivate our guys from pizzerias and to show that all of us are one team, and everyone knows how to work in the kitchen … and not to forget what's eight hours working shift when sitting in the office.[3]

Another interesting operational innovation suggested by Fyodor is the pleasant artificial voice that helps employees to inform about new incoming orders and guide them through the preparation process. In fact, it is a part of a complex IT system which Fyodor tried to build from the very start. The system is designed to monitor the pizza preparation process and is programmed to encourage employees to speed up when it is necessary or give them credit when they are doing fine. The voice belonged to Olga S., the director of one of the pizza shops. Once introduced, it was nicknamed "Olenka" and widely accepted by the employees as part of their team, notwithstanding its artificial nature.

Small incremental innovations paved the way for a huge innovation – the launch of the company's proprietary IT system. It was not an easy decision for the founder and his team. At that time, several Management Information System (MIS) solutions for restaurants and pizza shops were available that could be easily customized to meet the needs of Dodo Pizza. The DODO Information System (IS) is now a crucial element of the Dodo Pizza business and, probably, its unique competitive advantage.

Dodo's Way to Growth: How Digitalization Helped to Champion the "Get Big Fast" Strategy

The quick service restaurant (QSR) segment is booming globally. When building Dodo Pizza, Fyodor decided to scale up his pizza business via franchise. However, one of the biggest challenges of a growing QSR chain is keeping a permanent quality of food and services across all restaurants. First successes were coming to Fyodor and his team, and by the end of 2012 Dodo already comprised eight restaurants. After a careful consideration, Fyodor decided to make a bet on an IT system to ensure the transparency of business processes across the growing chain.

Another dilemma was choosing between buying and adapting an existing third-party solution available on the market and trying to develop a proprietary solution. There were several efficient solutions, including those from Bringg (www.bringg.com) and some other players. The conventional business logic suggested that Dodo should concentrate on its core competency – i.e. pizza making. In addition, it would be quite a challenge to build a professional IT team within a traditional QSR business. Finally, the growing company was cash constrained. Due to the challenging business environment at that time, it was difficult for the company to get a bank loan, and Fyodor had to finance the project through family, friends and eventually, crowdfunding.

Nevertheless, the founder decided to build Dodo's own IT system. At that time, such a decision seemed rather bizarre. It is only after several years of IT system development and implementation that nobody questions its ultimate success anymore. One of the reasons for this is that Fyodor used to run his fast-food business as retail or manufacturing rather than catering. This implies that the quality of his products and services should be standardized across the whole chain. Beyond a shared philosophy and business principles, only an IT system could ensure such standardization.

However, the way to the top was rather tricky. Once, the company almost ran out of money and survived only thanks to the heroic accomplishment of the company's IT developers. Several times failure of the IT system caused disruptions across the chain that led to losing opportunities. The early versions of the IT system caused painful decline in labor productivity leading to wasting foodstuffs and unhappy employees. Overall, over a period of eight years Dodo invested several million dollars in its IT system, but eventually it was worth doing and the payoff was huge.

First, over the years the company developed a smart cloud-based IT system that monitors almost all aspects of pizza production and delivery. The order tracking service is at the core of the Dodo IS. It starts with getting orders from customers via the company's website and integrated cloud-based mobile app solutions:

- *Production management.* "All the orders immediately show up on the iPads installed in our kitchens. The crew checks in the orders in the system to mark the beginning of every stage of the process: dough preparation, toppings, oven, packing, and delivery. We monitor the cooking time of every single pizza and compare it against the target value. The result is displayed on a separate screen in the kitchen. This helps us motivate the kitchen crew and adds some fun to the process."[4]
- *Benchmarking against best practices.* "Shift managers can see in the system how much time pizzas spend on the shelf waiting for delivery. If it's too long, they can take action and call in more drivers. Day/month stats provide management with an accurate assessment of how efficiently the delivery has been planned."[5]
- *Big Data.* "We store all the data and make forecasts about the workload of the kitchen. The system warns the shift manager if they assign too many or too few people to work in the kitchen for a certain hour."[6]
- *Productivity boost.* "Our smart order controller flexibly changes the sequence of orders on the line, taking into account our wait-time limits for different channels of sales. Sometimes, a delivery order can wait a while because the customers are expecting it in half an hour. In this case, the algorithm changes the sequence and makes a new dine-in order a priority."[7]

Thus, the IT system covers every aspect of Dodo's business, such as purchasing of food ingredients, monitoring their shelf life and best-before dates, managing employees and delivery couriers. It helps to manage micro-business processes, setting benchmarks, tracking performance of each individual employee, and quickly identifying potential losses and management pitfalls. That was the way to control standards of Dodo Pizza across the country. All processes were computerized by deploying tablets in the kitchen, at cashiers' desks and with couriers. Managers could easily control employees while directors could control managers. The head office could get relevant statistics across any of the franchise pizzeria literally within minutes. Clearly, Fyodor was inspired by Henry Ford's conveyor idea and tried to apply such a concept digitally to reinvent the pizza making process.

Second, over the years the IT system enabled the management to get big data on almost every aspect of the business routine leading to advanced analytics and performance prediction. For instance, it can now predict peak time and ensure far in advance that the stock of ingredients and the personnel headcount are sufficient at the restaurant at a given time to realise its full potential. Also, it helps to detect fraud, cheating or mismanagement in any pizza shop across 730+ entities.

Third, Dodo believes that efficient process management is a core capability of the company and software is instrumental in achieving production efficiency. Therefore, software development cannot be outsourced. By outsourcing key competencies, the company loses it in the long run. The web service solution proved to be a success: to get started, all franchisees simply need to log into the system from any mobile device. A cloud-based IT solution shows all the data in real time. Another advantage comes from the convenience of the system upgrading procedure, since it is a matter of a few minutes to update the IT system across the chain of hundreds of units.

Fourth, by continuously improving the processes (and its software), the company involves itself in the continuous learning and improvement cycle. The company runs experiments and implements features adapting its strategy on the fly.

Last but not least, by developing its proprietary IT system Dodo Pizza got an integrated all-in-one software solution for ordering, production, and delivery. Usually, a typical QSR chain would buy several of those solutions struggling to integrate them afterwards. Therefore, much of the productivity of a fast food chain will inevitably depend on whether the integration of multiple IT systems is successful enough.

Not surprisingly, Dodo Pizza considers itself a food tech startup in the QSR business rather than a typical fast food company (see Box 9.2)

BOX 9.2   SOME COOL FEATURES OF DODO IS

Dodo IS powers all of our brands in the Dodo family: Dodo Pizza, Drinkit, and Doner 42. And it consists of so many parts: a mobile app, a website, a contact center solution, a cash desk, tracking and motivation screens, shift scheduling, day and month overview, inventory management, dynamic menu and promotions, loyalty program, sales reports ... Basically, every aspect of our core business is covered, though the development is ongoing. It's hard to elaborate on everything, but let's highlight a few more cool features Dodo IS already has to offer.

Since every order is processed by Dodo IS, we see our sales in real time and are able to broadcast them online through APIs – for any particular pizzeria or across the chain. Our investors love this feature! (See also a post about our commitment to transparency, where we explain why we share our essential financial data with the public.)

If a customer in our home market calls Dodo Pizza, they can dial the same number in any city. The call is transferred to an available team member working remotely from their home office, which could be located thousands of miles away. Our CRM system provides the operator with all the information that is needed to process the order which immediately appears on a screen in the pizza shop closest to the client. This tech-driven solution allowed us to bring the efficiency of our contact center to a new level, which couldn't have been done even ten years ago.

Having a skilled team of software engineers and designers on board allowed us to make a mobile app with an excellent UI – a real cut above the market. This app also leverages the advantages of deep integration with Dodo IS. If an order is placed on a smartphone, we send a push notification asking customers to give feedback afterwards. Around a quarter of them seize this opportunity and give their pizzas a mark from 1 to 5 points. If it's not a five, we reach out to rectify our mistakes. Every pizzeria also gets a ranking based on this feedback.

Source: Company's website: https://dodobrands.io/post/dodo-is.

From Dodo Pizza to Dodo Brands – the Company Today and Tomorrow

The IT system, transparency policy, and unique business model have resulted in unprecedented growth rates of the company.

Eight years after the first Dodo pizzeria was launched in Syktyvkar, Fyodor was managing a pizza chain of 500 pizzerias. In 2016, Dodo became the largest pizza chain in Russia. By 2019, Dodo was one of the fastest growing pizza chains in the world (Figure 9.3). In the first eight years, the company experienced exponential growth reaching sales of USD 71m in 2017, USD 162m in 2018 (126 percent growth rate compared to previous year) and USD 263 in 2019 (80 percent growth rate compared to previous year). In 2019, Dodo rated third among the fastest growing restaurant brands in Europe and the fastest growing fast food chain in the world. Having started from scratch, Dodo Pizza dominated the Russian pizza market by 2020 being as big as three closest competitors – Papa John's, Domino's and Pizza Hut. Dodo Brand became the most recognized pizza brand in Russia with 37 percent of respondents naming Dodo pizza chain second to none.

However, the way to success was paved with many challenges. Especially hard were the years 2013–2015 when Fyodor was in desperate need to raise capital for expansion. He tried it with institutional investors – private equity funds – but none of them wanted to invest in an innovative pizza chain. A famous blogger, he was followed by thousands of people. After some thought, Fyodor decided to use crowdfunding as a source of capital attracting private individuals as investors:

> In 2013, I tried to attract investments from professional investors, but failure was behind the corner. No one believed in us and in our idea. Then I decided to attract private investors online through my blog – and we succeeded. In 2013–2015, we raised USD 3.5m from more than 150 private investors. Doubtlessly, it was a risky investment, and a lot of people considered our valuation to be too high. That's why I invented a way for our investors to get their money back with interest, should they be dissatisfied with our growth. Private investors gave our company loans under my personal guarantee, and in return, they got the opportunity to convert them into our shares in three years at a $30 million valuation. If we didn't live up to our investors' hopes, I would have to return $3.5 million. But we did. 99% of our investors converted their loans into shares in 2017. (Fyodor Ovchinnikov, 2021)[8]

The efforts of Fyodor didn't go unnoticed. In 2015, *PMQ Pizza Magazine* (USA) named Fyodor "the Steve Jobs of pizza". More than that, Dodo Pizza was recognized as the most innovative foodservice brand winning the Global Restaurants Leadership Conference (GRLC) Distinction Award, the industry's highest international tribute, in Singapore in 2019. The Award praised Dodo's innovation "for its pioneering efforts to develop and incorporate its own proprietary digital operating platform and its well-demonstrated commitment to transparency into all aspects of its business, from publishing monthly store sales to visibility into unit-level kitchen operations."[9]

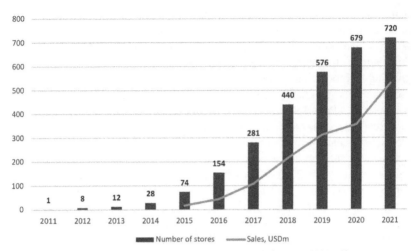

Source: https://dodobrands.io/files/dodo_company_presentation_sep_2021.pdf.

Figure 9.3   *Dodo Pizza growth by the number of pizzerias and sales (USDm), 2011–2021*

Two years later, in 2021 the company had more than 720 company-owned and franchised units in 15 countries including Russia, Belarus, Kazakhstan, Lithuania, Germany, Slovenia, the United Kingdom, the US, and even China and Nigeria. Nowadays, it is a truly global company growing rapidly across the world. During the COVID-19 pandemic of 2020, the company managed to add nearly 100 stores. The black swan event turned out to be very beneficial for the company since pizzerias have seen a great increase in the amount of online delivery services (people staying at home started to use the online order and delivery service more actively).

The Dodo IS continues to grow and expand as the company employs more than 120 software engineers with a plan to double its IT headcount by 2023. By the end of 2021, the company revenues are projected to exceed USD 500m, a remarkable number considering that just eight years ago the company couldn't raise USD 3.5m from institutional investors. Recently, Fyodor initiated his "Plan 333": 3 years, 3 brands, USD 30m EBITDA. The company plans to reach USD 1bn in sales within 2–3 years and plans to go to an IPO in 2024.

What's Next?

The company is striving to leverage its digital potential by creating an *ecosystem of products* in some of the market niches. The Dodo Brands consists now of a family of brands including Drinkit, a chain of digital-first coffee shops, and Doner42, a doner kebab chain (both brands launched in 2020). These brands are expected to become additional sources of growth for the company fully benefiting from its already existing technology ecosystem.

Currently the company is busy expanding Doner42, a "digital doner shop brand." The doner (kebab) market is not structured and is currently dominated by small producers while market potential is enormous. Dodo is planning to offer a completely new experience to customers via a digital mobile application: i.e., ordering in advance via the app, customization of kebab in the app, etc. Digital technologies offer a vast potential to transform consumer experience by customizing dishes, receiving special offers, avoiding waiting in line by paying for the order and taking it at the checkout.

Another product is the Drinkit coffee shop as Dodo is not afraid to compete against such leading companies as Starbucks. The company plans "to digitalize all the processes in the coffee shop so that we can track an order at a specific phase: from supply metrics to coffee machine settings for the certain order."[10]

It plans to experiment with "dodocoins" as a gamification method to provide cashback and to accept payments for other orders via its digital app. This is Dodo's promising attempt to switch to personalized marketing. Artificial intelligence methods combined with the big data will help to raise income from personalized marketing by an estimated 5 percent by the end of 2022.[11]

Although each innovation is incremental by nature and does not represent a breakthrough, taken together they significantly transform customer experience.

It would be interesting to see whether the company will be able to maintain its leadership on the digital market, more specifically in the fast-food sector, in the long run. As is the case with many other industries, digital technology changes the way of doing business in the fast-food sector.

Whether digital technology can provide a sustainable competitive advantage remains an open question. Although the digital experience of Dodo is not easy to replicate in the short-term, the nature of digital technology presumes easy transferability. Therefore, one might expect that key rivals will be catching up in streamlining their business processes with a digital approach. Some questions remain: How sustainable is competitive advantage from implementing a digital technology? Or is it only temporary? How costly is it to replicate it?

Besides the digital angle, what are the other competitive advantages of Dodo that ensure its success? Will the company be able to maintain such an impressive growth trajectory in the future? Where is the future of the company's business: Is it in the pizza market or in some other market niches, such as coffee or kebab, or even in some markets the company has not yet discovered? Is Dodo's digital expertise from pizza making transferable to other fast-food segments?

Fyodor likes to quote Marc Andreessen, a legendary US venture entrepreneur, who said, "Software is eating the world." The visionary founder of Dodo

Pizza managed to utilize software at its full potential. Nowadays, Fyodor likes to repeat that Dodo Pizza is actually "a software company producing pizzas." He thinks that every quick-service restaurant chain will become a software company eventually. It looks like we have to believe him.

STUDENT CHALLENGES: DISCUSSION QUESTIONS

1.   What are the key growth drivers behind the success of Dodo Pizza?
2.   How do you think the Founder of Dodo Pizza managed to achieve sustained growth in a traditional pizza business by leveraging digitalization?
3.   Can you identify and describe the "core competencies" of Dodo Pizza using the resource-based view framework? Is Dodo's competitive advantage robust enough? Can Dodo's competitors replicate its success?
4.   Can we claim that through digitalization of its business model Dodo disrupted the entire fast-food industry? Please explain.
5.   How might digitalization help in implementing "Get Big Fast" strategies?

NOTES

1.   See https://www.britannica.com/video/214809/Dodo-extinct-bird-island-Indian-Ocean-human-induced-extinction.
2.   See https://brandbook.dodopizza.info/index_EN.html#!brand/mission.
3.   Fyodor Ovchinnikov personal blog (in Russian). https://sila-uma.ru/2014/07/28/den-direktora/ (accessed December 20, 2021).
4.   See https://dodobrands.io/post/dodo-is.
5.   Ibid.
6.   Ibid.
7.   Ibid.
8.   See https://dodobrands.io/post/plan333/.
9.   See https://globalrlc.com/2019-grlc-distinction-award-winners-announced.
10.   Dodo Meetup 21: the key unveilings. https://dodobrands.io/post/dodo-meetup-2021-summary/ (accessed January 20, 2022).
11.   Ibid.

REFERENCES AND FURTHER READING

Barney, J., Wright, M., and Ketchen Jr, D. J. (2001). The resource-based view of the firm: Ten years after 1991. *Journal of Management*, 27(6), 625–641.
Bughin, J., LaBerge, L., and Mellbye, A. (2017). The case for digital reinvention. *McKinsey Quarterly*, February 19.
Fedor Ovchinnikov, founder of Russian chain Dodo Pizza, may just be the "Steve Jobs of pizza." *PQM Pizza Magazine*, June 2015. https://www.pmq.com/fedor-ovchinnikov-founder-of-russian-chain-dodo-pizza-may-just-be-the-steve-jobs-of-pizza.
Johnson, M. W., Christensen, C. M., and Kagermann, H. (2008). Reinventing your business model. *Harvard Business Review*, 86(12), 57–68.

Russia's Pizza King Wants to Use the Cloud to Take Over the World. https://www
.bnnbloomberg.ca/russia-s-pizza-king-wants-to-use-the-cloud-to-take-over-the
-world-1.1331120.
Teece, D. J., Pisano, G., and Shuen, A. (1997). Dynamic capabilities and strategic
management. *Strategic Management Journal*, 18(7), 509–533.

WEBSITES AND WEBPAGES

Company results for 2021 financial year. https://dodobrands.io/files/dodo_company
_presentation_sep_2021.pdf.
Information about the company, its brands, strategy, plans and annual results. https://
dodobrands.io/post/plan333/.
Information about the company's franchising opportunities and value proposition to its
global potential partners. https://dodofranchise.com/.

VIDEOS

Dodo partners and shareholders meetup 2021. https://www.youtube.com/watch?v=
GbyCkHUucAs&t=17437s.
Quick video story about Dodo Pizza. https://youtu.be/qnshI4dfP6E.

10. Digital entrepreneurship for influencer marketing: the case of Buzzoole

Gianluca Elia, Alessandro Margherita, Pasquale Del Vecchio, Giustina Secundo and Marco Valerio Izzo

LEARNING OBJECTIVES

- Understand the impact of digital innovation on marketing strategies and processes.
- Appreciate the importance of influencer marketing.
- Understand and apply key metrics to evaluate an influencer marketing campaign.
- Simulate the design and realization of an influencer marketing campaign going through the strategy, implementation, and measurement phases.
- Conceive and design an initiative aimed at enhancing market success of an organization by leveraging digital technologies.

INTRODUCTION ON DIGITAL MARKETING

Digital technologies such as social media, mobile apps, business analytics, big data, cloud computing, artificial intelligence, etc. can be leveraged to support entrepreneurial processes, ranging from idea generation and opportunity identification to market launch. Digital technologies are opening new opportunities to conceive new ideas, develop new processes, experiment with new products, explore new markets, and create value. This applies to both innovative and technology-intensive industries as well as to the more traditional ones.

The power of digitalization has been largely exploited by Buzzoole, an Italian fast-growing technology venture specialized in influencer marketing enhanced by artificial intelligence. In just three years, the company has captured a fair share of the growth of the influencer marketing business, whose global value more than doubled between 2019 and 2021, growing from 6.5 billion to 13.8 billion US dollars (company's internal source).

By leveraging sophisticated technologies based on artificial intelligence and semantic social networking, Buzzoole provides organizations with services and tools to identify the perfect matching between social media influencers and their strategic needs to gain visibility and social reputation. More specifically, Buzzoole helps its clients discover the best influencers, automatizing the influencer marketing activities, and optimizing the campaign via analytics-driven assessment of marketing actions. Artificial intelligence technology embedded in the Buzzoole platform performs a deep analysis of individual profiles and contents, by using natural language understanding and image recognition techniques. This makes it possible to search for the most suitable influencers for marketing campaigns among over 2 million social profiles. Besides, the platform provides access to various modules that allow customers to follow the progress of marketing activities in real time, assess the performance of the campaign, and manage the administrative process (e.g., billing, payment). In this way, Buzzoole provides brands with an attractive and unique value proposition, i.e., the ability to implement and adapt marketing strategies quickly, based on a deeper understanding of consumers' sentiment and satisfaction, and a new view of the consumer–brand relationship.

The Buzzoole case also illustrates how digital technologies empower entrepreneurial activities by favoring the emergence of a new profile of digital entrepreneur able to leverage the Internet to execute most of the processes required to launch a new venture.

The case starts with an introductory section on digital marketing and the new frontier of influencer marketing, followed by an overview of Buzzoole, and a section on how the company innovates influencer marketing with a new way of assessing brand affinity based on key performance metrics and a purposeful technological platform. Then, the case introduces the Digital Entrepreneurship Canvas, a tool useful to support the design of digital entrepreneurship initiatives through the definition of seven key elements. In the final section, lessons learned and managerial insights are extracted from the case and discussed.

THE MULTIFACETED NATURE OF DIGITAL MARKETING: FROM DIGITALLY ENABLED CUSTOMER RELATIONSHIP MANAGEMENT TO INFLUENCER MARKETING

Digitalization has amplified the relevance of marketing in achieving entrepreneurial success. Digital marketing leverages different digital technologies to create value for customers by supporting conception, pricing, distribution, and communication of an offering.

Indeed, digital technologies can extend the traditional marketing mix levers (product, place, packaging, and promotion), by:

(a) expanding products' features through the addition of intangible characteristics and services;
(b) supporting fine-grained price discrimination via dynamic pricing;
(c) improving packaging via smart attributes and providing customers with more product information;
(d) enhancing distribution, by creating disintermediation opportunities and new digital marketplaces;
(e) increasing the effectiveness of promotional activities by offering new solutions and venues for a multi-channel, interactive, and instantaneous communication.

By embracing a digital marketing strategy, digital entrepreneurs can focus on the creation and maintenance of relationships with their customers, by leveraging advanced techniques for data collection, monitoring, and analysis. More specifically, Customer Relationship Management (CRM) is a particularly effective approach to support digital marketing initiatives driven by the management of information flows and knowledge exchanges with customers. CRM is characterized by five key features:

1. Focus on the single customer instead of an entire market segment.
2. Adoption of a perspective based on customers' lifetime value instead of maximizing margins of single transactions.
3. Zero-in on the higher value market segments instead of growing market shares.
4. Pursuing dialogue with and active participation of customers.
5. Relying on the active role of customers instead of a passive one.

CRM leverages digital marketing to help build loyalty with existing customers rather than acquiring new ones, thus developing a continuous, transparent, friendly, and valuable dialogue grounded on four types of knowledge exchanges:

• knowledge for customers, i.e., all the information about a product or a company made available to customers;
• knowledge from customers, such as feedback, comments, explicit and other content that customers voluntarily disclose;
• knowledge about customers, i.e., information extracted via the analysis of the customers' online profiles and behaviors;
• knowledge with customers, i.e. the explicit exchange of information and experience between a company and its customers.

In the last decade, the explosion of social media platforms triggered the emergence of virtual communities of customers. Such communities represent digital spaces for interaction and exchanges of information and knowledge that may affect firms' reputation, brand, and image. In these communities, individuals can dialogue about companies or with them, and express positive or negative opinions about products and services, thus influencing the members' behavior and their purchasing choices. It is thus fundamental to monitor customers' feedback both to handle criticisms and to extract new insights aimed at improving customer experience.

At the same time, it is today crucial to identify influencers, defined as individuals with high visibility and a prominent position in online communities whose opinions about brands and products are trusted by many followers. Such authority conferred by other users in the network is proven to weigh significantly on fostering positive responses towards brand perception, purchasing decision, and lifestyles.

Thus, companies must:

(a)   appropriately select and incentivize online influencers to engage with their followers to promote specific offerings;
(b)   monitor influencers' content creation and provide them with feedback based on the achieved performance.

A key factor driving the choice of the right influencers is *brand affinity*. Put simply, brand affinity is a positive inclination of a customer towards a brand and represents what a customer feels while interacting with a brand. Brand affinity relies on feelings and emotions that bring people to choose a brand, a company, or a product. Brand affinity is fueled by the capacity of a company to understand customers' values, needs and expectations, and its ability to provide them with great service, excellent customer support, anticipation of their latent requests, and emotional feedback. For example, a survey made by a travel magazine discovered that Alaska Airlines registered the best customer service level, even if not all the respondents had used Alaska Airlines. This highlights the power of word-of-mouth and social marketing as strategies for influencing the meaning of the relationship between a company and its actual or potential customers. Therefore, a key challenge in influencer marketing is to match the right influencer to the right brand/product to maximize the brand affinity. The following section describes in detail how Buzzoole, a leading digital marketing start-up specialized in influencer marketing, accomplishes the right match.

BUZZOOLE: BUSINESS AND INDUSTRY OVERVIEW

Buzzoole is an Italian fast-growing venture specialized in influencer marketing enhanced by the adoption of artificial intelligence. The market of influencer marketing is on the rise. Statistics indicate that the value of this specific market doubled between 2019 and 2021, growing from 6.5 billion to 13.8 billion US dollars (company's internal source). From 2017 to 2019, the total number of posts has increased from 629,000 to 1,733,000. Fashion and Beauty dominate the scene in terms of posts (i.e. messages created) and engagement (i.e. inter-actions of people with content created in terms of shares, likes and comments). Fashion (38 percent) and Beauty (14 percent) accounted for almost half of the #ad posts created (52 percent). Influencer marketing is a woman's affair, since more than three quarters (76 percent) of the creators who produced #ad posts in 2019 are women. The industry generally divides influencers into three main types based on the size of their online audiences: micro-influencers (50 < 25,000 followers), mid-level influencers (25,001 < 100,000 followers), and macro-influencers (over 100,000 followers). Figure 10.1 shows the breakdown of posts by client industry in 2019.

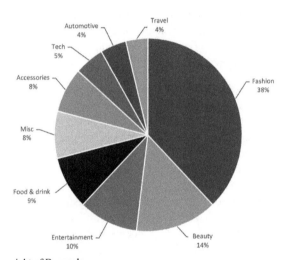

Source: Copyright of Buzzoole.

Figure 10.1   *Posts (messages created) and engagement (interactions of people with content created) by industry*

Large corporations belonging to different industries, including well-known com-panies such as Adidas, Audi, Burberry, Chanel, Fiat, Huawei, Lacoste, Oreo, etc. spend significant money on influencer marketing at the international level.

Buzzoole was established in 2013 with the idea of creating a technology-advanced player providing software and services to support brands in all the phases of influencer marketing campaigns. More specifically, the founders, being aware of the great opportunities offered by the emerging digital technologies like artificial intelligence and semantic social network-ing, ideated and conceived an innovative entrepreneurial project that can be represented by using the Digital Entrepreneurship Canvas (Elia, Margherita, and Secundo, 2020). It represents a framework that can be used to describe the strategy of a digital venture based on seven main pillars, which connect technological platforms, processes and people with the strategic purpose to generate outputs (performance and product) while creating a positive social and environmental impact, reputation, and responsibility (planet). Figure 10.2 provides a graphic illustration of the Digital Entrepreneurship Canvas, whereas Table 10.1 provides a description of the seven elements and their application to the case of Buzzoole.

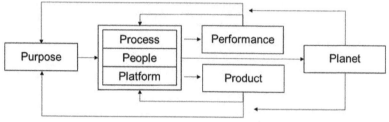

Source: Elia, Margherita, and Secundo, 2020.

Figure 10.2   Digital entrepreneurship canvas

Table 10.1   The digital entrepreneurship canvas of Buzzoole

Element	General description	Application to Buzzoole
Purpose	The grounding motivation and essence of the company's presence within the industry. It includes the business goal that the digital entrepreneurship initiative aims to achieve, properly aligned with the organizational and business strategy.	To realize a "perfect matching" among influencers and companies, thus leveraging the brand affinity and maximizing the impact of the social presence and reputation.
Platforms	The digital technologies supporting the operations of the enterprises in terms of digital artifacts and infrastructure.	A proprietary tool, based on deep learning algorithms and semantic social network analysis, which allows the rating and classification of individuals in terms of influence and provides companies with effective digital marketing choices.

Element	General description	Application to Buzzoole
Processes	The key processes that determine the value offered by the digital entrepreneurship initiative.	• Gathering information from the web to identify the most representative keywords; • Matching users to the best influencers for each topic; and • Delivering value-added recommendations to companies.
People	Both internal and external individuals and teams that are directly and indirectly involved in the digital entrepreneurship initiative, by including: the commitment and leadership necessary for leading the initiative; the digital skills; levels of autonomy and responsibility associated with roles; the professional profiles required; the key role of partners and stakeholders.	• Individuals working and/or acting as influencers on the web; • Highly trained and diversified team including software engineers, data scientists, digital marketing experts.
Performance	The value created by the digital entrepreneurship initiative, assessed through several dimensions including economic and financial growth, innovation, competency development, network of collaborations, and intellectual property.	Brand awareness, intention to buy, recommendation, favorability.
Product	The output deriving from the implementation of the digital entrepreneurship initiative, which may combine both tangible (e.g. object) and intangible components (e.g. service).	The best fit between the profile of influencers and their requests/needs in terms of brand visibility and loyalty.
Planet	The potential (positive) impact of the digital entrepreneurship initiative on the social and environmental dimensions (i.e. the earth), thus contributing to reinforce the organizational brand and image, and highlight the overall corporate responsibility.	Positive impact at societal and business level due to new opportunities offered to single individuals to get in touch with multinational companies.

Buzzoole is headquartered in Naples (Italy) with business offices in Milan and London, and it has received numerous awards and collected several investment rounds. At the end of 2021, the company revenues were 5.4 M€, with a total workforce of about 40 people. Buzzoole provides brands with complete management of influencer marketing campaign as outsourced service, or sells technology directly thus letting companies become autonomous in the implementation of influencer marketing campaigns. The Buzzoole technology supports the search of the most suitable influencers for a given campaign from over 2 million social profiles, and offers various modules that allow customers to follow the progress of activities in real time, verify the performance of the campaign, and manage the administrative process (e.g. billing, payment). All the activities are executed via the Buzzoole proprietary platform through which customers can take full advantage of the automation offered by technology. Figure 10.3 shows the homepage of the company's website.

Source: Copyright of Buzzoole.

Figure 10.3   Buzzoole's official website home page

Buzzoole Way to Innovate the Influencer Marketing

Building brand affinity is a big challenge for companies that want to have a relevant social media presence. In this perspective, brand affinity relies on feelings and emotions that bring people to choose a brand, a company, or a product. Despite the increasing attention to and importance of brand affinity for companies, there is no unique strategy and roadmap to maximize it.

An Innovative Approach to Assess Brand Affinity

There are two possible approaches to identify influencers with the right affinity with the brand: manually searching influencers via keywords through social media internal search engines or via software able to automate and optimize the scouting. Thanks to a proprietary algorithm based on artificial intelligence, the "Buzzoole's Discovery" app identifies the influencers that best match branding needs. The algorithm collects many data on influencers including topics they post about, gender, age, brand mentions, channel, location, performance, and biography, to name a few. Of particular interest is the *Health*

Check score, a grade from A+ to D assigned to the quality, authenticity, and performance of an influencer's profile.

Buzzoole's technology is based on artificial intelligence algorithms, more specifically deep learning algorithms based on neural networks able to recognize patterns in a large amount of data. The company's technology also uses statistical models, to identify probabilistic links among variables, and social network analysis techniques, to derive the architecture of the relationships among people. These allow the user to carry out an intelligent categorization and evaluate the brand affinity.

Artificial intelligence supports accurate analysis of profiles and contents, using the most innovative techniques of natural language understanding and image recognition. Buzzoole's platform can assess the degree of influence through an analysis of multiple web channels at two levels: (a) the first phase of the process concerns the analysis of the connections of an influencer's social graph; (b) the second step involves the analysis of individual posts on each channel. The output is a map where creators' areas of influence on the web are visualized. This graph is the basis through which a matching algorithm identifies the target influencers for a given campaign.

Each influencer is rated on 194 different topics, summarized in 20 macro-categories, of which 8 are selected as the areas in which he/she is most influential (and therefore potentially engaging for future campaigns). The large volume of data that Buzzoole can process allows customer brands to accurately estimate the success of a campaign. In relation to the availability of talent and human capital, Buzzoole leverages a highly trained and diversified team including software engineers, data scientists, digital marketing experts as well as experts in product, design and financial management.

Furthermore, Buzzoole collaborates with Nielsen, a world leader in the measurement of marketing activities to offer third-party certification of the data processed by its platform. In particular, the platform can be employed to carry out *brand uplift* studies applied to specific campaigns by measuring their contribution through metrics such as Awareness, Intention to Buy, Recommendation, and Favorability. Figure 10.4 shows a view of the Buzzoole Discovery tool.

Performance Metrics

Measuring the impact of a campaign is a marketer's single biggest challenge. Buzzoole has undertaken a solid analytical approach to the evaluation investments on influencer marketing. With Nielsen's help, the company has managed to develop a set of metrics and a new approach to help its clients meet the measurement challenge. One key indicator is engagement, a complex term that entails many dimensions and that requires multiple metrics to be assessed

Figure 10.4   Buzzoole discovery

correctly. In the following, the main metrics Buzzoole uses to assess engagement are briefly described:

- *Total Engagement* indicates the sum of the interactions (i.e. likes, comments, shares) generated by a given content during a campaign.
- *Engagement Rate* is defined in two different ways. If it relates to followers or fans, it is the ratio between the total interactions with the content and the number of followers of whoever produced the content. In this case, it is used to measure the degree of activity shown by fans/followers of a given influencer. If, on the other hand, the *Engagement Rate* is calculated as the relation between the total interactions with the content and its reach, it may be useful to calculate the degree of interest aroused among the people reached by the content.
- *Reach* refers to the number of people that are reached by a piece of content. More specifically, it refers to the people who have had the opportunity to see the content.
- The metric *Impressions* (usually translated as "views") refers to the number of times the content has been viewed or the number of times the distribution algorithm has included it in users' news feeds.
- To detect shifts in brand perception, the so-called *Sentiment* is evaluated in terms of the number of positive, negative, and neutral reactions to influencers' posts. Sentiment is a useful metric to collect and assess users' feedback, to drive subsequent product/service development actions.

Thanks to its collaboration with Nielsen, Buzzoole has developed a tool able to provide an accurate assessment of the success of influencer marketing actions. Companies that use Buzzoole have two new metrics available in their final report. *True Reach* indicates the number of people reached by the content produced by an influencer marketing campaign across different social media.

This metric is innovative in that it allows the reach to be estimated even for media channels that do not make any statistics available. While, for instance, Facebook and Instagram provide these metrics for business accounts, other media do not offer the same service (at the time this chapter was written). The True Reach metric is estimated based on: (a) social following, i.e. the number of followers of an influencer on each social channel; (b) effective readership, i.e. a visibility metric based on the data collected; (c) influencer interaction, i.e. the number of times followers interact with each individual post; and (d) influencer activity, i.e. number of posts published per month by each creator.

Ad Recall is a metric that estimates the percentage of people reached by a campaign and who remember seeing it. In addition to the interactions generated, it is very useful as an indicator to find out whether the campaign stuck with people. The two proprietary algorithms behind True Reach and Ad Recall are based on a comparison between the core social media performance indicators (i.e., number of followers, frequency of posts, involvement rate) and the information collected through periodic surveys on a diverse range of social media.

These metrics derived from social big data are used to provide companies with a comprehensive vision, on one single dashboard of the influencers' performance across all channels. In this way, they can analyze their progress and identify their best content to help Buzzoole's GAIIA (Growing Artificial Intelligence for Influencer Affinity) algorithm to identify the creators that are most suitable for a specific campaign.

Data Quality Assurance

Influencer marketing is subject to potential distortions and misbehaviors. Facebook has revealed to its investors that about 6–10 percent of accounts (around 200 million people) are duplicate and that about 3–4 percent are fake (60 million). A sample analysis revealed that 15–20 percent of Instagram accounts might have engaged in fraudulent activity.

Buzzoole uses large quantities of real-time data to improve companies' grasp of the authenticity of influencers' profiles. Given that there is no standard procedure to identify authentic profiles, Buzzoole uses several methods to achieve an accurate and comprehensive assessment based on the joint analysis of different parameters to establish whether a creator is authentic or not.

The most used fraudulent method for contaminating the market is buying followers and engagement (interactions). In some cases, companies use automated systems, namely botnets (fake accounts created ad hoc) to carry out automated actions such as following or interacting with a profile. In other cases, some companies pay individuals to make their account available in exchange for a little compensation (down to a few cents of dollar in some low-income countries). Whatever the technique used, brands end up using creators with fake audiences and paying for non-valuable interaction. In the absence of technological support, it is extremely difficult to detect such fraudulent activities.

To counteract this problem, creators joining the Buzzoole community are required to link their social media accounts and blogs, including access to all related information (e.g. Google Analytics data for their blog or Facebook and Instagram Insights for Zuckerberg's two social media platforms). Leveraging this information, Buzzoole's "fraud detection" system can identify with high accuracy influencers who adopt fraudulent practices. The technology draws on real insight data from social profiles and uses such data to assess the goodness of channels. It detects the presence of Bots and suspicious audiences, cataloguing the profiles based on their "state of health."

Conclusions

The shift of media consumption from traditional to online media, the different reactions of consumers to advertising when they are online, and the increasing amount of time that consumers spend on social media, contribute to enhancing the relevance of influencers as "socially trusted individuals" to the large community of consumers.

This is not a matter of a few people with very high numbers of connections; rather it is a very diffused phenomenon that involves relatively unknown individuals who are capable of moving masses of individuals towards one or another industry and business target.

When an influencer posts content, a brand's awareness and popularity are impacted. For this reason, the "perfect matching" between the influencers and companies that search for visibility and attention represents the killer application of modern digital marketing.

Buzzoole focuses on this business niche to provide a set of smart services that leverage artificial intelligence and modern data analytics techniques to discover potential influencers that provide a valuable contribution to enhance client companies' visibility and reputation, and eventually brand awareness and purchase intentions.

In this highly dynamic and competitive scenario, Buzzoole represents an interesting case of digital entrepreneurship. It shows how companies can extract value from digital data by exploiting opportunities created via digital technologies based on artificial intelligence to offer innovative and value-added services.

The successful undertaking of influencer marketing requires a strong alignment with the overall marketing strategy of the client organization and a brand affinity approach based on effective categorization and benchmarking methods and technologies. Besides, it is crucial to develop a comprehensive approach to performance measurement and to monitor the credibility of influencers to prevent fraudulent behavior.

Choosing the right technology is crucial when it comes to making data-driven investment decisions. Artificial intelligence and machine learning can help to find the best influencers for a brand. This implies that managers should carefully identify the best technology applications to serve the business and strategic needs of the organization. Moreover, committing to a pilot short-term influencer campaign is vital before embarking on a full program. Managers and practitioners should thus invest effort in designing proper pilot actions with careful monitoring of the same.

This case study also highlights the importance of identifying the right influencer by choosing among thousands of potential profiles. A lesson learned is that "micro-influencers" should be considered. If on one hand small businesses cannot afford to involve celebrity influencers (often costing upwards of £75,000 for a single post), they can leverage the more affordable long tail of micro-influencers to target more niche customer segments. A further recommendation for companies wanting to adopt influencer marketing is to rely on a trusted and experienced partner to support the influencer marketing campaign as opposed to a self-service platform, since an experienced service provider can provide the necessary strategic support and seamless control of campaigns on top of the data and the digital outputs generated by the platform.

Afterwards, practitioners should strive to analyze the customer journey as a whole and identify the best practices in each phase (i.e., awareness, consideration, purchase decision, etc.). Finally, it is crucial to understand that influencer marketing is not a one-off initiative to create temporary buzz, but rather something that must fit into a broader marketing strategy coupling different channels and tactics with the appropriate type of influencers.

STUDENT CHALLENGES: DISCUSSION QUESTIONS AND ASSIGNMENTS

1. Can you identify and briefly describe the five distinguishing features characterizing influencer marketing with respect to traditional marketing?
2. Why is brand affinity so critical? What factors or variables does your brand affinity depend on? What would you recommend considering, as a consultant, for a client company that wants to improve its brand affinity?
3. Can you summarize and discuss indicators you can use to assess the effectiveness of an influencer marketing campaign?
4. Based on the example described in the case, and with some extra research, can you list and describe the most important technologies supporting a digital marketing strategy?

5. Can you ideate and design a start-up initiative in the field of digital marketing by using the Digital Entrepreneurship Canvas?

REFERENCES AND FURTHER READING

Belanche, D., Casaló, L. V., Flavián, M., and Ibáñez-Sánchez, S. (2021). Understanding influencer marketing: The role of congruence between influencers, products and consumers. *Journal of Business Research*, 132, 186–195.

Byers, T. H., Dorf, R. C. and Nelson, A. J. (2010). *Technology Ventures: From Idea to Enterprise*. New York: McGraw-Hill.

Elia, G. and Margherita, A. (2016). A collective intelligence platform for developing technology entrepreneurship ecosystems. In G. Passiante and A. Romano (eds.), *Creating Technology-Driven Entrepreneurship: Foundations, Processes and Environments* (pp. 195–220). London: Palgrave Macmillan.

Elia, G., Margherita, A., and Passiante, G. (2020). Digital entrepreneurship ecosystem: How digital technologies and collective intelligence are reshaping the entrepreneurial process. *Technological Forecasting and Social Change*, 150, 119791.

Elia, G., Margherita, A., and Secundo, G. (2020). *Impresa Digitale, Scenari, Tecnologie e Percorsi di Trasformazione Digitale*. Milan: Egea.

Gawer, A. and Cusumano, M. A. (2014). Industry platforms and ecosystem innovation. *Journal of Product Innovation Management*, 31(3), 417–433.

Kraus, S., Palmer, C., Kailer, N., Kallinger, F., and Spitzer, J. (2019). Digital entrepreneurship. *International Journal of Entrepreneurial Behavior & Research*, 25(2), 353–375.

Leung, F. F., Gu, F. F., and Palmatier, R. W. (2022). Online influencer marketing. *Journal of the Academy of Marketing Science*, 50(2), 226–251.

Sussan, F. and Acs, Z. J. (2017). The digital entrepreneurial ecosystem. *Small Business Economics*, 49(1), 55–73.

Vrontis, D., Makrides, A., Christofi, M., and Thrassou, A. (2021). Social media influencer marketing: A systematic review, integrative framework and future research agenda. *International Journal of Consumer Studies*, 45(4), 617–644.

Ye, G., Hudders, L., De Jans, S., and De Veirman, M. (2021). The value of influencer marketing for business: A bibliometric analysis and managerial implications. *Journal of Advertising*, 50(2), 160–178.

11. How to stay agile while growing: (re-) designing the IT landscape of a digital gazelle in the online marketing industry

Nils J. Tschoppe, Jan K. Tänzler and Paul Drews

LEARNING OBJECTIVES

- Identify the stakeholders and their interests that are affected by the organizational and technical changes, and determine the strengths and weaknesses of a company's IT landscape.
- Develop a roadmap to drive the transformation of the IT landscape with a particular focus on software.
- Identify investment priorities based on the strategic analysis conducted in the previous points.
- Understand the challenges facing fast-growing digital companies.

INTRODUCTION

In 2012, the company "Marketing Beats" was founded by two friends, Stephen and Peter, in a medium-sized city in the immediate vicinity of the Munich metropolitan region. Originally, the two founders, who had already been in contact for many years through the local soccer club, wanted to earn some money on the side using Google Ads. The fact that the work was also fun was a bonus. After a short time, however, they both realized that there was enough potential for them to start their own business in online marketing. That was the starting point for the foundation of the company Marketing Beats. Although the metropolitan region of Munich was not far away, they decided to stay in their hometown, which is a sign of the founders' down-to-earth outlook and strong attachment to their roots.

In the early years, several factors ensured rapid company growth. First, Stephen and Peter worked almost around the clock. The money they earned was immediately reinvested. In this way, they were also able to hire staff early on in order to accelerate further growth. The two founders also tackled problems and challenges in a hands-on manner, which proved to be beneficial for the positive development of the company and saved valuable time. The two were also able to draw on the expertise of the university's startup network. In addition, two other factors played an important role in the rapid growth of the company. On the one hand, both founders managed to attract the right people to the company at the right time. For example, they hired an accountant early on who is still with the company after ten years. On the other hand, both founders complement each other very well. While Stephen is more of a salesman and excels at communicating with customers, Peter is more analytical and always keeps an eye on the company's figures, and he used to do some programming himself. Ultimately, however, luck with regard to the acquisition of customers and the development of the industry in general has also played a small role in the development of the company.

After completing some initial successful projects for customers from the region, the company positioned itself primarily in the sports sector and managed to acquire important clubs from the 1st and 2nd German soccer leagues as customers. However, this one-sided customer structure was also perceived as a risk, and so the company increasingly tried to acquire other customers outside the sports sector. Today, the sports sector still forms an important pillar for the company, but the customer structure now consists of around 150 customers from different sectors, such as food and beverage, online retail, and the manufacturing industry. This risk diversification and its ability to respond to changes in the market at short notice ensures that the company has been able to grow successfully even in times of crisis, such as at the height of the COVID-19 pandemic in 2020.

Since its founding in 2012, the company has always been able to grow by contracting about ten extra employees per year and now employs nearly 130 people, including many IT- and marketing-savvy students and graduates of the local university. With its digital business model, the company can be classified as a "digital gazelle," as it has been characterized by rapid company growth over a limited period of time (cf. Acs and Mueller, 2008; Birch, 1994; Henrekson and Johansson, 2010). Despite its rapid growth, the company has been able to maintain many positive characteristics that have contributed to its growth since the beginning. For example, it continues to cultivate its startup spirit (e.g., with regular sports and cooking events), has created positive conditions for remote working from the very beginning, and is still characterized by a high degree of agility and flexibility, which makes it possible to respond quickly to changing market conditions. Furthermore, the company is customer-oriented and very well connected in the region. The two founders have also been able to maintain their down-to-earth attitude despite the rapid growth.

The company's rapid growth has also led to major internal and external challenges that Stephen and Peter are now facing. However, the two founders are not alone in this. The constant adaptation of the strategy and organization of digital companies in particular to the changing environment is an important success factor, not only for young companies, and is discussed in the literature under the name of digital entrepreneurship (cf. von Briel et al., 2021; Nambisan, 2017; Recker and von Briel, 2019). Internally, it is important to meet the demands for optimized cross-departmental communication and project handling while taking department-specific requirements into account, without losing too much of the company's original agility through standardized processes. Externally, the company must respond to increased customer expectations, such as changes in project scope, at short notice, and adapt its processes accordingly, while building a suitable data infrastructure for this purpose. Basically, IT is seen as a strategic topic by the CEOs.

With these challenges in mind, Stephen and Peter are now asking themselves exactly what they need to do to pave the road for a successful future.

BUSINESS AND INDUSTRY OVERVIEW

Corporate Structure

Each of the department heads (e.g., search engine optimization (SEO), paid media marketing (PMM), social media management (SMM), web development, sales) reports directly to the two CEOs, Stephen and Peter, each of whom has an assistant. Some of these departments are also broken down into further areas. For example, the sales department includes key account management and business development, each of which is headed by a team leader. Nevertheless, the sales department is also a separate area with its own employees, who are not assigned to key account management or business development. Stephen and Peter emphasize that all employees can also contact the CEOs directly in urgent cases, which reflects the flat hierarchy of the company. Finally, there is the office management department, which is responsible for the internal organization (e.g., of company events).

The company is organized as shown in Figure 11.1.

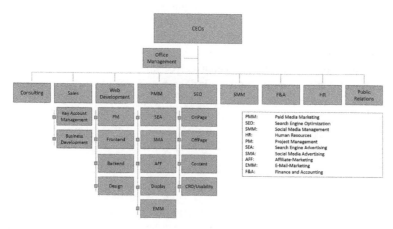

Figure 11.1   Marketing Beats' organizational chart

Market Position

With a turnover of approximately 8 million euros, Marketing Beats is one of the 50 largest German internet agencies. The 20 largest internet agencies have an average turnover of at least 20 million euros. In the digital advertising/ communication category, Marketing Beats ranks as number 8 in Germany (Figure 11.2).

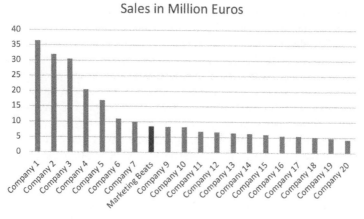

Figure 11.2   Germany's largest internet agencies (digital advertising/ communication)

Marketing Beats maintains good relations with other internet advertising agencies of a similar size and continues to be strongly anchored in the region with many local customers. Nevertheless, this provides only limited information about which new software solutions are suitable for the company. While some companies continue to use primarily free and poorly integrated solutions, others resort to highly individualized and fee-based software, or even a largely integrated IT landscape.

PROBLEM STATEMENT

Background

The company's IT landscape is in need of improvement. This was revealed as part of a previous situation analysis focusing on the company's environment and customer processes and the software solutions in use. In two workshops with the CEOs, among others, an overview of the status quo of the software used in the company was obtained, and its optimization potential was uncovered. The insights gained were condensed through semi-structured interviews with selected department heads and specialists. This had different objectives: On the one hand, against the backdrop of upcoming organizational and technical changes, employees were involved in the planning process, which led to an awareness of the transformation. It was also possible to draw on their expertise. On the other hand, several pain points were identified that affected both the entire company and individual departments. The company does not have a dedicated IT department. For example, backups or the setting up of IP telephony are carried out by an external service provider. In addition, two experienced employees from the web development department support the technical introduction of new software solutions. The focus of the redesign of the IT landscape is on the integration of existing software solutions or their replacement, as well as the associated process optimizations.

Missing software interfaces currently lead, among other things, to a lack of transparency and miscommunication in customer project implementation as soon as several departments are involved. In addition, master data are not managed centrally, relevant customer information is sometimes lost, and invoicing is more time-consuming than necessary. In addition, the recording of billable hours and the planning of effort (e.g., by using Microsoft Excel spreadsheets, hereafter referred to as "Excel") are largely independent of project communication and documentation. To save costs, group accounts in the Optimal Collaboration (OC) project management software are also used for project execution, which results in unnecessary spam and a lack of clarity in terms of project responsibilities, and slows down the company's performance.

Across the different departments, three software suites are used to coordinate communication with the customers and within projects. The individualized and outdated OC project management software is used by the online marketing departments (PMM, SEO, SMM). Because of this customization, an update would involve a great deal of effort and would still not fulfill the requirement of an integrated IT landscape. In this context, the integration of the Funnel customer relationship management (CRM) software, which is currently only used by the business development department and the CEOs, also comes into focus. The benefit of the second project management software Yeera, which is used exclusively by the web development department, also needs to be scrutinized. Although it fulfills the requirements of agile project management (e.g., with a kanban board to visualize and optimize the workflow), it is hardly integrated into the customer processes and the rest of the IT landscape.

Now, it is time to plan the redesign of the IT landscape with a focus on the implementation of new software, which is scheduled for the coming year. In addition to the condensing of information, promising software solutions are to be identified, a cost-benefit analysis is to be carried out, and the preferences of the individual departments are to be weighed up. To this end, a transformation roadmap must be developed for the upcoming rollout of new software solutions.

To accomplish this result, the following checklist was used in the analysis:

- identification of the departments involved
- survey of the current IT landscape
- interdepartmental collaboration on customer projects
- identification of the critical pain points
- identification of the requirements with regard to the new system(s).

Departments Involved

As part of the transformation, some departments are more affected by the redesign of the IT landscape than others. Accordingly, the main focus lies on the following departments.

- **Online marketing departments (PMM, SEO, SMM):** These departments are responsible for online marketing. For example, the SEO department alone is composed of more than 20 employees. As a full-service online marketing company, its services range from search engine advertising and optimization to native and display advertising and social media and content marketing. The OC project management software is primarily used for this purpose.

- **Web development:** This department deals with the design and maintenance of customer websites. It is the only department that works agilely
  in sprints and uses a kanban board. The Yeera software is used for this
  purpose. The OC project management software is only used to fill in
  invoice templates, which are later forwarded as PDF documents to the
  finance and accounting (F&A) department. Supplementary software, such
  as Masterplan and Bestfeature, are also only used in this department. With
  approximately 27 employees, it is one of the largest departments.
- **Business development:** Customer acquisition, as well as the planning
  and implementation of events, webinars, and other events, in which other
  departments may also participate, is the responsibility of the business
  development department. Initial customer communication is carried out
  via the Funnel CRM system, which also allows the statistical evaluation
  of the sales pipeline. This department is not involved in customer project
  execution. Due to missing software interfaces between Funnel, OC, and
  Yeera, valuable information is sometimes lost.
- **F&A:** This department is responsible for accounts receivable and accounts
  payable. The personnel structure and the software used in F&A have hardly
  changed in recent years. In particular, the associated automatic creation
  of dunning notices and monthly recurring invoices should be taken into
  account when redesigning the IT landscape.

In addition, the following departments must be considered as part of the
transformation:

- **Sales:** Sales is the link between customer acquisition (business development) and project execution (the web development and online marketing
  departments). Among other things, the department takes care of obtaining
  the final project approval from the CEOs, organizes internal kick-off
  meetings for the respective projects and handles the preparation of offers.
- **Consulting:** This department primarily provides consulting services.
  However, if two or more departments are involved in a project, one
  employee from consulting takes over the interdepartmental coordination.
  This person also takes care of the consolidation of the individual reports,
  ensures quality assurance and the documentation of the results, and creates
  the monthly invoice form for the online marketing departments in Excel,
  which he or she sends to the F&A department.

Overview of the Current IT Landscape

The following is an overview of the software used in the company that comes into focus when redesigning the IT landscape:

- **Optimal Collaboration (OC):** The version of this project management software is outdated and can no longer be updated, as it has been heavily customized over time. It is used by the online marketing departments as well as by the sales and consulting departments for documenting and executing customer projects. Many employees are dissatisfied with this software and find it time-consuming and impractical.
- **Yeera:** The second project management software is used exclusively by the web development department for customer projects because of its kanban functionality, among other things. According to the web development department, creating tickets is also easier than in OC and the software is best suited for project work. Other departments, however, find this software confusing; the use of this software by the entire company is therefore considered unlikely.
- **Funnel:** This CRM software was introduced by the CEOs to get a better overview of current leads. Currently, only the business development department and the CEOs work with this tool. An interface with OC does not exist. Although the information is relevant for the sales department, it continues to use OC in order to avoid additional hurdles in its close cooperation with other departments.
- **Debtware:** This software is used for accounts receivable (i.e., to create invoices for customers). An interface with the project management software to create an invoice directly based on the projects is not integrated.

In addition, other software is used, which may have an impact on the upcoming transformation of the IT landscape:

- **Credisson:** This software is used for accounts payable and was introduced a few months ago to simplify the accounts payable process. However, Credisson does not currently offer accounts receivable.
- **Masterplan:** This software is used solely by the web development department for internal resource planning.
- **Bestfeature:** This software is used exclusively by the web development department for the product backlog management.
- **Rocketchat:** This is a free chat program for internal company communication, which is used across departments and does not interface with other software.

The file server, Excel spreadsheets, and Google Drive are also used to exchange files across departments. In addition, essential processes, such as the calculation of projects, use Excel spreadsheets. The data protection-compliant use of Google Ads requires the Google Workspace as well, which is used intensively by the SEO department in particular.

Interdepartmental Collaboration on Customer Projects

Previous analyses revealed that 45 percent of the company's projects are exclusively realized by only one of the departments. These projects, however, make up only 17 percent of the total revenue. Most of the revenue (>70 percent) comes from about 40 percent of the customer projects, which are supported by 3–6 different departments. Therefore, interdepartmental projects, in particular, contribute to the success of the company (Figure 11.3). This also highlights the relevance of an integrated IT landscape that supports communication between the departments. In addition, the special requirements of the web development department (such as kanban boards) must be taken into account in the planning process, but these should not have a significant impact on the design of the entire IT landscape.

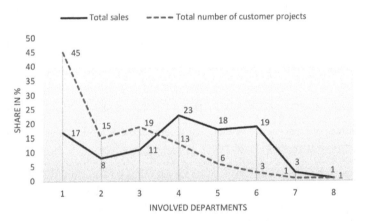

Figure 11.3   *Comparison of total sales with the total number of customers based on the departments involved*

The information collected during customer acquisition is entered into Funnel by the business development department. Invitations to events and the distribution of newsletters are also planned here. If customer acquisition is successful and customers request Marketing Beats for a project, a sales ticket is created in the OC software. Related documents are stored on the file server sorted by customer. In the next step, contact with the respective department, including a rough price estimate, is initiated by the sales department. For the purpose of a company-wide overview, the lead is simultaneously entered into Excel spreadsheets. The rest of the process differs according to the number of departments involved.

- **Only the web development department is involved:** If only the web development department is involved in the project, it is created in Yeera after an initial customer meeting together with the sales department. However, the initial sales ticket in the project management software (OC), which contains basic information about the customer project, still exists and is not connected to Yeera. Subsequent communication with the customer is documented in Yeera, and the progress of the project is recorded there. For internal departmental resource planning, a customer entry is also created in the Masterplan software. The completion of the invoice form is again carried out in OC (e.g., on a monthly basis depending on the project's progress). This is forwarded to the F&A department, which prints it out and enters the data into Debtware to send the invoice to the customer.
- **Only one of the online marketing departments is involved:** After the initial customer meeting together with the sales department, the project is created in the project management software (OC) by one of the online marketing departments. However, the initial sales ticket (in the OC) continues to exist and is also used for supplementary customer discussions, which means that valuable information can be lost. Relevant information is copied from the sales ticket onto the ticket of the respective online marketing department at the beginning of the project and at irregular intervals. Cross-departmental resource planning for project implementation takes place via Excel spreadsheets. Minutes of customer meetings and reports are stored on the file server. Invoices are generated via an Excel spreadsheet linked to OC and forwarded to the F&A department by email.
- **More than two online marketing departments are involved:** If a customer is served by more than one department, an internal consultant is usually called in to handle communication between the departments involved and to attend customer meetings. Action planning, as well as input on the strategy, is recorded in Google Drive; further arrangements are made via the project management software (OC), by email, or in person. Each department now creates its own OC ticket for this customer project (to document customer communication and internal departmental project progress). This is highly problematic as all project participants are required to subscribe to the respective projects of the other departments. There is no filtering option, so every piece of information (no matter how unimportant) is communicated to all the project participants, resulting in

spam. For example, an SEO employee receives the customer communication from the social media department, even if it is only the headline of a social media post. Quality assurance and the documentation of the (partial) results are also recorded in a separate OC ticket by the consultant. The consultant also carries out the reporting and saves it on the file server. Finally, he or she fills out an Excel invoice form and sends this by email to the F&A department.

- **More than two online marketing departments and the web development department are involved:** Building on the above process of when more than two online marketing departments are involved, the web development team also creates its own project in the Yeera project management software. Since master data cannot be maintained in Yeera, the contact persons from the web development department cannot be stored centrally. The web development team does not participate in cross-departmental action planning due to agile project execution in sprints. The documentation of the web development subproject is performed in Yeera. In order to assign a task to the web development department, the other departments have to create a ticket in Yeera themselves. Thus, integrating the web development team into the customer projects is another challenge. Also, a separate project report is created via Yeera by the web development department. The consultant fills out the Excel invoice form for the online marketing departments involved on a monthly basis and emails it to F&A. Once the web development department has also completed and forwarded its invoice form, F&A creates the invoice and sends it to the customer.

Identified Pain Points

The overarching goal is to design an integrated, clear, and easy-to-use IT landscape that supports sustainable growth and the original agility of the agency in the best possible way. Associated processes must be kept as lean as possible. These requirements are rooted in the rapid growth of the company. While in the early years non-integrated software solutions were quite appropriate and, for example, quality assurance was carried out by the same person who programmed the website, the increasing communication between customers and the departments involved now requires a certain degree of standardization. During the interviews and workshops, a set of pain points and optimization potential with varying degrees of relevance were identified, which need to be taken into account when designing the IT landscape. Some of the challenges uncovered are randomly illustrated in the pain point cloud shown in Figure 11.4.

Figure 11.4   Pain point cloud

Requirements Regarding the New System and its Implementation

From the preceding discussions, different wishes and priorities of the respective departments can be derived, and advantages and disadvantages of the software used can be identified. The use of on-demand cloud-based software (software as a service) should also be discussed in this context. Some central requirements become clear, which are presented in the following:

- **Information loss:** To prevent information loss and improve internal communication, the new IT landscape should enable better exchanges of information between Funnel and the project management tool(s). A lot of information is currently lost due to the lack of software interfaces, especially with regard to the business development department.
- **Project overview:** When designing the IT landscape, it should be taken into account that it is currently not possible to have an overview of the sub-project status in projects involving several online marketing departments and the web development team, especially since two project management tools are used.
- **Task assignment:** The transparent assignment of tasks (in the tool or by email) is desired by many employees and should be included in the decision. Rocketchat, the internal chat software, has certainly proven itself several times in the past. However, it is conceivable to integrate a chat function into the new software solutions.

- **Project evaluation:** The central evaluation of all projects according to the costs, status, involved actors, and priority, among others, should be supported.
- **Documentation:** The documentation within the projects is a central aspect. This takes up a lot of time and should be recorded in the software as intuitively as possible and with as little effort as possible. The linking of project files belonging to the project, whether internally within the software or on the file server, must also be taken into account.
- **Invoicing:** If the redesign of the IT landscape requires a replacement of the accounts receivable software Debtware, it must still be possible to automatically generate invoices for projects that run over several months. Currently, the web development department takes about 3–4 hours to create invoices at the end of the month, which are not billed. Since the tax advisor of the company also uses Credisson and it works well, there are no plans to switch here.
- **Master data:** Customer data should be managed as centrally as possible, so it can be used by all departments during projects.
- **Time recording:** Central time recording is desired. Currently, this is done both in OC and Yeera, depending on the department, which makes evaluation difficult.
- **Knowledge management:** Information on the implementation of projects, on customers, and, for example, on the storage of passwords should, if possible, be made accessible to all departments and collected in a wiki, for example.
- **Costs:** Against the backdrop of the grown structures and requirements, the CEOs are willing to invest more in the IT landscape. However, from the CEOs' point of view, introducing Yeera for the entire company does not seem to make sense and would also be very cost-intensive. In addition, other departments find this tool unclear, partly due to political reasons, and are reluctant to use it. The web development department, on the other hand, is convinced by this tool and justifies its decision, among other things, with the use of kanban boards or working in sprints. Overall, it is important to justify the benefits of new software investments. It should be taken into account that both bad investments and the retention of the widely outdated IT landscape could quickly result in six-digit costs for the company. "Ultimately, the added value must be right," say the founders. Accordingly, different scenarios have to be weighed up.

When planning the IT landscape and during its implementation, particular care must be taken to ensure that no (customer) data are lost. Performance slumps should also be avoided by piloting the changes in individual departments, if necessary. The cost of (internal) training and measures to raise awareness among employees affected by the upcoming transformation should be taken into account. Ultimately, the original agility based on the company's size must be largely maintained through lean process design, clear project responsibilities, and efficient software use. In this context, several solutions for designing the new IT landscape are conceivable, which can range from the replacement or new implementation of individual software solutions to a holistic integration, and they should be considered, in particular, against the background of a cost-benefit analysis. It is important to make a prioritized selection but, at the same time, to also show alternative paths that take into account the interests of the company as a whole, as well as the interests of the departments.

STUDENT CHALLENGES: DISCUSSION QUESTIONS

The following questions will guide students when working through the case:

1.   An overview of the strengths and weaknesses of the company with reference to the current IT landscape, as well as the opportunities and risks associated with its redesign, can help raise employee awareness and derive necessary measures as part of the transformation. Following this, what might a SWOT analysis look like?
2.   How do the interests expressed by individual departments affect the design of the new IT landscape? Point out organizational and technical challenges that need to be taken into account in the context of redesigning the IT landscape, and sort them according to their relevance to the upcoming transformation.
3.   The transformation can range from the selective replacement or procurement of software to comprehensive integration. Which software solutions come into question here and why? Analyze their pros and cons by developing a list of features for comparison.
4.   What could the transformation roadmap look like, and how would you proceed with the rollout of the new systems/software? In doing so, also consider the associated training efforts required with regard to the departments as well as the possible, temporary parallel operation of the old and new software. For this purpose, landscape models and "process support matrices," mapping departments in terms of processes and software, can be used complementarily, for example, to illustrate the as-is and to-be IT landscapes.

REFERENCES

Acs, Z. J. and Mueller, P. (2008). Employment effects of business dynamics: Mice, gazelles and elephants. *Small Business Economics*, 30(1), 85–100.

Birch, D. L. and Medoff, J. (1994). Gazelles. In L. C. Solmon and A. R. Levenson (eds), *Labor Markets, Employment Policy and Job Creation* (pp. 159–167). London, UK: Westview Press.

Henrekson, M. and Johansson, D. (2010). Gazelles as job creators: A survey and interpretation of the evidence. *Small Business Economics*, 35(2), 227–244.

Nambisan, S. (2017). Digital entrepreneurship: Toward a digital technology perspective of entrepreneurship. *Entrepreneurship Theory and Practice*, 41(6), 1029–1055.

Recker, J. and von Briel, F. (2019). The future of digital entrepreneurship research: Existing and emerging opportunities. Paper presented at the 40th International Conference on Information Systems, Munich, Germany.

Von Briel, F., Recker, J., Selander, L., Hukal, P., Jarvenpaa, S. L., Yoo, Y., Lehmann, J., Chan, Y., Rothe, H., Alpar, P., Fuerstenau, D., and Wurm, B. (2021). Researching digital entrepreneurship: Current issues and suggestions for future directions. *Communications of the Association for Information Systems*, 48(1), 284–304.

12. Lenali, the first audio social media: the Malian app empowering small-business owners

Katia Richomme-Huet and Odile De Saint Julien

LEARNING OBJECTIVES

This case reveals the value of looking at digital inclusion as a driving force to foster and encourage entrepreneurial talent through social media for illiterate entrepreneurs. This inclusive social network allows the community of people belonging to the Malian Base of the Pyramid (hereafter BoP) to improve the conditions for success of these previously digitally excluded local entrepreneurs.

Working on this case study will show the student how to:

- Describe and identify viable business models for social digital ventures.
- Relate the difficulty of starting and growing a digital venture in countries with low level of education and infrastructural problems.
- Explain the impact of digital voice technology on innovation and on BoP communities.
- Develop a business model for a sustainable and growing venture.
- Identify the entrepreneurial opportunities to contribute to closing the gap of illiteracy digital divide.

INTRODUCTION

Despite ongoing government instability, Mali is an African democracy that has put a lot of effort into creating a dynamic economy, including political reforms to boost its economy and stimulate investments. The Malian population comprises several sub-Saharan ethnic groups. Among these 20 million people,[1] whose median age is 16.3 years, only 35.5 percent are literate.[2]

While technologies such as Web 2.0 allow social network users to find, organize, share and create information and content in a personal and globally accessible way, they have created a world that operates in read-write mode. They induce a digital and social divide and thus generate user communities that are marginalized or discriminated against in the digital and market domains. Most Malian small business owners build their project from their own knowledge and by relying on people that they know, without any technology or education. Family, friends and word of mouth ensure their survival. Their objectives evolve as their entrepreneurial project progresses. These Malian BoP (Bottom of the Pyramid)[3] entrepreneurs (Prahalad, 2005), indeed digitally excluded, need to benefit from digital innovation.

Faced with this problem, Mamadou Sidibé created a voice-based application where BoP people can create new relationships that improve their quality of life. In February 2016, he invested his family savings in Lenali LLC.

Figure 12.1   Lenali's company logo

A tribute to his wife Elena (LENA) and his country (MALI), this application, also named Lenali, is the first Malian social and inclusive network based on audio technologies (Figure 12.1). Available since January 2017, Lenali speaks French and local languages (Bambara, Soninke, Songhai, Mooré, and Wolof) while considering regional habits in Bamako. The users can register online and communicate effectively without the need for writing.

Sidibé positioned his solution as a social intermediary capable of creating mutual value in correlation with local economic, social and environmental needs. The entrepreneur quickly realized that for these illiterate populations, the value of Lenali lies in what users could do with it rather than in the technical characteristics of his offer. He initiated a change in the rules of the game of the social networks by developing an inclusive and scalable approach that emancipates people and allows the development of local value chains.

In line with the BoP 3.0 approach,[4] local entrepreneurs can reach out beyond their immediate social network and attract a wider net of customers through the voice app and its sharing network.

BUSINESS AND INDUSTRY OVERVIEW

Via the internet, social networks, such as Facebook, are functioning as multi-sided marketplaces connecting various categories of users through platforms and applications. Despite limitations to access due to infrastructure deficiency or lack of literacy, they have become vital tools of communication for many Africans for news, elections and, of course, selfies.

The potential impact of social media in Africa is enormous but largely unexploited. As shown in Table 12.1, Facebook remains the most popular with an 83.46 percent market share (against 76.55 percent worldwide), far ahead of their competitors or other platforms (YouTube, Twitter, Pinterest, Instagram, LinkedIn, Tumblr or Reddit) even if fewer than 10 percent of Africans have a Facebook account.[5]

Table 12.1   *Social media market share by platform in Africa (percent)*

2021	Social media platforms in Africa						
	Facebook	YouTube	Twitter	Pinterest	Instagram	LinkedIn	Other
January	67.51	16.51	8.32	6.48	0.83	0.16	0.19
April	54.23	28.98	10.53	4.41	1.3	0.18	0.37
July	63.21	10.83	21.16	2.54	1.61	0.12	0.53
October	74.88	10.96	7.12	4.13	2.2	0.16	0.55
December	83.46	9.11	3.06	2.34	1.6	0.13	0.3

Source: Adapted from Statcounter GlobalStats – December, 2021.

Education in Africa is overpriced. Over one-fifth of children between the ages of 6 and 11 and one-third between the ages of 12 and 14 are out of school.[6] Consequently, it is difficult for them and more broadly for the uneducated to access fast-advancing digital technologies. African governments need to support this digital transformation through effective social media and digital policy to reap its full benefits. For Vera Songwe, United Nations Under-Secretary-General, women and people from rural areas need access to the internet to take advantage of technologies.

The low literacy rate may be the main reason why the number of digital users in Mali has stagnated around 20 percent despite the falling price of mobile phones and increasing internet access and 4G connections. A second reason is the multiplicity of ethnic groups.[7] While the official language of Mali is French, 80 percent of people speak Bambara and there are at least 40 local dialects in use. A third reason relates to the importance of the agricultural sector, which accounts for almost 40 percent of GDP and employs 73 percent of the population.[8] This may also explain the low literacy rate and the limited use of the web. What is more, existing platforms are largely centered on written posts and conversation, as well as video and pictures. Indeed, they are mostly inaccessible for BoP communities, composed of people from oral and spoken language cultures, with little formal education and predominantly illiterate.

Already established apps, like Viber, allow users to communicate by recording voice. Some projects are developed such as Foroba Blon[9] in Mali (a W4RA – Web Alliance for Regreening in Africa – project and a voice-based service to support citizen journalism). Foroba Blon allows rural residents to call radio stations and leave audio messages from basic mobile phones to a web interface without being connected to an internet connection.

DIGITALLY-ENABLED SOCIAL ENTREPRENEURS AND SOCIAL INNOVATION

Founder Mamadou Sidibé spent years developing social networking apps that he hoped one day would rival giants such as Facebook or WhatsApp in his native Mali, each time realizing he was always one step behind. One day, he clearly perceived his users' pain points. Even with smartphones, mobile banking and social networks, many trade features are text-based, leaving users out, or relying on friends, family and neighbors to create accounts, change settings and read non-audio messages. The Eureka moment occurred during a visit to a supermarket when a shop manager asked his help to read a message in French on the chat application Viber. "That's when it clicked: I was running after the wrong tools."

Sidibé completely changed his approach. "I decided Lenali should be a vocal social media app, in the local language. I needed to help people like him (the shop manager) to understand what they were doing when they try and install it," he explained. "You can do everything vocally, right up to do up your profile. If you know how to write you can put it in writing and, if not, you speak into the application and record it. And after that you can publish vocally, you can comment vocally and really you can do everything in this application without ever having to write a single word," Sidibé added.

With this mission in mind, he gave up his career in French start-ups to devote himself fully to the development of Lenali (Figure 12.2). His biggest challenge has been limited access to funding as he has bootstrapped the project himself, with the help of his family and friends for more than 160,000 euros of love money.

Figure 12.2   Presentation of the Lenali application by its creator

First, this application is positioned in the booming voice services market. This inclusive technology allows the most disadvantaged users to create, share and discuss information to express their entrepreneurial tendencies. Once logged in, users have the option of recording a message in a language of their choice. An audio guide directs the user on how to record a message. To publish a post, the user simply needs to record the message and send it. Lenali has many options and functional capabilities available to the user (Figure 12.3).

Figure 12.3   Lenali's features

Second, Lenali is contextualized and grounded on the respect of the local culture and environment while allowing local entrepreneurs to establish their digital presence on the local markets and providing value for a broader audience, as shown in Figure 12.4.

Figure 12.4   Lenamarket, a selling and promoting marketplace in local languages

LENALI, A BUSINESS AND EDUCATIONAL ENGINE

Providing Economic Opportunities at a Large Scale

Through audio technologies, Sidibé wanted to help illiterate entrepreneurs to develop the local market by reaching more customers: "Everything is done without the need for writing skills," Sidibé says, though the application does accept written posts as well. For the millions of Malian uneducated citizens, it has the potential to change the way business is done.

Far from the wealthy and Western-educated entrepreneurs behind such initiatives, thousands of business people are flourishing despite their lack of education. Offline, they are adapting to an increasingly competitive business environment and demanding more rights from a government they say marginalizes them. In the Dabanani market, especially in Bamako, the almost habitual handing down of shops from father to son is a lucrative alternative to education. The traders take advantage of the business owners' illiteracy. In the formal economy, they benefit from helpers, young graduates or their own children, who act as intermediaries between the traders and the administration.

The main problem remains that even the solutions offered by local start-ups require knowing how to use a smartphone and to understand basic French. So, the illiterate entrepreneurs stick to subsistence trading in a very informal way. Lenali is a real solution. A mango vendor could post a photo, add audio that tells his or her location and ask people who want more information to comment by voice posts.

Ada Tembely, Sidibé's house cleaner who also runs a fruit and vegetable stall, volunteered to test the application to advertise her business. She had not previously invested in a phone – which cost a month's salary – or an internet connection. Uneducated and a non-French-speaker, she is able now to attract customers with Lenali by sending a voice message in her language, Bambara. She can show the location of her stall, pictures of the fruits and vegetables she is offering that day. "Here are your lovely fruits. We have nice ripe oranges, apples, bananas. Not to mention fantastic pineapples. Today we have almost everything to keep you satisfied. To find us go to the third bridge and you will see me." Her earnings have tripled since she started using the app, which like Facebook provides users with options such as "likes" and "posts." "A lot of people heard of me through the app," she said. She advertises services and produce such as vegetables on the platform, as well as using it to host her CV.

Motorbike sales at Boubacar Sidiki Goita's shop in Bamako went up after he started using this application to promote his goods and share information with customers who cannot read. "Since I have been using Lenali, my turnover has gone up 400 percent and now I can sell 20 motorbikes a day whereas before it was hard work selling just 5 a day." Goita is literate but many of the people he is trying to reach are not. As his motorbikes are mainly aimed at young people, he says that Lenali has become popular with them.

Improving Digital Inclusion While Fighting Illiteracy and Empowering Communities

In this day and age, when Africans are gradually adopting foreign cultures, Lenali revives communication in local languages. Oral communication is part of Africa's culture, used for passing their history (oral epics) from one generation to another but also as the primary source of information for people in West Africa.

For Sidibé, this application is a response to economic and social problems. Embedded in a strong social mission, his aim is also to stimulate digital inclusion, first in Mali and later in other countries in Africa. "Because the problems in Mali are the same as in the majority of countries in Africa, the app could work anywhere, and in the future, we can add many languages," he says. Lenali has helped to reach offline people through public debate on issues including democracy, economic policies and health. This sharing of information coupled with the creation of content related to both the personal and professional interests and goals of Lenali's participants and learners, "as a sign of empathy," encourages these learners to engage in the use of digital technologies (Sheridan and Kelly, 2010). They begin to participate in the production and consumption of information, enabling discussion on topics of local or specific interest. Through citizen journalism and reader comments, they create content and are engaging in literate practices.

Currently, some local non-governmental organizations (NGOs),[10] such as the National Network for the Development of Young Girls and Women of Mali, are using Lenali for social mobilization. "An essential part of the information we publicize is about reproductive health, gender-based violence and literacy," say Hawa Niakate and Aminata Camara, who work for the organization. "We use Lenali social network to reach everyone." Thanks to Lenali, they mobilize and educate the public on social topics but also on economic empowerment. A similar phone-to-web system created in nearby Ghana, Viamo, provides advice about health, rights, and news. Collaborating with network providers such as the French mobile giant Orange, Viamo has conducted phone surveys in remote communities to get their views on the legitimacy of the summer 2018 Malian election or on incidents of sexual violence.

Develop an Inclusive Social Network for Inclusive Business Models

Unlike Facebook and classical social networks, which are mainly driven by profit maximizing via the monetization of online traffic, Lenali contributes to a virtuous circle of increased usage, skills development, improved livelihoods and, overall, greater digital inclusion. The app allows users to take an active and leading part in the development of their own BoP community (Chelekis & Mudambi, 2010). It helps and supports local entrepreneurs in the digitalization of their economic activity and thus improves and increases their productivity. This also fosters "word-of-mouth" marketing, in local language, with culturally appropriate community interaction and eventually the emergence of community influencers.

As an inclusive and social network, but oriented towards the BoP market, Lenali is:

1. *A connecting channel within a BoP community*: since conventional media channels are often absent in BoP communities, Lenali improves the flow of information, resources and skills that make it possible to connect supply and demand. For example, without Lenali, Ada Tembely was unable to connect her supply to demand because she could not reach enough consumers interested in her fresh products.

2. *An online and technical vocal facilitator for illiterate entrepreneurs*: the voice commands, humanizing the electronic environment, enable the integration of illiterate people previously excluded from the digital marketplace by promoting the understanding of "who is who," who does what and how.

3. *A BoP hub for an inclusive marketplace*: it is a trusty and tangible point of reference (O'Kelly, 1987) for the BoP population seeking to develop entrepreneurial activity with confidence and to expand its customer base. On the client side, it offers a wider range of products and services. It catalyzes new business opportunities by bridging the silos, exploiting connections, sourcing novel solutions and transforming the value chain.

4. *A network of "business friends"*: it offers the BoP community the possibility to project itself into the future through education, support and empowerment. With Lenali, in accordance with African culture, exchanges are not limited to economic transactions but enhanced by humanized links motivated by both personal and professional interests. The BoP actors become "business friends" (Uzzi, 1997), with a "business intimacy" (Simanis & Hart, 2008) that promotes the co-creation of mutual value and establishes trust across the value chain.

5. *An inclusive business model booster*: digitally equipped entrepreneurs improve their connectivity to their customers, boost their efficiency, and build their confidence and status. These close interactions and interdependencies between BoP local entrepreneurs and communities, building upon local and indigenous knowledge, culture and environment, enable the development of native capabilities as well as a responsible and sustainable growth.

Involving low-income customers and entrepreneurs, Lenali offers an inclusive and scalable business model that is fully guided by the founder's social mission and has its roots in the Malian BoP. The main goal is to generate sustainable and decent income opportunities for communities with little or no labor market mobility (Likoko and Kini, 2017). Value creation is generated through the impacts of Lenali's social and inclusive activities. To support this process, Lenali focuses on "what's needed" for these digitally excluded entrepreneurs to build a local business that helps them get out of poverty and shamelessly get online.

PROBLEM STATEMENT: NEXT STEPS

Evolving the Business Model or Waiting for the Market to Tip

To recover his initial investment (linked to the creation, development, launch and promotion of Lenali) and generate revenue, Sidibé planned to implement an advertising-based revenue model. Because of its easy implementation and widespread acceptance by mobile application users, it was the chosen strategy to monetizing Lenali. The second complementary option was the freemium model, with basic services to consumers for free, while charging for premium services (advanced features and perks) to paying members. This matches with a classical strategy for bootstrapping networks – "come for the tool, stay for the network" – which attracts users with a single-player tool and then, over time, gets them to engage in and develop the network. For both models, it is expected to become profitable when it reaches 200,000 users in a nation of more than 20 million people. Since it was launched in 2017, the number of users has consistently grown. Lenali had 27,000 users in 2017, 60,000 in 2019, 75,000 in 2020 and over 100,000 in 2021. While most of Lenali's users either are in Mali or are part of the diaspora, Sidibé believes the application can gain traction across the continent. "Francophone Africa's underrepresented in terms of contributions and headlines on the tech front, despite the work of countries like Ivory Coast, Senegal and Cameroon."

In the meantime, he had to cover both the initial costs (one-time expenses for long-term assets such as major equipment, or upfront costs for permits, licenses, logo and website design, communication tools or support and incorporation fees, insurance, taxes, etc.) and the ongoing costs (rent, payroll, taxes, legal services, loan payments, insurance payments, operating and marketing expenses, etc.). To support run-up and development activities, he participated actively in a variety of research projects in collaboration with universities and institutions to get grants. He sold four custom software developments, performed by his in-house development teams: "PAMON" and "PAAR" for the World Bank; MFC for the NGO "Mali FolkCenter" and "Mali Health" for the NGO "Mali Health." In addition to his team (3 developers and 7 trainers, data collectors and local languages translators), he is delighted to count on active production and participation from highly motivated volunteers in Mali but also from the outside Malian diaspora.

Further Develop the Economic Opportunities Within the BoP Communities

By exploiting hidden local entrepreneurial opportunities, Lenali fosters development and initiates new businesses and value streams from which other entrepreneurs can profit. This solution-driven innovation is part of the answer for BoP markets in Mali and in other places in Francophone Africa: (1) it overcomes infrastructure and resource deficits; (2) it mitigates distance and institutional voids; (3) it correctly tackles the social problems to compensate for the insufficiencies, failures, or absence of basic fundamentals to economic development.

Develop New Tools Against Illiteracy to Better Empower BoP Communities

Vocal social media has the potential to bridge formal and informal learning through participatory digital cultures. "First, you need to create the need for

L'application TOTALEMENT VOCALE Gafé d'*Alphabétisation Numérique, Standard* et *Fonctionnelle* est conçue par **Lenali** pour **rendre accessible en LANGUES LOCALES et en FRANÇAIS les services numériques** aux populations non alphabétisées (surtout en zones rurales), **réduire l'inégalité Hommes/Femmes** et poser les bases de l'autonomisation par le numérique.

Figure 12.5   Google play GAFE App

literacy and for digital tools. If the internet helps people make more money, they will invest in it," Sidibé said. "Then quickly they'll realize they need to read and write and will want to take literacy classes." This is why he decided to develop Gafé, a new application (Figures 12.5 and 12.6).

Figure 12.6   *Design of the digital interface for the mobile version of the app*

Gafé stemmed from a two-pronged approach: simultaneously work on improving the education, literacy and digital skills of users, as well as design relevant and usable digital solutions that are inclusive of a full range of skill levels. It enriches the literate environment in offering motivations and opportunities for learning and practicing digital skills and literacy, answering to aspirations and social pressures to get online. Using this inclusive digital solution, BoP communities develop their digital and literacy skills.

As powerful tools that add value to people's lives, Lenali and Gafé stimulate and evolve the entrepreneurial and educational system in Mali.

STUDENT CHALLENGES AND DISCUSSION QUESTIONS

Based on the descriptions of the problems and Sidibé's questions, students will answer the following questions and/or instructions.

Situational Analysis (Past and Present)

Learn about describing and identifying viable business models for social digital venture

Using the Social Business Model Canvas, identify the information in the text and map Lenali's current BM.

A. *Social value proposition*: What are the main motivations of the founder to launch Lenali (vision)? What differences is Lenali making with existing solutions? What could be the social value proposition in one sentence? What social impact measures could Lenali use?
B. *Market*: Who are the main users/customers, early adopters, etc.? What is the macroeconomic environment and what are the changes affecting the market? Who are the competitors?
C. *Implementation*: What does Lenali do? What resources does Lenali have? Who helps Lenali to carry out its activities? What is its sales and marketing plan? How does Lenali reach its users/customers?
D. *Finance*: What are the main costs? What are the main revenue streams? Where does Lenali intend to reinvest its surplus?
E. *Impact*: What are the impacts of this social value proposition?

Understand the difficulty of starting and growing a digital venture in countries with low levels of education and infrastructural problems

A. Identify what can help or did help Lenali to overcome low levels of education and infrastructural problems and perhaps leverage some local assets. What are the points of strength and weakness of the company? What are the major opportunities and threats? Answer the above questions through a SWOT analysis matrix.

Explain the impact of digital voice technology on innovation (opportunities and technologies), on BoP entrepreneurs and on BoP people in general (exclusion and inclusion)

A. As audio is becoming the new frontier for user digital experience (boom of digital voice recognition and digital speech market with podcast, smart speakers, etc.), what are the opportunities for innovation?
B. What are the main impacts of Lenali on the Malian BoP entrepreneurs and communities?

Business Model Evolution (Future and Diversification)

**Discuss how the business model could evolve to make Lenali
a sustainable and growing venture**

A. How is Lenali going to become profitable? Should its business model be changed?
B. Given its social mission, how can Lenali make the business sustainable and even profitable?
C. Lenali is currently a not-for-profit company. Should the founder consider changing it to for-profit?

Identify the opportunities for the company to contribute to closing the gap of the illiteracy digital divide and to go beyond the local market of illiterate users

A. What is new with Gafé (how is it different from Lenali)? What are the main objectives of Gafé?
B. What could be other opportunities to go beyond the local market?
C. How does Lenali optimize the user experience and how may it become more attractive?

NOTES

1. Mali's population is expected to surpass 50 million by 2058 and 80 million by 2099, due to a fertility rate of 5.92 births per woman (https://worldpopula tionreview.com/countries/mali-population).
2. The Malian literacy rate among the population aged 15 years and older in 2018 is about 46.2% for males and 25.7% for females. Even more alarming, the rate reaches 50.1% among 15- to 24-year-olds, with a less unequal distribution between men (57.8%) and women (43.4%) (http://uis.unesco.org/en/country/ml).
3. This economic term "refers to the poorest two-thirds of the economic human pyramid, a group of more than four billion people living in abject poverty. More broadly, BoP refers to a market-based model of economic development that promises to simultaneously alleviate widespread poverty while providing growth and profits for multinational corporations (MNCs)" (Encyclopedia Britannica, https://www.britannica.com/topic/Bottom-of-the-Pyramid). The concept evolved from BoP 1.0 to BoP 3.0. The BoP 1.0 has been criticized for mainly adopting the Western large companies' perspective and objectives, neglecting the local communities.
4. Recent approaches included the active engagement of the poor, local empowerment and entrepreneurship in business activities (BoP 2.0), as well as more inclusion and collaboration with local businesses and enterprises (BoP 3.0).
5. Stats are based on aggregate data collected by Statcounter on a sample exceeding 10 billion page views per month on 2 million websites (https://gs.statcounter .com/social-media-stats/all/africa).

6. See http://uis.unesco.org/en/news/263-million-children-and-youth-are-out-school.
7. The largest is the Bambara, accounting for 37% of the population. The Bambara, Sonike, Khassonke and Malinke are part of the larger Mande group, which accounts for 50%. Other large ethnic groups include the Fula (17%), Voltaic (12%), Songhai (6%) and the Tuareg and Moor (10%) (https://worldpopulationreview.com/countries/mali-population).
8. Food and Agriculture Organization (2017), *Country fact sheet on food and agriculture policy trends, Mali*, Report I7617EN/1/07.17, July.
9. Foroba Blon is a community radio station in Africa and on the Web (https://w4ra.org/foroba-blon-community-radio-in-africa-and-the-web/).
10. NGOs are non-profit associations, of public interest, which play an essential role in meeting the needs of vulnerable populations, going where other actors do not. They are at the origin of the emergence of ecosystems characteristic of the BoP where acting together and creating wealth are achieved in a symbiotic relationship (Prahalad, 2005).

REFERENCES

Chelekis, J. and Mudambi, S. M. (2010). MNCs and micro-entrepreneurship in emerging economies: The case of Avon in the Amazon. *Journal of International Management*, 16(4), 412–424.

Likoko, E. and Kini, J. (2017). Inclusive business: A business approach to development. *Current Opinion in Environmental Sustainability*, 24, 84–88.

O'Kelly, M. E. (1987). A quadratic integer program for the location of interacting hub facilities. *European Journal of Operational Research*, 32(3), 393–404.

Prahalad, C. K. (2005). *The Fortune at the Bottom of the Pyramid: Eradicating Poverty through Profits*. Upper Saddle River, NJ: Wharton School Publishing.

Sheridan, K. and Kelly, M. A. (2010). The indicators of instructor presence that are important to students in online courses. *Journal of Online Learning and Teaching*, 6(4), 767.

Simanis, E. and Hart, S. (2008). Beyond selling to the poor: Building business intimacy through embedded innovation. Johnson School of Management. https://www.researchgate.net/profile/Stuart-Hart/publication/265874360.

Uzzi, B. (1997). Social structure and competition in interfirm networks: The paradox of embeddedness. *Administrative Science Quarterly*, 42(1), 35–67.

Chapter 1: teaching notes

Cesar Bandera and Katia Passerini

CASE SUMMARY

This case is based on a true story. Steve is a digital entrepreneur whose company JITTEI seems to be on the right track. JITTEI has prototyped and patented a technology that broadcasts short instructional and logistics videos to the cell phones of emergency responders. Think of it as a public messaging service that sends out videos instead of just text messages. In the fall of 2010, the Centers for Disease Control and Prevention (CDC) awarded JITTEI a $1M two-year contract to develop the technology into a formal product and install it at their new Emergency Operations Center (EOC) in Atlanta, Georgia. However, at the start of the project, CDC requested help from JITTEI in the response to the Haiti cholera epidemic. Steve complied with the humanitarian request, but also for business reasons: if the deployment of the prototype to Haiti was successful, JITTEI and CDC would enjoy a strong relationship during the two-year project, and afterwards. The deployment in Haiti was a success, and in the ensuing two years, the CDC successfully used the proto-type in several other emergency incidents.

Given the close working relationship between JITTEI and the CDC, Steve assumed the delivery of the system to the EOC at the end of the two-year con-tract would go smoothly. However, in December 2012, CDC announced that it would not accept the system, and instead use JITTEI as a video messaging service provider. This resulted in a dramatic change of JITTEI's business model, from being a product provider to being a service provider. Steve had not taken note of four facts. First, the CDC had used JITTEI as a service provider during the two-year period and simply preferred to continue that type of relationship. Second, digital business models in general were gravitating towards software-as-a-service. Third, pilot projects and demonstrations are not the same as commercial sales. Fourth, digital entrepreneurship facilitated technology development and client engagement, but also made business model validation more difficult.

Target Audience

This case is intended for undergraduate and graduate students with prior knowledge of basic business concepts, such as the definition of a business model. The case is appropriate for students learning about de-risking digital entrepreneurship, and for courses that use the lean startup methodology. Prior knowledge of telecommunications, software design, or project management is not required.

TEACHING OBJECTIVES

- Students learn differences between a product-based business model and a digital service-based business model, and the challenges unique to each.
- Students learn how a digital entrepreneur can pivot from a product to a service.
- Students learn the perils of misreading the market when developing digital services.

TEACHING STRATEGY AND ASSIGNMENT SUGGESTIONS

This case study is well suited for group research and reflection. The suggestions below include supplemental activities for graduate students.

Discussion Question 1: Describe and contrast product-based business models from service-based business models. What are their advantages and disadvantages from the point of view of the user and of the provider? Why are service-based models becoming dominant in the software industry?

This case study discusses a specific type of pivot: a company cannot sell a tool but can sell the service of the tool. It is like a company that cannot sell novel efficient accounting software but is able to use that very same software and sell accounting services. As a low-tech example, consider a carpenter who cannot sell an innovative vise for building furniture, but is able to sell furniture that he makes with said vise. Ask students to find examples of such product-to-service pivots. Graduate students can research the growing popularity of the software-as-a-service (SaaS) business model, and answer the question, "did JITTEI become an SaaS company, or just a service company?"

Discussion Question 2: What changes should Steve introduce to the JETTEI business model to pivot from a product-based to a service-based business model? How could he implement this change quickly and cost-effectively?

Discuss with students the concept of the pivot, and its importance. Students will likely realize the need for pivoting but underappreciate the business model uncertainty that drives pivoting. Stress to students that a company rarely pivots because the product fails to work – a company pivots because the product fails to sell. Graduate courses can discuss the first-mover myth, which states that the more innovative the offering, the more uncertain the business model becomes because there is no precedent.

Discussion Question 3: Before changing the JETTEI business model, should Steve confirm that a pivot is necessary? Would more pilots help this decision?

The company in the case study survives because it pivoted. What is surprising is that a pivot was necessary in spite of an excellent relationship with a client that paid for a successful pilot. Where did our protagonist get it wrong? The most recommended start to validating the product-customer fit is discussions with potential customers about their needs, and there are protocols for conducting such discussions that maximize the entrepreneur's collection of actionable and unbiased information. Ask students to identify which transgressions in the appendix "Screwing Up Customer Discovery" of Giff Constable's book *Talking to Humans* (2014) were committed by the protagonist.

Assignment 1: Steve may have to pivot JETTEI from a product-based business model to an SaaS business model. Draft a business model canvas for his new business model. Note that the payer and the consumer of emergency public health communications are not the same.

Undergraduate students should use Osterwalder's traditional 9-block canvas. Graduate students can use the 11-block canvas, which is the traditional 9-block canvas, plus two more blocks: competitors, and regulatory requirements (i.e., legal requirements that JETTEI must follow). Figure TN 1.1 presents a good example of the JETTEI SaaS business model canvas. Things to look for include:

1. The value proposition and customer segment blocks distinguish between the payer and the consumer.
2. The model includes traditional SaaS offering (access to the platform) or optional turnkey support (labor billed by the hour).
3. Regulatory requirements obligate consumers to opt into a campaign; otherwise, the messages are considered spam.
4. For campaigns that require only text and involve consumers with broadband access, JETTEI competes with well-established text and email messaging services.

Business Model Canvas for: JETTEI (SaaS) by Steve

Regulatory Requirements				
In the United States, a messaging service cannot push messages to someone without their consent.				

Key Partners	Key Activities	Value Proposition	Customer Relationships	Customer Segments
Public health consortia. Responder consortia. Wireless carriers. Cloud hosting providers.	Outreach (sales). Client relations. Platform maintenance. Special services: Content creation, campaign mgmt., analytics gen.	Client/Payer: (1) Ease of campaign creation and management. (2) Reach vulnerable audiences lacking Internet. (3) Help with content creation, campaign management, and analytics.	Your reliable partner in public health emergency and outreach campaigns, whether you need just a tool or turnkey support.	Client/Payer: Emergency response and public health administrators, non-governmental organizations.
	Key Resources Patents for mobile multimedia broadcasting. Operational pilot-tested system.	Consumer: Relevant health information that is easy to receive and view on any cell phone or carrier.	**Channels** (Advertising, Sales, Delivery) How will you reach your customers? How will you target your advertising to your customer segment?	Consumer: Civilians and responders without Internet access.

Cost Structure	Revenue Streams Account setup (one time);
Servers, gateway to wireless service providers, staff (sales, software developers, content creators, admin)	Subscription (monthly/annual); Messages sent and received (per campaign); Content creation, campaign management, advanced analytics, training (optional, hourly rate)

Competition
Twilio (SMS), Mailchimp (email)

TN Figure 1.1   Example JETTEI system as a service business model canvas

Assignment 2: Assuming the JETTEI pivot to an SaaS business model is successful, what new markets might Steve consider pursuing? Can he leverage the CDC pilot?

Students traditionally associate pivots with nascent startups seeking to validate their business model assumptions. Explain how pivots are also part of validating the expansion of a successful company into new markets where the business model has not yet been proven to work. Encourage students to be creative in this assignment, and to think "outside of Steve's box." New markets to consider include mobile news and entertainment channels, distance learning, and targeted advertising. Graduate students can either identify funding sources for this expansion, and/or draft the canvas for the new business model.

ADDITIONAL READING

atotaldisruption (2012, October 19). Eric Ries explains the pivot. *YouTube*. Retrieved March 21, 2022, from https://www.youtube.com/watch?v=1hTI4z2ijc4 (Eric Ries explains The Pivot).

Constable, G. (2014). *Talking to Humans*. N.p.: Giff Constable. Retrieved March 21, 2022, from https://www.talkingtohumans.com/.

Google (n.d.). *Rehydration of Cholera Patients – Google drive video*. Google Drive. Retrieved March 20, 2022, from https://drive.google.com/file/d/1ESJxHb0w0Rgh2wnplfv-Dv1-I3Iz4LRi/view (One of the cholera patient rehydration videos sent by the protagonist to Haiti).

Richter, J. (2020, September 30). What is a pivot? Top 10 best tech pivot examples [case study]: Winnona partners blog. Blog. Retrieved March 21, 2022, from https://blog.winnonapartners.com/what-is-a-pivot-top-10-best-tech-startup-pivots-case-study/ (A description of emblematic pivots).

The half-truth of first-mover advantage. *Harvard Business Review*, August 1, 2014. Retrieved March 21, 2022, from https://hbr.org/2005/04/the-half-truth-of-first-mover-advantage (A discussion of the business model uncertainty that comes with innovation).

The SaaS founder's journey – what matters at each stage. *For Entrepreneurs*, December 8, 2017. Retrieved March 21, 2022, from https://www.forentrepreneurs.com/saastock-2017/.

YouTube (2018, November 6). The SaaS business model & metrics: Understand the key drivers for Success. *YouTube*. Retrieved March 21, 2022, from https://www.youtube.com/watch?v=5RR6M_d6eKc (Web Summit).

Chapter 2: teaching notes

Michael Dominik

CASE SUMMARY

This case helps instructors who want to convey a balanced perspective between the appeal and the risks of entrepreneurship. Based on a real-world story about John, a US student entrepreneur who launches a mobile app targeted toward fellow students, including video and actual content from four years of operation, students will learn about common mistakes or critical aspects that are often overlooked by entrepreneurs trying to monetize app development such as lack of adequate testing, cybersecurity threats, and legal issues that are particularly relevant in the digital domain.

TEACHING OBJECTIVES

The primary emphasis for learning from this case is to increase knowledge and respect for the risks of becoming an entrepreneur, especially a digital entrepreneur where the barriers to entry are so low that students may be tempted to accept risks that they do not understand or are prepared to face. This case is intended to help students with modest life or business experience to learn that digital entrepreneurship can be a risky career and life path, and that the journey can end in a shutdown failure and the loss of time and money. This is particularly important for students – or anyone with little to modest understanding of the risks of digital entrepreneurship – who might seek to create a startup that breaks new ground, which represents additional risk. Becoming an entrepreneur necessitates students gain a basic understanding of the risks and associated implications of such a choice. It is the responsibility of educators to uncover for their entrepreneurial-leaning students the potential dark side of their choices.

TEACHING STRATEGY AND ASSIGNMENT SUGGESTIONS

Undergraduate Course

As preparation, the instructor could assign advance reading of the case along with additional readings or materials related to entrepreneurial risk such as those identified in the references.

The instructor might assign students to identify what they see as John's personal sacrifices for nearly five years of his young adult life, as stated in the case and others that are implied or assumed. This may be readily identified by undergraduate students who are the same age as John when he founded Stunited. Actual sacrifices made by John include the dedication of thousands of hours of unpaid time during days, nights and weekends when he could have been hanging out with family or friends; putting off the pursuit of relationship opportunities; increased personal stress compared to working for someone else; and loss of money that came from himself, family, and outside investors. Students in their young adult years should be able to speculatively identify more sacrifices made by John if they consider Stunited was a job that consumed an average of 20 hours per week for John while he was still a college student.

Students might also explore something that John did not entertain: the value and utility of partners and formal advisors and mentors. John had a strong sense of independence, and with a tendency to want to make his own decisions, thus he had little propensity for answering to a partner. John may have benefited from a strong and qualified partner, the value of which should be explored in evaluating this case. However, such discussion may also lead to a focus on entrepreneurial personality self-awareness, which is often still evolving in persons until the age of 25. If John had attempted the Stunited venture starting at age 30, he might have taken a different approach to many of his decisions with a different outcome for the company.

To engage in deeper exploration of entrepreneurial risk, students could be assigned in teams or individually to answer the case questions and prepare a multi-page written report or ten-minute briefing to the class. A rubric for such an assignment might be to include multiple additional references that explore entrepreneurial risk and how they relate to this case.

Graduate Course

This case could be coupled with Pittz and Liguori's (2020) short guide to risk and decisions for entrepreneurs, which would provide opportunity for a more comprehensive analysis approach, such as identifying in which topical areas John from Stunited fell short (e.g., insufficient financing, was a SAFE agreement best, product testing scenarios such as anticipating malicious actors and how to deal with them).

An MBA course might explore this case and evaluate the potential success for John as an entrepreneur using a SWOT (strengths, weaknesses, opportunities and threats) analysis. John's strengths were in his salesmanship and communication, with weaknesses in not more actively seeking mentors and advisors, in not gaining deeper competencies in programming and managing the technology elements of the app. John's opportunities included being young and able to take personal and professional risk, because he did not have bills to pay and a family to support, while threats included his business inexperience, and the distractions of having another startup already underway while Stunited was struggling.

The case could be evaluated using one or more theoretical constructs around entrepreneurship, including opportunity recognition, entrepreneurial intention, entrepreneurial effectuation, prototyping, experimentation, and the business model.

The following are possible answers to the questions posed in the case.

Discussion Question 1: What should be a twenty-one-year-old student's realistic expectations for success of an online startup?

Answers to this question are intended to elicit discussion around career and life choices for the prospective student entrepreneur. Discussion should yield grounded and realistic views about the breadth and depth of competition for many types of digital apps. Discussion should also reveal how John's youth and inexperience with technological and legal remedies in dealing with the threat actors caused him to be under-prepared to respond to crises. Students may need to overcome an illusion of expertise because college students use apps so frequently, wherein they may think they can easily understand how software should be developed and managed, that prospective customers think like them, and that optimism is the best response to evaluating risk. Another source of risk for many young digital entrepreneurs is cybersecurity, meant in a broad sense as any risk of outside hacking of the application, but which can also be behavioral and social engineering (as Stunited experienced with its threat actors). To increase the probability of success, students might be encouraged to be open to and even solicit deep-experience mentorship, which John did not seek or solicit. Success when investors are involved may also warrant or call for investor management oversight, whether informal (Board of Advisors) or formal (Board of Directors). Additionally, students may benefit from reflection and investigation/research into the value of some technical or functional business experience that could be later leveraged for benefit in a future entrepreneurial endeavor.

Discussion Question 2: What are the types and magnitude of risks that a student entrepreneur might face when considering a digital entrepreneurial venture?

The obvious risks that should be identified are John's loss of his own money, measured in the low tens of thousands, and his sacrifice of his own time, measured in the low thousands of hours. John also incurred collegiate opportunity costs in terms of distractions from his academic commitment by pursuing Stunited while finishing his undergraduate degree with potential poor academic performance. Career opportunity costs should be very prominent in the discussion, with John's example of having forgone an opportunity to take a finance job on New York's Wall Street representing an annual income sacrifice of one hundred thousand US dollars. Students should be expected to dig deep and identify potential hidden consequences, such as possible legal action by Stunited users who were threatened, and John's reputational risk with investors whose monies were lost. There were risks to his personally driven pride and reputation, which required John to continually refuel his internal motivations. He was clearly self-motivated to keep Stunited moving forward for its first three years, and after investors were brought on, there were risks associated with the fear of letting them down. There was also a personal emotional toll, which is difficult to quantify, and John did publicly acknowledge the stress and strain that came with early self-imposed pressure to keep Stunited moving forward.

Discussion Question 3: What should investors – whether angels, venture capitalists, institutions, or family and friends – expect when considering an investment in a student-led startup?

This question may be difficult to answer for students who have no experience with high-risk investments, but the learner should attempt to understand this perspective. Some possible answers include:

- An expectation that the student entrepreneur should be able to demonstrate basic financial literacy, including an understanding of revenue and cost projections, and how to read, understand, and even prepare pro forma accounting statements, which was never a requirement imposed upon John. Such understanding may be represented in the preparation of a detailed business plan with forward projections, including projection of additional financial metrics such as cost of acquiring and retaining a customer.

- Investors should also understand their own risk tolerance, especially if they are family or friends and not a sophisticated or accredited investor. Entrepreneurs seeking startup financing arrangements should have an understanding of multiple options for sources of financing, such as family, friends, banks or other sources of small business loans, angel investors, venture capitalists, and institutional investors.
- Entrepreneurs should also become familiar with the variety of legal agreements whether pre-equity or for equity such as non-disclosure agreements (NDA), simple agreements for future equity (SAFE), vesting terms, equity options, and terms of liquidity events.
- Investors may have insisted on the formation of a formal governance, through a Board of Advisors or even Board of Directors to provide experienced guidance and advice to John, who remained fiercely independent and did not solicit or welcome such counsel. Investors may have insisted on shared management with John, where they may have been able to be aware of the threat actor problems and bring advice and resources to bear. There are also a series of investor materials provided as digital resources, including an investor pitch deck and an investor financial agreement, that could be used for discussion and/or analysis.

Discussion Question 4: What might have been the nature of a productive relationship between Stunited and John's undergraduate university both before and after he graduated?

This question is particularly pertinent for universities with entrepreneurship centers and those who directly or indirectly support and nurture student entrepreneurs. Possible answers for an improved relationship include mandatory advising from the university, which also required willingness on John's part to receive that support, which was lacking. This raises the challenge of how assertively the student entrepreneur should pursue seeking advice from the university if they initially feel unsupported, and conversely how proactive universities should be in encouraging student entrepreneurs to receive their support. In this case, both John and the university were willing to leave each other alone if either party demonstrated lack of interest, which resulted in a modest collaborative relationship, which, if it had been better, may have forestalled some of the problems that eventually led to the shutdown of Stunited.

Discussion Question 5: How should John have anticipated and dealt with the threat actors who were threatening Stunited users?

This episode revealed a weakness in John's base of experience, and in his lack of anticipation and testing of possible user scenarios. Students venturing into app development should strive to become deeply aware of the cybersecurity risks they can face, including both technological risks (hacking) as well as social engineering / behavioral threats, as seen in this case. Deeper and more thorough testing of the app prototype – even while in its earliest stages of development while still at university – may have exposed this scenario and aided in preparedness. John did casually investigate with law enforcement authorities if there were criminal inquiry options when faced with a legal and ethical challenge that threatened the viability of Stunited when malicious actors posing as students seek to extort money from unsophisticated students. But the anonymity provided to sophisticated actors by the internet was difficult to overcome without significant cyber research resources, and law enforcement was not ready to dedicate resources to any effort. John might have sought and implemented alternative software approaches in the app to avoid obscured identities, but he suspected identity verification would have turned off his target audience of college students. He may have sought advice and counsel from experienced entrepreneurs and advisors who have faced similar challenges. To some extent, this challenge that eventually led to the shutdown of Stunited was a final breaking point for John, who felt strained by the slow traction of Stunited and the associated financial and emotional burdens and risks, which were less appealing than his alternatives, including moving on to another startup idea.

Discussion Question 6: How should John have explained the shutdown of Stunited and the loss of $75,000 to his investors?

There are no perfect answers here, but just thinking about having this communication should force students to think seriously about difficult conversations that can evoke stress. What John did was to call and talk on the phone with each investor individually and separately, and explain what had occurred with Stunited, and explain his firm conclusion that the firm should shut down. Some weeks following these calls, John did provide written documentation to each investor that their investment was worthless. Alternatively, John could have convened a meeting to allow the investors to ask questions, and he might have solicited perspective from the investors as mentors regarding options other than shutting down. He might also have offered investors some pre-equity investment opportunity in his already-underway next online startup.

ADDITIONAL MATERIALS

Startup Materials

The following materials serve as reference to Stunited's startup. For instructional use, these materials could be used for discussion regarding investor pitching and investor agreements.

1. **Stunited One-Pager** (https://www.e-elgar.com/textbooks/iandoli): A brief summary of Stunited as prepared for its investors in late 2020.
2. **Stunited Pitch Deck** (https://www.e-elgar.com/textbooks/iandoli): Investor pitch deck for Stunited as of October 2020.
3. **Simple Agreement for Future Equity** (SAFE) (https://www.e-elgar.com/textbooks/iandoli): This agreement was used to structure the first and only pre-seed round of investment between Stunited and its first outside investors.

Multimedia Materials

The real-world student entrepreneur in this case utilized social media as a channel to reach users, including video and audio content that was granted with approval for use in this case. The multimedia material is intended to help students gain a deeper understanding and relationship with John as the student entrepreneur. This should also help students relate to Stunited's journey, and to visualize and appreciate the activities of a young digital entrepreneur.

For instructional use, many of these materials could be used to evaluate pitching, marketing, and product design.

1. **Opportunity Recognition** (https://www.e-elgar.com/textbooks/iandoli): John's recollection of the first time he experienced the problem that eventually led to him creating Stunited.
2. **Pitching** (https://www.e-elgar.com/textbooks/iandoli): John's actual pitch at his university's new venture competition in 2017, at which he and Stunited won first place and the $4,000 he used to fund the functional prototype.
3. **Product Marketing** (https://www.e-elgar.com/textbooks/iandoli): A high-quality promotional video depicting the app and its value proposition, with animation and music that appealed to a younger audience.
4. **Product Marketing** (https://www.e-elgar.com/textbooks/iandoli): A university-setting vignette that was an effort to be humorous in promoting the Stunited app including student actors.

5. **Product Marketing** (https://www.e-elgar.com/textbooks/iandoli): A personal explanation by John to promote the second version of the Stunited app with a personal appeal and relationship model.
6. **Customer Engagement** (https://www.e-elgar.com/textbooks/iandoli): John attempts to deal with the Stunited threat actors by providing advice to users on how to know if the other party is credible.
7. **Customer Engagement** (https://www.e-elgar.com/textbooks/iandoli): John provides his input on the types of things Stunited users can barter.

Chapter 3: teaching notes

Ada Scupola

CASE SUMMARY

The case tells the story of a Danish digital social entrepreneurship venture, E-BRO APS, and the development of its main digital solution, JobIntra, whose purpose is to help disabled people to find a job faster than current praxis in the job centers. The case focuses on the early stages of the formation and establishment of the company in the market. The case illustrates (1) how the idea for the company was born in partnership with the public and private sector and the founder's motivation; (2) how digital technologies can be used in social entrepreneurship ventures and how they can create public value; (3) the barriers that digital social entrepreneurs may face in the early stages of their venture.

TEACHING OBJECTIVES

The main objective of the case is to contribute to understanding how digital technologies can be used in social entrepreneurship and the difficulties that companies adopting such technologies may experience in the initial establishment stages. The main instructional objectives of the case are to:

1. Provide examples of difficulties of being a digital social entrepreneur and different perceptions of the term "social entrepreneurship" among different official bodies.
2. Provide an example of how digital technologies can be used for social entrepreneurship.
3. Provide an example of how the idea for a digital social entrepreneurship venture was born and the motivation for starting the company.

Target Audience

The case is recommended for senior undergraduate and graduate students on a variety of courses including digital entrepreneurship, innovation management, entrepreneurship, social entrepreneurship and social innovation, digital innovation, public administration, and public–private innovation networks.

SUGGESTED TEACHING STRATEGY

A suggested sequence of instructions providing both mandatory and optional steps is given in TN Table 3.1 The case can be delivered in a typical three-hour class, assuming students read the case in advance. The case may also be suitable for a two-hour class, if only selected teams make presentations, thus decreasing the overall presentation time and/or focusing on one or two of the proposed challenges.

TN Table 3.1   Suggested instructional sequence

Step	Suggested duration	Setting execution
Preparatory activity (before class)		• Students read the case before class. • Some student independent research on social entrepreneurship, digital entrepreneurship, and adoption and diffusion of innovation is recommended but not necessary. • Create teams of three or four students. • Select a couple of discussion questions for the in-class discussion, depending on the instructional objectives and the type of audience (remaining questions can be assigned for follow-up homework).
Intro	10 min	Create PowerPoint presentations with the list of the steps to follow and the questions to address.
Analysis	45 min	Students work in predefined teams to discuss the case and prepare answers to the questions.
Student visual presentation: Visualize the answers	15 min	Ask students to create a visual presentation through a PowerPoint presentation, a poster, or a visual map using markers and post-it notes to illustrate their conclusions.
Presentation by the teams of students	60 min	Ask each team to give a 10-minute presentation of their visualization (or selected teams if there are too many students in the class).
Class discussion	30 min	Class discussion of the case and the analysis.

SUGGESTED SOLUTIONS TO STUDENT CHALLENGES

Discussion Question 1: Based on the E-BRO case, can you identify critical challenges that a digital social entrepreneurship venture has to face? How do these critical aspects differ from a company operating in full for-profit markets?

The case illustrates three main types of barriers that E-BRO APS encounters in the early phases of establishing the company, namely acceptance of digital technology, digital divide with some stakeholders, and outdated or non-digitally prone organizational culture (see TN Table 3.2 for details). In particular:

- The difficulty of collaborating with public actors and other stakeholders who do not have a digital mindset, digital platforms, or skills.
- The difficulty of integrating the social venture technology (the digital solution JobIntra) with those of the partners.
- Cultural factors determining resistance to innovation and adoption of new technology.

From a more theoretical point of view, these challenges can be analyzed and addressed by classical theory on social entrepreneurship (see, for example, Dees's (2001) definition also reported in the Appendix to the case) as well as the Diffusion of Innovation Theory by E. Rogers (1995) and/or Adoption of Innovation by Tornatzky and Fleischer (1990). According to Rogers (1995), the stages a person/organization follows in adopting an innovation, and whereby diffusion is accomplished, include awareness of the need for an innovation, decision to adopt (or reject) the innovation, initial use of the innovation, and continued use of the innovation. According to Rogers (1995) there are five main factors that influence such adoption:

- Relative Advantage – The degree to which an innovation is seen as better than the idea, program, or product it replaces.
- Compatibility – How consistent the innovation is with the values, experiences, and needs of the potential adopters.
- Complexity – How difficult the innovation is to understand and/or use.
- Trialability – The extent to which the innovation can be tested or experimented with before a commitment to adopt is made.
- Observability – The extent to which the innovation provides tangible results.

Another important model with which to address and analyze this question is the Technology-Environment-Organization (TOE) model developed by Tornatzky and Fleischer (1990). Briefly, according to the model, the decision to adopt a technological innovation by a potential adopter depends on three broad sets of factors, namely those related to the environment, the technology, and the organization (see TN Figure 3.1).

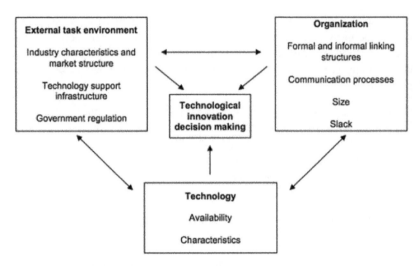

TN Figure 3.1   The TOE framework

Discussion Question 2: How should the company diversify its business to be less dependent on public finances (for instance, what would happen if the budget allocated to the policy is cut by the government or the reform is altered)?

Some answers to this question can be found on the company's website, at https://www.E-BRO.dk/, where the company has started diversifying its software solutions so that one targets the employment agencies and the other the job centers.

Another option is for the company to adapt the system to create a marketplace for regular jobs as well, perhaps with a focus on certain applications or customers such as nursing services and schoolteachers.

Earlier on, the company attempted to develop a system for unemployed new graduates, although it appears that this system has not been launched yet.

One possible approach to answer this question is through the following role play:

(a)   Divide the students into small brainstorming groups.
(b)   Each group is asked to come up with at least three different ideas about how the company can innovate and diversify. Innovation can be technological or just at the business-model level.
(c)   Discuss pros and cons of each idea, identify the best idea, and come up with a plan for its implementation.
(d)   Then, each group presents the best idea to the instructor, pretending to be consultants pitching the idea to the company.
(e)   The instructor acts as if s/he is the E-BRO chair and eventually decides what is the best idea and whether the company wants to pursue it.

In this exercise, students can also be assessed in terms of quality of presentation and professionalism.

Discussion Question 3: What can the company do to favor JobIntra adoption by other job centers and employment agencies?

The answer to this question can be found, for example, in the two models of innovation and diffusion mentioned under the challenge (a).

TN Table 3.2   Summary of E-BRO analysis

Social issue: Finding permanent flexi-jobs for disabled citizens Country: Denmark	
Objective	Development and adoption at Job-Center level of a digital solution "JobIntra" with the aim of 1. Increasing the number of flexi- jobs available to disabled citizens and 2. Substantially reducing the time to find a suitable job for disabled citizens The context is the Reform of the Disability Pension and Flexi-Job Scheme (2013) targeting citizens "with a complex set of problems, for whom social-, employment- and health-related challenges create barriers to entering the labour market, and where the lack of an interdisciplinary initiative means that they are at risk of ending up on a permanent disability pension." The flexi-job scheme targets people, in any profession, with permanently and significantly reduced ability to work. In many ways, a flexi-job is a normal form of employment, except that tasks and working hours are adapted to what the individual flex-job employee can handle.
How was the idea born?	The idea behind the ICT innovation "Job Intra" and company E-BRO APS was spontaneous and involved extensive discussion between Jacob and his manager, but its adoption required a lot of planning and collaboration between different actors.
Barriers	Three major types of barriers: barriers concerning JobCenter Brøndby; barriers related to the company E-BRO; and systemic barriers at the municipal/society level.

Social issue: Finding permanent flexi-jobs for disabled citizens Country: Denmark	
Barriers	Barriers in JobCenter Brøndby: integration of JobIntra into the existing IT system and solutions; ease of use of the IT system.
Barriers	Barriers to E-BRO's growth: diffusion of the IT solution to other job centers in Denmark; the feeling of being "stuck in the middle" concerning the status of the company as a social-economic company. In fact, E-BRO has difficulty in being recognized as a "social-economic company" by some funding bodies, although it was listed as a "socio-economic" company by the National Board of Social Services.
Barriers	Systemic barriers: the complexity of the municipal ecosystem; availability on the local/municipality job market of both recruitment agencies and companies/organizations with the need and will to employ flexi-jobbers. JobIntra is born at operational level. The distance between the operational level and the policy level makes it difficult to get policy people involved in spreading the IT solution in the other municipalities.
Drivers and motivation	The institutional and political factor: the "Reform of the Disability Pension and Flexi-job Scheme" introduced by the government in 2012. E-BRO's founder's keen interest in helping people with disabilities to have as high a quality of life as possible. E-BRO's aim to be economically viable as a company by the end of 2019.
Diffusion	Potentially, JobIntra could be adopted by all Danish municipalities. In practice, it takes a lot of effort to navigate the public eco-system and get in contact with other job centers.
Observability on provision of services (Values)	JobIntra, by increasing competition between the different actors, has increased the number of flexi-jobs available and contributed to Brøndby Municipality becoming one of the Danish municipalities with the lowest unemployment rates among flexi-jobbers.
Observability on the quality of public services (Values)	JobIntra has increased the service quality concerning flexi-jobs in JobCenter Brøndby by decreasing the time required to find a job and increasing the number of available jobs.
Observability on types of values (Values)	JobIntra has contributed to generating several types of values at the individual, organizational, and socio-economic level. 1. By reducing the amount of time it takes to place a disabled unemployed person in a job, it has increased the satisfaction and decreased the frustration of citizens who, for one reason or another, fall into this category over the course of their life, thus contributing to increasing their "happiness." 2. JobIntra has substantially decreased the amount of time that employees in JobCenter Brøndby spend on each specific flexi-job, thus generating resources that can be used to take care of the most complicated cases or on other types of activities within the job center. 3. By speeding up the process of finding jobs and decreasing the number of disabled unemployed, JobIntra decreases the amount of public subsidy paid to the unemployed by saving on public unemployment expenditure.

REFERENCES AND ADDITIONAL READING

Alford, J. and O'Flynn, J. (2009). Making sense of public value: Concepts, critiques and emergent meanings. *International Journal of Public Administration*, 32(3), 171–191.

Benington, J. (2011). From private choice to public value? In *Public Value: Theory and Practice*, ed. John Benington and Mark Moore (pp. 31–49). Basingstoke: Palgrave Macmillan.

Dees, G. J. (2001). The meaning of "social entrepreneurship." The Center for Advancement of Social Entrepreneurship (CASE), Duke University. https://centers .fuqua.duke.edu/case/knowledge_items/the-meaning-of-social-entrepreneurship/ (accessed November 20, 2021).

Hansen, A. V., Fuglsang, L., Gallouj, F., and Scupola, A. (2021). Social entrepreneurs as change makers: Expanding public service networks for social innovation. *Public Management Review*. https://doi.org/10.1080/14719037.2021.1916065.

Rogers, E. (1995). *Diffusion of Innovations*. New York: Free Press.

Tornatzky, L. G. and Fleischer, M. (1990). *The Processes of Technological Innovation*. Lexington, MA: Lexington Books.

Chapter 4: teaching notes

John DiMarco

CASE SUMMARY

This case helps students to visualize the process of product development through the lens of design thinking utilizing technology. It provides an agile case that highlights multiple real stages in an entrepreneurship process and how accessible technologies played a role in bringing a product idea to tangible form. Students are introduced to entrepreneurial tasks that can be facilitated using technology tools to help research and develop problem definitions, product ideations, design iteration, intellectual property research, and brandmark development. The case provides a scaled learning experience to move students from initial research through to iteration and presentation on a product development.

Ask questions of students to foster open discussions:

- How could the process used in the case (technology driven, agile) be adopted to update other existing physical or digital products?
- What technology methods from your skillset can you think of that can be used to improve the design and production process of a product?

TEACHING OBJECTIVES

The main objective of the case is to show how design thinking and product development can be accelerated with an array of technologies across a wide range of product development duties. The text highlights online digital tools including Adobe applications for ideation, USPTO tools for research, and Thomson tools for manufacturing data. These resources can be used by students in course exercises and projects in their respective design labs and learning environments.

The case also provides an opportunity to explain design thinking from an inductive approach, based on the spiral of agile development from initial lightbulb or pie in the sky concepts through real user problem identifications. The case shows how the startup experience cannot be solely defined by business plans or formal approaches, but in a way to teach students about the necessity of ambiguity and how it can be addressed with the use of technology tools and design thinking. The case encourages student exploration of materials and processes through experiential and do it yourself (DIY) methods.

A third use is to show the tasks in a product development situation, without having extensive resources. Students are presented instances in the Shape Stretch product journey that followed an entrepreneurial spiral beginning with a lightbulb moment, where the inventor saw a better way to do something, followed by intense research on existing solutions and prior intellectual property. This was followed by a period of agile design and development, focusing on digitally driven experimental approaches to understanding the user and what they expect against what they are currently getting from the market.

After reviewing the case with the class, the instructor will be able to:

1. Present different stages in the design thinking and product development processes to students.
2. Provide examples of online tools and technology resources to research patents and trademarks (see Google Patents, USPTO website, Shopify free trial sites).
3. Introduce digital prototyping and Frankenstein prototyping for physical products.
4. Facilitate research and ideation of a new physical product.
5. Critique final product ideas, IP reports, and product presentations.

TEACHING STRATEGIES

Using actual live products to teach product development allows students to see the design and innovation process from a more inductive perspective. To enhance this, allow students to seek out other products and have them break down the information they find to reveal patterns in process, pitfalls, and successes.

Suggested Answers to Discussion Questions

Discussion Question 1: Why is "ideation" a fundamental keyword in the digital product design? How can you use digital tools and technologies as the author did in his case to experiment with product designs?

After reading the case, students should be able to grasp which technology tools can be used for ideations and intellectual property searches. Students should understand that products are developed with a cross section of traditional tools such as pencil and paper for sketching to a wealth of applications for 2D and

3D designs for physical product manufacturing, which are DIY in nature. The instructor can demonstrate Adobe, AutoCAD, Fusion 360, or USPTO search tools (PAIR and TESS) that they are familiar with to show students how to use or allow students time to freely explore how to use the tools they need to complete entrepreneurial tasks in ideation and IP research. They can also demonstrate DIY tools such as Canva to create simple brandmark mock ups.

Discussion Question 2: What do you think was the role technology played in the development and eventual patent issuance of Shape Stretch?

After reading the case, students should be able to identify and define how various technology tools were used to meet critical tasks in the entrepreneurial process such as costing with Thomas Register, designing with Adobe and AutoCAD Apps, and securing IP applications using the USPTO Pair and TESS systems.

Students should inventory their own technology skills and establish how they can use design thinking to iterate, fail, and create solutions rapidly by using technology tools that they are already familiar with and don't require extensive experience.

Student Challenge Spiral

The student challenges are broken into spiraling assignments that can be used individually or together as a sequence for a semester long project. For undergraduates it is recommended for all levels of students that the above stages are broken into separate units to allow them to explore each step with rigor and curiosity, enabling a wider view of the invention and product development journey. These skills are transferable to students who seek to not only invent and develop products on their own, but also to serve as innovation analysts and product managers in manufacturing and consumer product companies.

Approaches to the Challenges

Encourage students to seek out new product ideas by going to retail stores and online shopping sites such as Amazon to explore product options and discover how other product managers are positioning and presenting products in the space.

Encourage students to create digital mockups and Frankenstein physical materials into mock products through exploration of materials including foam, cardboard, wood, clay, metals, and plastics. Let students hand craft extensions to existing products and then translate them into digital composites after understanding proportion, scale, and physical forms.

Let students free play with names, taglines, and layouts in DIY or professional applications such as Canva, Fusion, and Sketch Up to develop mock creations that extend from product to brand.

Chapter 5: teaching notes

Rubén A. Ascúa, Andrea Minetti and José A. Borello

CASE SUMMARY

Agroads.com, a digital start-up founded in Rafaela (Argentina) in 2007, is a digital marketplace where farmers can find all kinds of agricultural-related products and services, new or used, and sellers can gain customers and increase their business. The digital transformation of agriculture is a long-term trend that the COVID pandemic accelerated.

Agroads provides an interesting example of how this trend unfolded in a country such as Argentina, where agriculture and related activities are key in terms of exports, production, and employment. Agroads is a case of a small firm that shows how digital technology can become the vehicle to channel entrepreneurial spirits and actions. Although it is based in the city of Rafaela, in the middle of the Pampas plains, its operations cover a large portion of the center provinces of Argentina.

Agroads' vision is to create a digital market where business opportunities are more accessible to all operators. It is a virtual place where farmers find everything they need easily and quickly, along the whole supply chain. In this platform the profile of each customer is used to personalize his/her user experience. The system offers the opportunity to find new suppliers throughout Argentina. Any product or service connected to the agricultural sector may be traded conveniently: the platform offers financing options in a secure trading environment.

Currently, Agroads' main challenge is to digitize its customers as well, by encouraging farmers to use data for decision-making through the incorporation of e-commerce in their sales operations.

Target Audience

The case is recommended for senior undergraduate and graduate students on a variety of courses including innovation management, entrepreneurship, new product development, e-commerce, internationalization, and digital transformation. Students with previous knowledge in Industry 4.0, organizational behavior, innovation, and internationalization of companies can analyze the case from different angles, including strategy, knowledge management, disruptive innovation, and business models, among others.

TEACHING OBJECTIVES

- Learn how digital technology is transforming agribusiness.
- Identify the most relevant technological vectors of Industry 4.0 that the company uses in its products.
- Understand how e-commerce is affecting internationalization opportunities for small businesses.

TEACHING STRATEGY AND ASSIGNMENT SUGGESTIONS

A suggested instructional sequence listing both mandatory and optional steps is given in TN Table 5.1. The case can be taught in a typical three-hour class, assuming students read the case in advance. For the sake of time and depending on the instructional objectives, students' discussion may be limited to the first set of questions, leaving the general point/ questions planned for a later class or for homework.

TN Table 5.1   Suggested instructional sequence

Step	Suggested duration	Setting/execution
Preparatory activity (before class). Divide class into groups of 3 or 4 people.		Have students read the case beforehand. In addition, it may be useful (but is not a requirement) to get some background information on the agricultural activities typical of the Pampas of Argentina.
Introduction	10 minutes	Create slides with a synthesis of the case and the questions for group discussion (see text for example questions).
Students work in teams to discuss the case and elaborate answers to the assigned questions	45 minutes	
Visualize the answers	15 minutes	Ask students to develop visual presentations through a board or visual diagram using color markers and post-it notes to illustrate their responses.

Step	Suggested duration	Setting/execution
Present topics discussed	10 minutes	Ask each group of students to give a 10-minute presentation of their discussion.
Break	10 minutes	
The whole class discusses the results of each group's results.	70 minutes	Class discussion.
Two more general questions may be added to the whole class discussion	20 minutes	Class discussion based on two new additional questions.

Assign each group one of the following sets of questions. (If the class is small or some questions are not very pertinent for the audience or content of the specific course, some questions may be used to guide follow-up homework.)

1. Why do you think agriculture is considered to be a traditional sector? Why would the introduction of digital technologies be particularly disruptive?

Example of possible responses:

As opposed to manufacturing or services where digital tools have a longer history of implementation, digital tools are newcomers in the context of agricultural activities, more so in a less-industrialized country such as Argentina. Moreover, before the emergence of digital tools, agriculture and related activities had, in general, a slower rate of incorporation of innovations. One of the reasons for agriculture to be refractive to new ideas and instruments is the lower presence of technical personnel with respect to other economic activities such as manufacturing or services.

Digital technologies such as those on which Agroads bases its business are making a profound change in routines and processes and making it possible for farmers to access more easily useful data for production purposes. Yet, the particular context in which these technologies are deployed adds an extra challenge to Agroads.

2. What factors were key in the development of Agroads?

Example of possible responses:

Major factors in the development of Agroads were: early entry, local and regional knowledge, concentration on fundamental aspects of the business, and incorporation of a small group of technical employees devoted to their work.

The early entry of Agroads in the market coincides with the surfacing of several hundreds of small and very small software firms in cities and towns of the Pampas after the financial crisis of 2001–2 (Albornoz, 2006). This expansion followed the commercial deployment of the internet in Argentina.

The founder of Agroads had worked for some years at an IT firm in Rafaela, and that experience gave him the local and regional insight about firms' commercial and service needs. Though smaller than some of the other cities in the region, such as Rosario or Buenos Aires, since the early twentieth century, Rafaela has had a particular productive lure observers attribute to the hard work of the descendants of immigrants from Piemonte, in Northern Italy. Rafaela is also well situated, in the center-north of the Pampas.

As it is described in the case, early efforts were concentrated in fundamental aspects of the business and in developing tools that would be valued highly by users. At the same time, in the initial years of development, the small group of people who made up Agroads had to undertake multiple tasks: this gave them a wide and systemic view of the platform and of the needs of users. Working many hours shoulder to shoulder gave the group cohesion and strength to face complications and downturns.

3. **Which of the Industry 4.0 vectors do you see applied in the case of Agroads? Ask students to determine what other products the organization could market using other Industry 4.0 vectors, such as cloud computing or robotic process automation.**

Example of possible responses:

The case mentions the following Industry 4.0 vectors that Agroads applied or will apply in the products it offers: big data, business intelligence and artificial intelligence.

Although electronics were initially incorporated into manufacturing equipment in the 1970s, a wider utilization of these devices is a more recent phenomenon, more so in Latin America. Technologists in Germany began talking about Industry 4.0 around 2010. This catchall phrase refers to the fourth technological revolution and includes a number of technologies that are transforming products, processes, and organizational forms. Internet of things, or IoT, involves the interconnection of objects through several devices (as in smart TVs). Advanced robotics, for example, connects machines on the production floor with input stocks in the warehouse of a manufacturing firm. The availability of enormous amounts of data (in many different contexts) has fueled the emergence of both new business services (such as data mining) and new academic fields (such as data science). Cloud computing is widely available and will eventually enable firms, governments, and households to dispense with heavy investments in computers while, at the same time, having permanent access to data and archives. A number of expert systems (of varying complexity) underline a process of diffusion of instances of artificial intelligence and machine learning. Technologists and practitioners are experimenting with additive printing in several fields: medicine, construction, manufacturing, etc. Virtual reality is being applied to a variety of problems that go from urban planning to medicine and from road design to education.

Some of these technological tools are embodied in Agroads' products and services. For example, the firm generates commercially useful information through hundreds of daily transactions and inquiries (big data). Agroads is also able to systematize the behavioral pattern of firms and can make explicit those patterns in both new products and consulting services (business intelligence).

4.   What alternative business models might the company consider adopting? Is business model-driven innovation an option for the company? Discuss why or why not.

Example of possible responses:

Business model innovation entails an approach where the leaders of an organization are, literally, ready to bite their own tail, if needed, and reshuffle an organization from its foundations. Business model innovation is normally oriented to follow market trends and to perceive opportunities for change and growth. Business model innovation goes beyond partial innovations such as those that may be undertaken in product, process, or organization.

The company could venture into business models leveraged on other Industry 4.0 vectors, e.g. artificial intelligence and cloud computing. Offering services leveraged by these vectors could be an interesting alternative.

It could also expand its activities in regions outside of the Pampas where other agricultural and agro-industrial activities are present such as viticulture in Mendoza, San Juan and other provinces, sugar cane in the north, etc.).

5.   How can e-commerce be a form of internationalization of the firm? Discuss.

Example of possible responses:

Digitalization plays an important role in the growth of medium and small companies that want to internationalize, so the use of a digital strategy is presented as a great opportunity for the success of companies that want to operate in foreign markets. E-commerce provides one of the most important advantages for companies that decide to internationalize, since it facilitates the sales of their products or services anywhere in the world, and one of the alternatives is the creation of a marketplace. Yet, even in a virtual world, other problems emerge.

As we have underlined in the case study, Agroads has the potential to expand not only into other regions of the country but also into neighboring countries where Spanish is also spoken. The firm would not even need to develop a completely new site as it has done in the case of Brazil. Other issues will need to be addressed such as the morphology of markets, legal regulations, logistics, and differences in business practices.

To facilitate the interpretation of the business model the instructor can use Osterwalder's Business Canvas Model.[1]

To close, the whole class can have a general discussion based on a response to the following questions/points.

* How would a similar situation unfold in the context of your country or region? Choose another example of a marketplace/industry and discuss the internationalization opportunities enabled by digital technologies that it offers.

NOTE

1. A template to guide students is available at https://www.strategyzer.com/canvas/business-model-canvas. A template in Spanish is available at https://docs.google.com/drawings/d/1EybSXFTXfqlQaEusOw2iQe0N3OrNxmPfvE1-TJsflUA/edit.

REFERENCES AND ADDITIONAL READING

Agroads + (n.d.). Retrieved May 1, 2022 from https://blog.agroads.com.ar/.

Albornoz, I. (2006). "Software para el sector agropecuario." Universidad Nacional de General Sarmiento, LITTEC. https://www.academia.edu/19783502/Software_para_el_sector_agropecuario.

Censo Industrial Rafaela 2000 – icedel.rafaela.gob.ar (n.d.). Retrieved May 1, 2022 from http://icedel.rafaela.gob.ar/archivos/ORDICEdel/Censo%20Industrial%202000%20(1).pdf.

FAO (n.d.). *The Future of Food and Agriculture – Trends and Challenges* (Summary version) and *Global Perspectives Studies*. Retrieved May 1, 2022, from https://www.fao.org/global-perspectives-studies/resources/detail/en/c/1156611/.

Grandes Historias de Pymes Industriales. Universidad Nacional de Rafaela (n.d.). Retrieved May 1, 2022, from https://www.unraf.edu.ar/index.php/editorial-unraf/1703-noticia-6.

Chapter 6: teaching notes

Roberto Parente, Rosangela Feola and Ricky Celenta

CASE SUMMARY

The case of Santomiele concerns a small firm in southern Italy engaged in the transformation and commercialization of figs. Products made in the small town are appreciated and sold worldwide. The firm was founded by two friends, intent on relaunching a typical local product which was of little value and was slowly disappearing.

In the late 1990s, Antonio and Corrado got together in an old farmhouse that they call their "garage." There they decided to set up a business to make excellent dried figs, based on an eco-sustainable approach and chemical-free processing.

In over 20 years of business activity, the two friends have succeeded in making the "Cilento" fig renowned worldwide while enhancing the product and its area of origin. Santomiele products are targeted at a specific niche of consumers for whom price is not an issue but attention to detail is. The first part of the case recounts the story of the two start-up entrepreneurs, the evolution of the firm, and the reasons for its success. The business's success unfolds through an analysis of the positive trend in turnover and the international awards obtained.

The second part of the case is set in recent years and tells of the critical issues that the firm has had to face (and is still facing) and how digital technology has made it possible to transform a critical issue into an opportunity.

In recent years, generational change within many supplier companies has resulted in Santomiele having to tackle major problems in procuring its raw material: dried figs. In order to overcome the problem, the two partners sought to internalize the entire supply chain, but this could not be achieved in the short term. Investment in digitalization offered Santomiele a short-term solution to the problem and also opened up numerous opportunities. Through a collaboration project with the university, Antonio and Corrado were able to develop and patent a smart oven powered by solar energy and equipped with an IoT system.

This solution has allowed them to upgrade the fig drying process while at the same time enhancing the firm's value chain.

Digital technology has enabled Santomiele to innovate a traditional industry. The two partners are aware that the technology they have developed has great potential, although they are undecided about how best to use it. They could differentiate their range by introducing new products and, at the same time, could lease the ovens to their suppliers to consolidate their loyalty and manage supply. Recognizing that they have developed a product not currently available on the market, they are also thinking about the possibility of opening a new firm for the manufacture and marketing of smart ovens.

This challenge is still open as Antonio and Corrado have not yet reached a decision.

TEACHING OBJECTIVES

The main objective of the case is to show how digital transformation offers traditional businesses opportunities for different types of innovation. Furthermore, the case offers students the opportunity to analyze the role of the university in supporting the digital transformation of an SME.

In particular, the case of Santomiele can be used to illustrate how collaboration with a university can generate a successful digital transformation even for a small company operating in a traditional sector.

The case study provides students with the opportunity to think critically about the opportunities that digital transformation offers SMEs operating in traditional sectors, and also to understand how digital transformation can requalify and innovate ancient crafts.

The educational objectives of this case are to:

- Highlight how the digitalization of a process has generated previously unimaginable business opportunities: entering a new market sector, achieving product innovation, innovating the supply chain.
- Stimulate critical thought on collaboration between universities and SMEs, to implement digitalization processes. In studying the case, students are encouraged to think about the reference context, i.e., the role played by the university in supporting the digitalization of local SMEs.
- Put students in the entrepreneurs' shoes when making strategic business choices. Process digitalization has offered Santomiele numerous opportunities for innovation and growth, but Antonio and Corrado still do not know which decision to take. Students are thus asked to address the same critical issues facing the owners of the company in real time.
- Highlight how digital technologies can play an important role in enhancing traditional know-how, which risks being lost.

Target Audience

The case study is recommended for senior undergraduate students and graduates on a variety of courses including innovation management, entrepreneurship, digital innovation, business, and administration.

Students with previous knowledge of digital transformation, organizational behavior, and innovation management can analyze the story from different angles, including strategy, open innovation, disruptive innovation, and partnership strategies.

SUGGESTED TEACHING STRATEGY

A suggested instructional sequence listing both mandatory and optional steps is given in TN Table 6.1. The case can be delivered in a typical three-hour class, assuming students read the case in advance. For the sake of time and depending on the instructional objectives, the analysis should be limited to two questions chosen from those proposed.

TN Table 6.1   Suggested instructional sequence

Step	Suggested duration	Setting/execution
Preparatory activity	Before class	• Get students to read the case before class. • Get students to conduct independent research of Santomiele's web information. • Create teams of 3 or 4. • Select a couple of questions for the in-class discussion, depending on the educational objectives and the type of audience (the remaining questions can be assigned for follow-up homework).
Intro and housekeeping	15 min	Create slides with the list of the steps and questions.
Students work in teams to discuss the case and prepare answers to the questions	75 min	Encourage students to use the internet for further research.
Visualize the answers	30 min	Ask students to create a visual presentation through a PowerPoint, poster or visual map using markers and post-it notes to illustrate their conclusions.
Presentation and discussion	60 min	• Ask each team to give a 10-minute presentation of their visualization. • Class discussion.

SUGGESTED ANSWERS TO DISCUSSION QUESTIONS

Discussion Question 1: Summarize the business challenges and the key management features that enabled digital innovation at Santomiele. Analyze traditional (non-digital) SMEs operating traditional and/or artisanal businesses in your city/region. How could digital technologies be used to solve problems and/or improve their business?

Through an analysis of Santomiele's history, the case describes the social and economic context in which the company operates and how it has evolved. The company's supply chain has been developed over more than 20 years of activity and farmers are key partners in the company's business model.

The quality of the raw material is fundamental for Santomiele, and their relationship of trust and esteem with the fig producers plays a crucial role.

The high perishability of the produce and logistic needs led Antonio and Corrado to outsource the drying process, entrusting it to the fig producer. As a result, the producers are responsible for production quality and management of the drying process.

Unfortunately, the new generations of fig producers have not inherited the same values as their parents and do not respect commercial agreements in terms of both quality and quantity. The case shows that fig processing and sales in Cilento had almost disappeared until a few years ago. Today, the sector is experiencing steady growth and demand for figs has been increasing. Consequently, fig producers are seeking to increase production by using chemicals which compromise the quality of the figs. At the same time, Santomiele's competitors are sometimes willing to pay suppliers a higher price for the dried figs.

The critical issues that led Antonio and Corrado to develop the smart oven (or solar oven) are as follows:

- New generations of producers do not respect business deals: suppliers have often sold figs destined for Santomiele to other companies.
- The increasing demand for figs has resulted in producers not complying with the production rules agreed with Santomiele. To increase production and speed up the drying process, producers are adopting practices that affect product quality.
- The company cannot internalize fig production in the short term, and it is also unlikely to achieve this in the long run.
- Fig drying is a process that has had to be outsourced up until now because of the high perishability of figs. The natural drying method made it impractical for the company to internalize this activity as it might have entailed the loss of several hundred kilos of fresh produce.

- Ovens available on the market could not be adapted to Santomiele's fig drying process. The case study explains that the white figs produced by Santomiele must be dried using heat and sunlight. None of the solutions on the market were suitable for Santomiele's production.
- Fig drying is a complex process that requires a lot of experience. The Smart oven makes it possible to standardize the drying process as it allows the progress of the fig to be monitored, even without a great deal of experience.
- The demand for Santomiele products is growing rapidly, as shown by the growth in turnover. The company needs to make the drying process scalable so as to step up the quantity produced while maintaining quality standards. The ovens available on the market would not have allowed the "natural approach" to be maintained, which would have negatively affected the quality of the end product.

The key management features that have enabled digital innovation in Santomiele can be summarized as follows:

- A strong attachment to their homeland. Antonio and Corrado began their journey as entrepreneurs because they love their land. Their dream was to enhance the Cilento and the tradition of the Cilento fig. They have never considered choosing suppliers from other areas because their goal is to enhance the white fig of Cilento and develop the local economy.
- A willingness to seek innovative solutions to improve the quality of the products made. On several occasions Antonio and Corrado have collaborated with research groups from various universities to develop new products and/or innovate processes.
- An attention to detail. The case study highlights how Antonio and Corrado are able to satisfy their needs: their attention to detail led them to reject the solutions available on the market because they could not meet their requirements and to seek an ad hoc solution.

Students are asked to assess traditional and/or artisanal businesses in their own area, perhaps (but not necessarily) identifying IT companies as well. The student is asked to think critically about the processes of these businesses and to identify the opportunities offered by digital technologies. TN Table 6.2 describes the main technologies.

TN Table 6.2   Example of trending digital technologies

Technology	Description
Artificial Intelligence (AI)	AI refers to the simulation of human intelligence processes by machines. It automates complex decision-making tasks so as to mimic human thought processes. Encompassing Machine Learning (ML), AI algorithms can learn, understand, analyze, and act on new rules-based data to reach approximate or definite conclusions.
Augmented Reality (AR)	AR is a technology that superimposes a computer-generated image on a user's view of the real world, thus providing a composite view. When set up properly, the user experience is seamless, opening a new realm for businesses across the board to explore. It has already been successfully implemented in the manufacturing and entertainment industries.
Blockchain	Essentially, Blockchain is an open, distributed ledger that can record transactions between two parties efficiently and in a verifiable and unalterable way. Originally devised for the Bitcoin digital currency, the business community has found other potential uses for the technology. Insurance, supply chain, energy and ad-technology are a few industries where Blockchain applications are already being used.
Drones	Drones are UAVs (Unmanned Aerial Vehicles) used in situations where manned flight is considered risky, difficult or expensive. Types of drones can vary significantly based on their design and application. Surveillance, surveys, sport, cinematography, and delivery are some examples where use of drones is becoming commonplace.
Internet of Things (IoT)	IoT works on the premise that everything that can be connected will be connected to the internet. It is a system of interrelated computing devices, machines, objects, or vehicles able to transfer data over a network without requiring human-to-human or human-to-computer interaction. Logistics, appliances, packaging, security industries are making headway in industrial automation and the possibilities for IoT are endless.
Robotics	Machines with improved sensing, control and intelligence used to automate, augment, or assist human activities are growing in a broad range of service applications. These technologies help develop machines that can substitute for human beings or replicate human actions. This is widely used to reduce human resource costs and increase efficiency.
Virtual Reality (VR)	Virtual reality (VR) is a simulated experience that can be similar to or completely different from the real world. A person using virtual reality equipment is able to look around the artificial world, move around in it, and interact with virtual features or items. Gaming, entertainment, education, and defense are some industries that are benefiting from VR.
3D Printing	3D Printing builds a three-dimensional object from a computer-aided design (CAD) model, usually by successively adding material layer by layer, which is why it is also called additive manufacturing. It is being used in manufacturing, the medical sphere, industry, and socio-cultural sectors, and it is becoming a successful commercial technology. More recently, 3D printing has also been used in the humanitarian and development sector to produce a range of medical items, prosthetics, and spare parts.

Instructors can use the case to show how digital technologies represent an opportunity for traditional businesses. After analyzing the Santomiele case, students are invited to "look around" and think about SMEs operating in traditional and/or artisanal sectors in their own city/region. Through this analysis, students are invited: to think critically about the opportunities that digital technologies can offer these companies; to put themselves in the shoes of the entrepreneurs of their own area; to think about a concrete application of digital technology.

Discussion Question 2: Analyze the case and summarize the successful elements of the collaboration between the university and Santomiele. Analyzing your university (especially the technology transfer center) and the entrepreneurial ecosystem in the area, what do you think are the opportunities for collaboration in the digital transformation of SMEs? What would be the benefits for SMEs? And the benefits of research?

In order to understand the successful elements of this collaboration, the entrepreneurs and some members of the research group were interviewed on this specific topic. The key factors identified are indicated below:

- The company had previous experience of collaboration with research groups. Antonio and Corrado were aware of the opportunities that collaboration with universities could offer in terms of the quality of the final result.
- The research team had a good understanding of the context and business needs, which made it possible to develop an ad hoc solution.
- There was a good time alignment between academia and business needs. Usually, the academic world and the corporate world "travel" at different speeds, as they have different objectives. According to Antonio and Corrado, one of the successful elements of this collaboration is that the research group tailored the management of the project to the company's time needs.
- It was possible to see beyond the criticalities known to the entrepreneurs and inform them of the opportunities offered by research. Corrado and Antonio had initially envisioned the development of a solar oven. The application of the different IoT solutions was proposed by the research group, based on the knowledge already available in the literature.
- The developed solution can be adapted to fit business needs and economic resources. It would have been possible to develop better performing hardware and software solutions in terms of computing accuracy, time optimization, etc., but these would have been economically unsustainable for the company. The research will remain ongoing for an indefinite period. When it is applied to a concrete case, it is important to balance the effectiveness and the actual applicability of the solution.

Both parties agree that the key to the collaboration project's success was the ability to fully grasp the problem and business context and to understand how the daily activities carried out by the research group could help to overcome the business challenges.

The benefits for SMEs can be summarized as follows:

- Companies can receive support from researchers seeking new frontier solutions on a daily basis. The literature does not stand still and evolves at a faster innovation rate than companies, especially if they are small. Companies can therefore interface with researchers studying frontier technologies.
- As the university comprises different departments, collaboration with the technology transfer center enables the company to draw on a range of professional skills.
- The researchers' experience allows entrepreneurs to overcome the problems facing them. As highlighted in the Santomiele case, the researchers have a vision that goes beyond the single business problem so that they can offer a broader perspective and propose digital solutions that the company may not even imagine.
- According to the specific regulations in force, companies can draw on the research and development services offered by universities and thus obtain tax advantages.

To understand how research can benefit from supporting the digital transformation of companies, we interviewed some researchers directly involved in the Santomiele project and managers from the technology transfer center at the University of Salerno. Their comments are summarized below:

- Stimulus to research. The co-understanding of real business problems stimulates researchers to observe certain problems from other perspectives, thus stimulating their creativity beyond the boundaries of the scientific literature. Curiosity is the energy that drives research: stimuli from beyond the academic world can only be good for researchers.
- Understanding business problems. As noted above, SMEs have practical needs (finance, timing, etc.) that differ from those of researchers. Comparing business problems with state-of-the-art research stimulates the researcher to develop applicable solutions that balance effectiveness and economic sustainability. The researcher is required to go beyond academic abstraction. As in the Santomiele case, the research had to be tailored to company needs.

Instructors can use the case to show how collaboration projects between universities (especially technology transfer centers) and SMEs provide an opportunity to facilitate the digital transformation of SMEs.

After analyzing the Santomiele case, students are invited to think about the opportunities that this collaboration offers to SMEs and researchers. Specifically, students are invited to analyze their university's technology transfer center and the activities it carries out in relation to the third mission.

Resources for the second question are as follows:

- Arenas, J. J. and González, D. (2018). Technology transfer models and elements in the university–industry collaboration. *Administrative Sciences*, 8(2), 19.
- Ungureanu, M., Pop, N. and Ungureanu, N. (2016). Innovation and technology transfer for business development. *Procedia Engineering*, 149, 495–500.
- Introductory video on technology transfer: https://www.youtube.com/watch?v=ygX5zcU5vdg.

Discussion Question 3: The entrepreneurs have identified three different ways of exploiting the developed innovation (differentiating the offer; restructuring the value chain; enlarging the business activity by selling the innovation). Antonio and Corrado have not yet decided what to do. Put yourself in their shoes and try to answer the following questions as a consultant:

(a)   What are the benefits and risks of each option?
(b)   How could each option be implemented?
(c)   Have all possibilities been considered?

1.   *Differentiating the offer.*

Antonio and Corrado have used the oven to dry other products, achieving excellent results. As highlighted in the case study, the fig drying period runs from early August to mid-September. As a result, the oven would only be used for a month and a half and would remain unused for the rest of the year. Should Antonio and Corrado decide to internalize the drying phase, it would be convenient to increase the productivity of the ovens by expanding the range of products offered.

   (a)   As highlighted above, the main benefit of this would be the reduction of machine downtime. The introduction of new products would allow the company to expand its offer, taking advantage of the brand and the same commercial network currently used. The main risk would be the loss of brand identity linking Santomiele to the white fig and the Cilento area.

(b) The company would opt for this decision if it decided to internalize the fig drying process. As a result, it would be obliged to purchase several ovens or have them built. At the same time, the company would have to hire additional staff for fig processing. It would also be necessary to invest in the development of new workshops. At present, the workshops, and employees of Santomiele are entirely dedicated to fig processing.

2. *Restructuring the value chain of figs.*
   (a) Antonio and Corrado are also considering whether or not to restructure the value chain by supplying the ovens directly to their suppliers, either on free loan or with a rental fee. The free loan strategy would allow Santomiele to count on a supply of standard-quality dried figs (their raw material) and ensure greater supplier loyalty. However, Santomiele would have to bear the initial cost of purchasing / manufacturing the ovens. At the same time, the new generations have proved to be unreliable partners and it is unclear whether they could be relied upon to comply with business agreements. The strategic option to rent the ovens to producers is one part of a broader strategy, the development of the "Cilento Fig District." As highlighted in the case study, Corrado hopes to create the Cilento Fig District: a network of producers and fig transformation companies in which everyone adopts a single quality standard. The district is used in other Italian food chains. According to Corrado, offering all producers the possibility of leasing the oven would be a first step in defining a new quality standard for the entire ecosystem of the white fig. This entrepreneurial vision is far from an exclusively profit-oriented approach but is, instead, inspired by a strategy that rewards an ecosystem vision and territorial development. Regardless of whether or not the district is created, the choice to lease the ovens to all producers would allow the company to obtain a source of revenue without having to set up a new ad hoc company to produce and market the ovens. However, unlike the free loan option, leasing would not create loyalty among producers, who could continue to supply the figs to other companies.
   (b) However, the creation of a fig district is an ambitious plan and Corrado is still unsure about which strategy he should pursue to fulfill this "dream." The second organizational problem concerns oven manufacture: if they opted for this choice, they would need to find a solution.

3. *Enlarging the business activity by selling the innovation.*

    (a)   Antonio and Corrado are evaluating the possibility of setting up a new company dealing exclusively in the manufacture and marketing of ovens. As highlighted in the case study, the drying of fruit takes place mainly in Spain, North Africa, and South America: countries with a great deal of sunshine which could use the solar oven to innovate their drying processes. It would be a costly and time-consuming operation to set up a new company and Antonio and Corrado would also have to bear the risks of launching a new company from scratch.

    (b)   In order to implement this solution, it would be necessary to set up a new ad hoc company dealing in the manufacture and marketing of the ovens.

Instructors can use the case to show how digital transformation can enable new growth opportunities for companies. The goal is to put students in the shoes of entrepreneurs and think critically about the strategic choices to be made. To date, Antonio and Corrado remain undecided, so there is no correct answer to this question. The goal is to make students think critically about the complexity of strategic choices and the impact of the digital transformation of a process within an SME in terms of the strategic options generated.

FURTHER READING AND ADDITIONAL RESOURCES

Garzoni, A., De Turi, I., Secundo, G. & Del Vecchio, P. (2020). Fostering digital transformation of SMEs: A four levels approach. *Management Decision*, 58(8), 1543–1562.

Kane, G. C., Palmer, D., Phillips, A. N., Kiron, D. & Buckley, N. (2015). Strategy, Not Technology, Drives Digital Transformation. MIT Sloan Management Review and Deloitte University Press, https://www.cubility.com.au/wp-content/uploads/2018/11/dup_strategy-not-technology-drives-digital-transformation.pdf.

OECD (2021). The Digital Transformation of SMEs, OECD Studies on SMEs and Entrepreneurship, OECD Publishing, Paris, https://doi.org/10.1787/bdb9256a-en.

Pelletier, C. & Cloutier, L. M. (2019). Conceptualising digital transformation in SMEs: An ecosystemic perspective. *Journal of Small Business and Enterprise Development*, 26(7), 855–876.

Video: An employee shows the firm's process. https://www.youtube.com/watch?v=0mjH3bPSe64 (Video in Italian, but English subtitles can be activated on YouTube).

Video: Interview with Antonio Longo. https://www.youtube.com/watch?v=47QIlkbNdno (Video in Italian, but English subtitles can be activated on YouTube).

Chapter 7: teaching notes

Anna Sörensson and Maria Bogren

CASE SUMMARY

Jamtland Farm is a family farm that is run by Anna and Stefan. Like many other farms they own the animals that live on the farm such as cows, pigs and sheep. The farm's main income comes from selling milk, produced by their cows, to a milk dairy. They also sell meat that comes from slaughtering their livestock, where they send the animals away for slaughter and later sell it to private individuals.

The food for the animals they grow themselves, except protein supplements for the cows. The protein supplement is an important part regarding the milk, but it also represents a large cost for Jamtland Farm to buy.

The farm covers 1,100 hectares, which also contains forest land. Therefore, the farm sells timber to a timber company. Jamtland Farm also offers a moose hunting experience for individuals. This business is concentrated at certain times of the year and the meat from the hunt is also for sale. In addition to themselves, Jamtland Farm have one full-time employee on the farm, as well as two employees who work as needed.

Today's customer base is relatively small and consists mainly of regular customers and acquaintances. Anna says that they would like to expand the business but that they currently do not have any farm shop or any major interest or knowledge of the marketing required for this.

Jamtland Farm is divided into two individual companies, where Stefan is the owner of one part, related to the income from the cows and pigs, and Anna owns the second part regarding the income from sheep breeding. The reason for this divide is because larger farms are subject to a permit requirement, and the maximum limit for a company was 200 animal units. The Jamtland Farm had at that time more than 200 animal units and therefore the farm was divided into two companies. The maximum limit today is 400 animal units. However, Jamtland Farm has chosen to continue with two companies.

Diversification means investing in new products or services for a new market. The Jamtland Farm has several empty buildings on the property. There are plans for the future to use them for various purposes, including restaurant, farm shop and bed and breakfast. These investments would differ from the previous products and can therefore be seen as an investment.

One empty building is an old barn and the other is a residential building that has been uninhabited for almost 30 years. The old barn could be refurbished to run a café combined with a farm shop. A business like this can be open during the summer and also weekends with both sales of own products such as sausages, meat products and wool for visitors. The café could also have a direct connection for example, lambs and rabbits that children could feed and pet, which would also make it a pleasant experience. The house which is located on the same land could be used for private rental all year round as a "stay at farm" or bed and breakfast.

The idea with the case is to examine a traditional business (like nature-based businesses) and how they can use digitalization to reach their customers.

TEACHING OBJECTIVES

The students should gain a deeper knowledge about:

- how a traditional industry can use digitalization to diversify its value propositions;
- how a traditional industry can reach its customers with the help of digitalization;
- how a traditional industry should step into the digital age;
- how a traditional industry can create new ways of distributing its products.

TEACHING STRATEGY AND ASSIGNMENT SUGGESTIONS

The idea of the case is that it should offer many different aspects of entrepreneurship in a traditional industry. Many students perhaps think of IT companies when it comes to digitalization. The purpose is thus to broaden the students' perception of how to work with digitalization in a traditional and old industry such as nature-based business. The case does not intend to offer a correct answer, but the case can lead students in different directions depending on their level of prior knowledge.

Undergraduate Courses

The case is based on three different dimensions that you as a teacher can make them focus on, namely:

- **Who is the customer?**
  - What different customer segments can the farm have?
  - Depending on which segment you turn to, how does it affect the price picture?
  - Are there different customers depending on which product and service the farm sells?
- **Diversification of the farm**
  - What new different business ideas can you create on the farm?
- **Marketing via digital channels**
  - How should the farm reach its existing customers?
  - How can the farm reach new customer segments?
  - What is the value for the different customer segments?
  - How can the farm investigate what the customers demand and are willing to pay for?
  - What prices should the farm set for its various products? Here, it is appropriate for students to do competition analyses to create an image of the market.
  - How can they use social media?

Graduate Courses

The case is based on three different dimensions that you as a teacher can make them focus on, namely:

- **Who is the customer?**
  - What different customer segments can the farm have?
  - Depending on which segment you turn to, how does it affect the price picture?
  - Are there different customers depending on which product and service the farm sells?
  - What has research in the field shown in terms of customer segments in nature-based businesses?
- **Diversification of the farm**
  - What new different business ideas can you create on the farm?
  - What has research in the field shown in terms of diversification?
- **Marketing via digital channels**
  - How should the farm reach its existing customers?

- How can the farm reach new customer segments?
- What is the value for the different customer segments?
- How could the farm interact with the customers both physically and digitally?
- How can the farm investigate what the customers demand and are willing to pay for?
- What prices should the farm set for its various products? Here, it is appropriate for students to do competition analyses to create an image of the market.
- What has research in the field shown in terms of marketing in digital channels?
- How can they use social media?

With regard to graduate students, a strong connection should be made to **existing research in the field**. A starting point should be to let students search for research articles that can be used as arguments for how the case can be developed. Then the case will not only be a practical application, but there will be a clear connection to research in the field.

With regard to graduate students, there is the opportunity to broaden the potential market for the case's products by conducting a discussion on **regional, national and international markets**. Depending on which market you turn to, you should use, for example, different digital channels and different symbols and expressions. Where is the customer segment that you turn to?

FURTHER READING

Vadana, I. I., Torkkeli, L., Kuivalainen, O., and Saarenketo, S. (2020). Digitalization of companies in international entrepreneurship and marketing. *International Marketing Review*, 37(3), 471–492.

Chapter 8: teaching notes

Davide Gamba, Tommaso Minola and Matteo Kalchschmidt

CASE SUMMARY

Marlegno is an Italian small to medium-sized family firm that operates in the green building construction industry, designing and manufacturing customized timber houses, buildings, and structures. The case can illustrate the importance of digitalization as a driver for process innovation, servitization of the business model, and organizational change by analyzing the adoption of digital innovations by a company in a traditional industry. In addition, the case demonstrates how open innovation approaches can boost the innovation process. Finally, it is a learning resource that helps understand the evolution of the green building construction industry and real estate from the financial crises in 2008 to the advent of smart homes.

TEACHING OBJECTIVES

The educational objectives of this case are to:

- Show how digitalization was the source of innovation opportunities and competitive advantage in a small-medium sized company that operates in a traditional industry. The story provides application cases of digital technologies such as the internet of things, artificial intelligence, and virtual reality in the green building construction industry.
- Introduce students to servitization strategies in small-medium manufacturers. Compared to large companies, small-medium sized companies lack internal financial and managerial resources, capabilities, and experience helpful for a compelling servitization journey.
- Present innovations enabled by open innovation strategies, following Chesbrough's theory (Chesbrough, 2006).

Target Audience

We recommend the case for undergraduate students at an advanced stage (third year), Master's students, and executive classes of various courses, including innovation management, strategic management, and entrepreneurship. The case makes a good fit also for operations management students, especially for classes on service management. The case may be of interest also for an audience without or limited previous knowledge in business modeling.

SUGGESTED TEACHING STRATEGY

TN Table 8.1 provides a recommended instructional sequence that includes necessary and optional elements. If students read the case ahead of the class, the teaching case can be given in a regular three-hour lecture. The analysis should be confined to two or three questions among the ones provided for the sake of time and based on the instructional objectives. The first question can be considered a warm-up stage of the teaching strategy, which should be answered by mostly analyzing the teaching case's content. The authors suggest selecting this question jointly with one or more of the following questions according to the student audience and the pursued teaching goal. The last question can be used to conclude the class by prompting students to forecast challenges that the company will face in the future (TN Figure 8.1).

TN Table 8.1   Suggested teaching strategy

Step	Suggested duration	Execution
Preparatory activity		Students read the case before class. Create teams of 3 or 4 students each. Depending on the educational objectives and the type of audience, the instructor will select a couple of discussion questions for the in-class discussion.
Introduction	10 min	The instructor creates slides with a list of the steps and questions that have been chosen.
Students discuss the case in groups and develop responses to the questions	45 min	
Groups' answers definition	15 min	Ask groups to prepare a presentation to illustrate their conclusion. The instructor should stimulate non-standard presentation methods.
Discussion	90 min	Ask each group to present answers in 5 minutes maximum, adopting an elevator pitch approach. Class discussion.

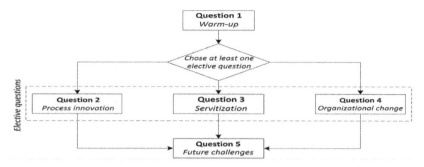

TN Figure 8.1   Suggested questions selection process

SUGGESTED ANSWERS TO DISCUSSION QUESTIONS

Discussion Question 1: How would you describe the SME strategy before the financial crisis? What were the drivers that led the SME to the decision to innovate its business model? Can this business model innovation be replicated in other industries?

Marlegno started as a B2B subcontractor of prebuilt timber roofs for local construction companies. Due to the 2008 financial crisis, Marlegno's customers became insolvent which prompted the company to shift to a B2C target selling directly to final customers. The instructor can ask students to reflect on the transaction from a B2B to a B2C strategy through the business model canvas (Osterwalder and Pigneur, 2010). A suggested solution is presented in TN Table 8.2.

The financial crisis started as an endogenous factor that impacted the building construction industry in 2010, serving as a driver to the business model shift.

Other industries can replicate the shift from a B2B to a B2C, mainly thanks to digital transformation and servitization opportunities. A couple of good examples to stimulate reflections are as follows:

- Volvo started to sell its cars directly to final customers without dealerships through the program Care by Volvo (Volvo, n.d.) in the automotive industry.
- HP started to sell ink for its printers directly to final customers through the Instant Ink (Hewlett-Packard Company, n.d.) program in the computer hardware industry.

The instructor can then ask students to suggest other cases, especially in manufacturing.

TN Table 8.2   Suggested analysis of Marlegno's transaction from B2B to B2C business model

Building block	B2B strategy	B2C strategy
Value proposition	*Price leadership*	*Sustainability, differentiation, innovation*
Revenue strategy	*Prebuilt timber roofs one-off sale*	*Buildings one-off sale; services sold through long term contracts*
Customer segments	Construction companies	Households
Customer relationships	Discrete	Continuous (i.e., loyalty)
Channels	Direct contact	Internet channels, events (e.g., open house)
Cost structure	*Production and operations activities; workers and employees; raw materials*	*Production, operations, design, R&D, and marketing activities; employees; raw materials*
Key resources	Production workers	Designers, project managers, production machineries
Key activities	Production, and on-site operations	R&D, design, on-site operations, marketing, customer service and aftersales
Key partners	Raw materials supplier	Raw materials suppliers; tech and institutional partners

Discussion Question 2: How does digitalization influence process innovation in a traditional industry SME? What were the factors that played a fundamental role in the innovation process?

The instructor should start guiding the class by reflecting on Industry 4.0[1] practices and technologies that the teaching case does not explicitly mention (e.g., 3D printing) to stimulate possible other digitalization applications for process innovation. Digitalization impacts the manufacturing process through Industry 4.0's technologies by introducing novel fabrication methods that allow more flexibility while still granting low-cost, low-volume production (Savastano et al., 2019). Because SMEs have fewer resources than large companies, managing the innovation process is the most challenging task. Digitalization necessitates a mental change in how current processes and re-engineered activities are seen based on facts rather than appearance. The shift from a process-oriented to a data-oriented emphasis underlies the transformation from data scarcity to data abundance, which transformational technologies like IoT and AI may facilitate. As in the case of "Oikos x," new datasets based on replicated and distributed structures enable innovative processes to enhance competitive advantage.

In most cases, SMEs are not "early adopters," mainly because of the fear of investing in the wrong technologies or adopting inapt practices. Due to the lack of hard skills related to the technology adopted and the potential risk of failure, institutions can incentivize SMEs' process innovation through partnerships and inter-firm collaborations based on open innovation strategies. In that sense, the teaching case describes the EU's Level-Up project in which Marlegno collaborated with SCM to adopt "Oikos x" in its production plant.

Discussion Question 3: How does the servitization of the business model gain from digitalization? What could be the main challenges faced by SMEs in adopting such a business model?

The instructor can encourage students' reflection by revisiting answers about the transaction from a B2B to a B2C business model provided for question 1. Product-centric SMEs adopt servitization to gain a competitive advantage, as well as improved flexibility, cost and time savings, product reliability, increased sales and profitability, and improved customer satisfaction (Kaňovská and Tomášková, 2018). Digitalization and technologies usage play an essential role in new services creation. The teaching case shows that adopting technologies such as the IoT, VR, and AI can create opportunities or completely transform the features of delivered services, such as Marlegno's preventive maintenance system developed with a local start-up. At the same time, SMEs need an appropriate management information system as a base to exploit data collected from customers. Data collected from products can be the input for developing new, value-adding services and optimizing the existing ones.

Unfortunately, SMEs usually experience a shortage of skilled personnel and a lack of organizational mindset. These barriers are also present in large enterprises, but they are perceived more intensely in SMEs because of their smaller size and lack of resources. On the other hand, hard skills related to technology can be insourced through partnerships and collaborations based on an open innovation strategy. In addition, SMEs could face significant financial barriers to servitization, the so-called service paradox (Gebauer et al., 2005). The latter says that companies that invest heavily in extending their service business enhance their service offerings and incur higher costs (e.g., because of digital transformation implementation), but this does not result in the expected correspondingly higher returns.

Discussion Question 4: How does digitalization shape the company's organizational transformation and corporate culture? Is employees' reskilling and upskilling a consequence of technologies adopted, or, vice versa, a propaedeutic to innovation?

Digitalization shapes a company's organization through the introduction of new roles. In fact, along with technology advancements, the organizational structure undergoes numerous significant changes, helping businesses to become more adaptable in the face of rapidly changing markets. The teaching case illustrates that Marlegno introduced HR and marketing functions. Each of them is horizontal with respect to the existing ones. This horizontal coordination mechanism allows new interactions between different functional areas for continuous improvement (both formal and informal). Data favors and enables interaction between departments. The HR department can use data collected to analyze all workers' and employees' performances to manage resources reskilling and upskilling. On the other hand, the marketing department uses data collected from external sources to help the sales function in the lead acquisition and commercial opportunity processes. De facto, the organizational structure of Marlegno assumed a matrix configuration with the introduction of the two abovementioned cross-functional departments, as shown by TN Figure 8.2. Hence, the firm experiences a passage from a hierarchical structure to an organic and adaptive one. Digitalization guides businesses toward more flexible organizational structures that allow continuous adaptation (Hanelt et al., 2021).

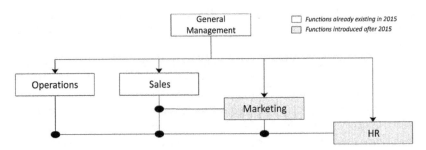

TN Figure 8.2   The TOE framework

The instructor can stimulate additional analysis at the individual resource level. Possible triggers of discussion connected to digitalization are as follows:

1. Employees' involvement in the continuous improvement process thanks to data sharing.
2. Collaboration between workers and machines.
3. Single resource and team evaluation as a result of data collected.

Incidentally, Industry 4.0 is not just a wave of disruptive technical innovation: it's a cultural shift as well (Savastano et al., 2019). The instructor can stimulate analysis of digitalization's impact on corporate culture based on the following triggers:

1. Introduce top managers and middle managers with a strong drive towards digitalization to tackle cognitive inertia.
2. Add an innovation manager who can spread the digital culture within the company and introduce new technologies to older resources. SMEs can select a middle manager with a strong orientation towards digitization to spread digital culture among resources.
3. Share objectives with workers and employees.

Finally, the last question is intentionally open to stimulate class discussion. The instructor should guide the debate highlighting the different innovations mentioned in the teaching case and the open innovation strategy adopted by the company. Process innovation started by an EU project that allows creating a partnership with SCM Group, while the servitization of the business model began by identifying firms that collaborated with Marlegno to implement pre and aftersales technology applications, such as IoT. Hence, it seems that Marlegno started from technology adoption through expert partners; then, it began to upskill and reskill its workers and employees to cope with technologies usage and business implications.

Discussion Question 5: What do you think the company should do in the future to stay ahead and maintain an edge in the digitalization of its business?

The instructor should guide students to think about future challenges stressing the dimension related to elective questions selected. The authors suggest using easy strategic tools (e.g., SWOT analysis focusing on opportunities and threats quadrants) to stimulate thoughts about possible scenarios. For the benefit of the instructor, the authors suggest a not exhaustive list of three different future challenges to stay ahead and maintain an edge in the digitalization of its business (TN Table 8.3).

The first future challenge regards 3D printers for highly customized components production at accessible costs. Unfortunately, this opportunity led to different design and production processes, requiring new digital capabilities compared to the existing ones. The second challenge refers to insourcing the production of smart objects (e.g., humidity sensors). This choice can benefit from economy of scale with existing production, enhancing the performances of Marlegno's remote monitoring of their buildings. Investments could be very high, both for the new production lines required and the new capabilities needed to design these products. Last, students should reflect on introducing c-level managers within Marlegno's organizational chart. The new manager should effectively promote and implement digital opportunities (i.e., CIO, Chief Information Officer). Such a role can enhance product production and services delivery by helping Marlegno understand the usage of new digital technologies. On the other hand, conflicts with Marlegno's owners and existing IT figures could arise.

TN Table 8.3   Future challenges

DIMENSIONS				
DIGITAL OPPORTUNITIES		Process innovation	Servitization	Organizational change
New technologies 3D Printers	*Opportunities*	Optimization of raw material consumption	Customized components at accessible costs	-
	Threats	Different design and production processes	-	New digital capabilities are needed
New services Production of smart objects	*Opportunities*	Economy of scope	Enhance remote monitoring	-
	Threats	New production lines	-	New capabilities are needed
New c-level roles CIO	*Opportunities*	Enhance existing production processes through a better understanding of the technologies used	Enhance existing services provided through a better understanding of the technologies used	Resources managerialization
	Threats	-	-	Conflicts with Marlegno's owners and existing IT figures

NOTE

1. For more information about Industry 4.0, see: https://en.wikipedia.org/wiki/Fourth_Industrial_Revolution.

FURTHER READING AND ADDITIONAL RESOURCES

Chesbrough, H. (2006). Open innovation: a new paradigm for understanding industrial innovation. In H. Chesbrough, W. Vanhaverbeke, and J. West (eds.), *Open Innovation: Researching a New Paradigm* (pp. 1–12). Oxford: Oxford University Press.

Gebauer, H., Fleisch, E., and Friedli, T. (2005). Overcoming the service paradox in manufacturing companies. *European Management Journal*, 23(1), 14–26.

Hanelt, A., Bohnsack, R., Marz, D., and Antunes Marante, C. (2021). A systematic review of the literature on digital transformation: Insights and implications for strategy and organizational change. *Journal of Management Studies*, 58(5), 1159–1197.

Kaňovská, L. and Tomášková, E. (2018). Drivers for smart servitization in manufacturing companies. *Agris On-line Papers in Economics and Informatics*, 10(3), 57–68.

Osterwalder, A. and Pigneur, Y. (2010). *Business Model Generation: A Handbook for Visionaries, Game Changers, and Challengers* (Vol. 1). Hoboken, NJ: John Wiley & Sons.

Paschou, T., Rapaccini, M., Adrodegari, F., and Saccani, N. (2020). Digital servitization in manufacturing: A systematic literature review and research agenda. *Industrial Marketing Management*, 89, 278–292.

Savastano, M., Amendola, C., Bellini, F., and D'Ascenzo, F. (2019). Contextual impacts on industrial processes brought by the digital transformation of manufacturing: A systematic review. *Sustainability*, 11(3), 891.

WEBSITES AND WEBPAGES

Hewlett-Packard Company (n.d.). *HP Instant Ink*. https://instantink.hpconnected.com/us/en/l/.

Volvo (n.d.). *Care by Volvo*. https://www.volvocars.com/us/care-by-volvo/.

Chapter 9: teaching notes

Dmitry Katalevsky

CASE SUMMARY

The case study describes how Dodo Pizza, a traditional fast-food company, leveraged its growth strategy by digital transformation. Digitalization has helped the company to get a dominant position on the Russian market and to pursue a successful international expansion strategy. The case introduces students to the company's growth drivers and sources of competitive advantage. We use a resource-based view (RBV) and core competence concept to get insights about the role of digital transformation in the company's spectacular success. The concept of increasing returns and self-reinforcing growth loops (systems thinking perspective) is applied to explore the mechanism of Dodo's fast growth. The benefits of the "Get-Big-Fast" strategy are discussed. Finally, the case is a learning resource that helps to assess the disruptive potential of Dodo's digital transformation for competitors (whether Dodo's model of digitalization is disruptive for the industry or not).

TEACHING OBJECTIVES

The main objective of the case is to show how digitalization can reinvent traditional and conservative industries. Digitalization increases the speed of business operations on the one hand, and makes all business processes completely transparent on the other. Increased speed and transparency enhance customer experience and drive consumers' interest and loyalty. Digital technologies (in the case of Dodo, its IT system) helped the pizza chain to scale up quickly both domestically and internationally maintaining the same level of quality of product and service which would be difficult otherwise (if possible). As a result, traditional business models of domestic and international rivals are being challenged by newcomers who reinvent the traditional ways of doing business with the help of digital technologies.

The aim of the case is to:

- Show how traditional businesses can be transformed through digitalization.

- Discuss the sources of competitive advantage in digitalized businesses.
- Improve understanding of whether digitalization is a disruptive factor for traditional businesses.
- Teach how to use the RBV to identify the potential of and opportunities for a high growth startup.
- Find out if digitalization can be useful in implementing "Get-Big-Fast" strategies.

This case emphasizes that even in traditional industries the sources of competitive advantage are changing due to digitalization opportunities.

Target Audience

This case can be recommended for bachelor students majoring in business studies or MBA students studying strategic management, strategy analysis, innovation management, entrepreneurship, digital technology, etc. The case might be helpful in studying such concepts as disruptive innovation, business model, corporate growth management, and Get-Big-Fast strategies. The case might be also useful in product development and digitalization studies. The case might also be interesting to students with a technical background studying artificial intelligence and big data with no or limited business background as it shows the benefits of unified data. Finally, the case could be helpful in examining international business experience and business models relevant to emerging markets (Russia and the East European countries).

SUGGESTED TEACHING STRATEGY: SETTINGS AND INSTRUCTIONAL SEQUENCE

The suggested instructional sequence listing both mandatory and optional steps is reported in TN Table 9.1. The case is to be delivered in a typical three-hour class, assuming students read the case in advance. For the sake of time and depending on the instructional objectives, the analysis should be limited to three or four questions from those proposed.

TN Table 9.1   Suggested instructional sequence

Step	Duration	Setting/Execution
Preparation (before the class)	30 min	• Students read the case before the class • Students watch one of the founder's interviews, if possible • Some research on fast-food industry business model is recommended but not obligatory
Introduction & goalsetting	7–10 min	• Class gets into teams 3-4 students each • Instructor sets goals of the teamwork and provides questions for discussion, sets timeline and work objectives
Team work; Presentation of results (visualization)	25–30 min	• Group work in teams • Teams prepare a poster outlining results of their work
Debriefing	30 min	• Class discussion • Discussion of new entrepreneurship models made possible through digitalization
Total:	90 min	

SUGGESTED ANSWERS TO DISCUSSION QUESTIONS

Discussion Question 1: What are the key growth drivers behind the success of Dodo Pizza?

Traditional industry analysis tools (e.g., PESTEL or Michael Porter's Five Forces Industry Analysis Model) are not always able to explain the nature of a sustainable competitive advantage considering that industry incumbents are likely to prevent newcomers' growth via barriers to entry, economies of scale effects, access to supplier and customer networks, as well as capital mobilization opportunities. However, there is evidence, and the Dodo business case clearly shows, that newcomers manage to make a difference even on established and highly competitive markets such as fast food.

In fact, even a quick industry analysis based on Porter's Five Forces methodology (Porter, 1980) shows that the industry is unattractive to newcomers given its slow growth, low entry barriers, low switching cost from one pizza brand to another, and availability of fast-food substitutes (i.e., hamburgers, sandwiches, hotdogs from both recognized international players and domestic chains).

Clayton Christensen's theory of disruptive innovation has a limited explanatory power in the case of Dodo Pizza. Christensen's theory of disruptive innovation is based on the assumption that newcomers usually challenge incumbents by attacking the market niche of lower profitability where typically price sensitive customers are ready to switch to a cheaper alternative (Christensen and Raynor, 2003; Christensen et al., 2015). Winning these niches (usually neglected by the industry leaders) first, the newcomer gradually improves the product or service eventually targeting the core customers of the incumbent by offering the same or more of a product or service for (significantly) less.

Yet, the winning strategy of Dodo was quite different. It did not offer the cheapest pizza to challenge the established pizza chains. Instead, Dodo offered its pizzas at average market prices, the same as those of the industry leaders, such as Domino's Pizza, Pizza Hut, etc. In addition, there are no clear economy-of-scale advantages in the fast-food industry like, for instance, in semiconductors, automaking or telecom industries.

Let us examine Dodo's success factors in more detail.

From the very start, the founder of Dodo worked hard to implement an aggressive growth strategy. First, Dodo successfully exploited the traditional growth loop typical for fast-food companies – the number of restaurants opened. The early success of Dodo's own restaurants coupled with the founder's marketing activity generated interest from potential investors in Dodo's franchise program. Once launched, this franchise program helped to generate additional revenue stream from royalty payments. The pace of opening of new restaurants was impressive – the company nearly doubled the number of restaurants each year in 2014–2018.

Second, the early success was amplified by the founder's marketing and PR activities carried out through *digital communication channels* (the most important was his personal blog read by tens of thousands of people, as well as several viral videos, e.g., the title "First Drone Delivered Pizza Globally" that generated a lot of buzz). It helped not only to build brand awareness, but also to bring early investors in Dodo's franchise network from the founder's blog readers.

Third, the digital channels enabled the founder to secure the much-needed equity financing via crowdsourcing to support the company's high growth rates in a very cash constrained and turbulent economic environment (after some consideration, VCs and PE funds refused to take the risk and to finance the company). Having numerous readers of his blog, Fyodor communicated his needs in financing and soon managed to raise the necessary amount.

However, the key growth accelerator for Dodo was *digitalization* – in particular, its unique IT system that helped to standardize the sales, purchasing, HR, and even management processes along the whole pizza chain (TN Figure 9.1).

A useful explanation of the company's success is offered by the concept of growth accelerators based on self-reinforcing feedback loops (Achi et al.,

1995; Sterman, 2000). Achi et al. (1995) studied the growth patterns of more than 9,000 publicly listed companies and found out that the fast-growing companies intelligently exploit *increasing returns economic effects* that help to drive company growth in an unprecedented way.

> Under increasing returns, returns from marginal investments go up rather than down. Some firms continue to invest, their profitability grows, and eventually one or two firms can dominate the market. Other firms are unable to keep up the necessary investments … fast growth fuels itself. Multiple reinforcing feedback loops conspire to create a "virtuous cycle," unleashing a momentum that competitors are powerless to stop. (Achi et al., 1995, p. 7)

Multiple reinforcing feedback loops help to create "growth accelerators" that drive the company at a much faster speed that competitors are not able to sustain.

> A combination of three, four, or more accelerators are usually needed to establish a powerful growth cycle. The reason is simple. Each reinforcing loop is inherently self-reinforcing. But when they are combined, loops with a common element become mutually reinforcing as well. … And since each reinforcing feedback loop in isolation leads to exponential growth, mutually reinforcing loops produce not just faster growth, but exponentially faster growth. (Achi et al., 1995, p. 15)

The diagram of Dodo's key growth accelerators is presented in TN Figure 9.1.

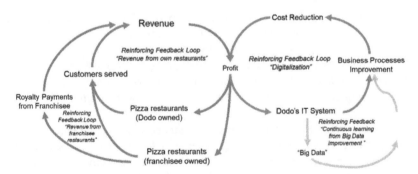

TN Figure 9.1   Multiple reinforcing feedback loops fueling Dodo's expansion (restaurant chain, digitalization and "big data")

Such reinforcing loop accelerators help the company to grow faster than competitors. As a result, the company can pursue a "Get-Big-Fast" strategy to capture the market share and to lock in their leading position (see Discussion Question 5 for more details).

Discussion Question 2: How do you think the Founder of Dodo Pizza managed to achieve sustained growth in a traditional pizza business by leveraging digitalization?

As the company was expanding quickly, the key question for the management was how *to ensure the high standards of quality* and *consistency of service delivery across the whole chain.*

Dodo's IT system was a much-needed solution to this problem. The quality issue was exacerbated by the fact that the franchisees were typically young entrepreneurs attracted by the company's high growth rates and revenue opportunities, while lacking necessary skills to run a pizza restaurant. The IT system played a crucial role in cementing the universally shared rules of conduct and service provision for all franchisees across the country and the world at a later stage. It enabled the fast growth of the company without eroding its service quality and standards. Once the issue was resolved, the company started growing quickly and seamlessly.

Also, digitalization helped to lower the company's costs through optimization of business processes and better assets utilization – i.e., making the employees more efficient by automating some routine operations (i.e., pizza ordering though the website rather than a call center, etc.).

Generating "big data," the IT system also enables a continuous learning process that drives further improvements in the company's operational efficiency (i.e., better forecasting of customer demand, more efficient product and waste management, etc.). As Moeller et al. (2018) mention, digital technology "reduces the need for physical assets ... Digital systems accumulate data and, through machine learning, they continually improve the performance of the new business models, thereby accelerating their impact." The continuous improvement cycle translates into *a self-reinforcing loop* helping to drive further business efficiency.

Overall, successful digitalization helped Dodo to grow in double digits over the period of 2011–2019.

Discussion Question 3: Can you identify and describe the "core competencies" of Dodo Pizza using the resource-based view framework? Is Dodo's competitive advantage robust enough? Can Dodo's competitors replicate its success?

(a) What are the core competencies of Dodo Pizza?

A **resource-based view of the firm** can also shed some light on the company's outstanding performance compared to its traditional peers. The resource-based view assumes that the success of the company lies in the resources it can mobilize and create to fuel its growth. Not all resources, though, are of equal importance. The most important are the resources that are hard and costly (if it is possible at all) for the competitors to replicate.

It is not so difficult for a competitor to copy a successful marketing campaign; however, it's difficult to replicate a corporate culture (Peter Drucker used to say, "Culture eats strategy for breakfast") or, in the case of Dodo Pizza, *its tailor-made IT system* that manages nearly all of its business processes from sales and ordering to supply chain management.

To a large extent, Dodo's success can be explained by the "sticky resources" it managed to create. In the case of Dodo, it is a unique IT system that was built from scratch and customized to meet the company's needs. It was a hard decision for the founder to build an IT system from scratch. At first, it was not even supported by his own team members. At the time the decision was taken, the company was cash constrained. The founder even struggled to support the two IT specialists he had hired as the first effort to create it. The market was abundant in specialized IT systems offered by various IT companies and integrators, but Fyodor rejected them all due to their "failure to meet Dodo's needs." He had a vision of something unique that none of his competitors possessed at the time, reflecting the company's need to be fully transparent for both the customers and franchise partners.

Later, the IT system, once built, became an invaluable source of big data that enabled *continuous improvement and learning*. Big data enables ongoing optimization of the supply chain, sales and marketing efforts, sales seasonality, early notification of changing consumer demand, and other important factors. As of 2021, the company employs more than 150 IT specialists to support and develop Dodo's information system, and plans to increase this number by another 100 people within the next 1–2 years.

To conclude, it is not pizza recipes, unique pizza making equipment or creative marketing campaigns but a sophisticated tailor-made IT system and big data that emerged into a real *core competence* of the company (Prahalad and Hamel, 1990).

(b)   Is Dodo's competitive advantage robust enough? Can Dodo's competitors replicate the company's growth model?

It's rather unlikely that the competitors will be able to replicate the success of Dodo soon due to their lack of "sticky resources" (company culture and team spirit, IT system) and inability to imitate them. However, nothing lasts forever. Some researchers claim that in the era of digital technology there is no sustainable competitive advantage – any advantage can only be temporary. There is a difference between catching an opportunity and converting an opportunity (acquiring competitive advantage). Some companies grow successfully by leveraging growth factors in a favorable market environment (i.e., overall market growth, stronger consumer purchasing power, favorable consumer spending trends), but later they fail to protect their positions from competitors. This is well exemplified by LEGO, a company that experienced high growth rates in the 1970s and 1980s but struggled in the 1990s because of increased competition from their rivals on the toys market and changing consumer preferences arising from the video gaming industry (Robertson and Breen, 2013).

We can speculate that Dodo has some competitive advantage over its rivals in the short run but not in the long term. Moreover, such advantage is partial as the company coexists with big international players (i.e., Domino's Pizza and others) that continuously improve their internal business processes and pursue their own digitalization strategies.

Dodo will likely outrun smaller domestic and international competitors. The success of the company on the international arena will not only require streamlined and efficient business processes but also other tangible and intangible resources, such as access to capital to fuel its growth (the company is considering going to an IPO in 2024), investments in strong brand and reputation to attract talents, and knowledge of local traditions and demands (i.e., the company tried unsuccessfully to enter the Chinese market in 2019–2020), etc.

(c)   Can Dodo's rivals replicate its success?

Like any successful company, Dodo is quite special in terms of its business path, corporate culture and values. However, Dodo's business model, albeit quite efficient, is not unique. The fast-food market is competitive and fragmented, offering plenty of opportunities to successful and growing companies cannibalizing the market share of smaller and less successful rivals.

However, one might expect that other companies, inspired by Dodo's success, will also invest heavily in digital transformation. As discussed in the previous section, the competitive advantage of Dodo will probably weaken over the years as other companies will be catching up. Besides, some rivals may have additional sources of growth, such as brand, funding, etc. that will provide them with good chances of catching up.

At the same time, it is important to mention that Dodo may have another important and rather unique feature that helps it to stand out from the crowd of competitors – transparency. The company's transparency is a distinctive feature that makes it especially appealing to customers. For instance, the company was the first to install webcams in its kitchens. Every customer may have a kitchen tour upon request. Dodo broadcasts its company meetings on YouTube.[1] While many other fast-food chains keep their sales data secret (sales of each restaurant/store), Dodo has made it absolutely transparent on the company's website. Dodo continuously promotes transparency internally (to its workers) and externally (to its customers).

These unique features of corporate culture are even more difficult to replicate than the IT system. We cannot measure how and to what extent transparency translates into the sales and reputation of the company; however it is, definitely, an important factor of the overall success of Dodo. The company's philosophy and way of doing business are not replicable and remain truly unique.

To conclude, it is likely that the growth patterns of the company can be copied (at least, to some extent) by competitors. However, it is unlikely that the overall success of the company can be replicated due to the company's unique corporate culture.

Discussion Question 4: Can we claim that through digitalization of its business model Dodo disrupted the entire fast-food industry? Please explain.

The theory of disruptive innovation provides for two different types of innovation – sustained innovation and disruptive innovation. According to Christensen, "sustained innovation" is about making a good product better for the existing customers. Such improvements intended to sell more to existing customers can be either incremental or radical. On the contrary, disruptive innovation usually targets currently unprofitable or low-margin market segments (the bottom of the market). A disruptive product has a mixture of attributes that appeal to smaller customer groups, i.e., it is cheaper, more accessible, or more convenient than those of the incumbents. Usually, established companies do not invest in such markets until it is too late (e.g., the case of competition between Blockbuster and Netflix).

As a result of disruption, established market leaders are usually ousted by new entrants; however, this is not always the case. Sometimes incumbents just move into higher-end and more lucrative markets. Christensen et al. (2015) explain that the disruption process varies across the industry and may affect firms differently. Disruption usually restructures the industry in such a way that former leaders may end up in niche businesses while entrants may grow into new leaders or win a noticeable market position.

We should not think of Dodo's case in terms of "radical" innovation or "disruptive" innovation. Dodo Pizza does not disrupt the business model of the industry. As we can see, Dodo has not come up with a brand-new product or technology, or even a business model. Dodo used digital technology *to optimize operations and customer experience*, but those operations and experience did not change much. However, it significantly *transformed its business processes* by making them more transparent, faster, and more streamlined for both insiders (workers) and outsiders (customers). This enabled *high and fast scalability of the business* since digital technology helped Dodo's management to control its business efficiently (in near-real-time), both throughout the country and across borders to manage its franchised stores.

For instance, Dodo was the first to introduce the concept of "one hour delivery or pizza for free," as well as to install webcams in the kitchens and stream video to consumers in real time. In doing so, Dodo efficiently used digital solutions to optimize its business processes throughout its organization. In addition, digital technology helped Dodo to eliminate inefficiencies to make its business transparent and cost effective.

Thus, the success of the company can be attributed to fast digitalization of the traditional pizza-making business that enabled consistent growth across many geographies simultaneously. It helped the company to grow aggressively and eventually become the biggest pizza chain in Russia (2018–2019), as well as to expand to international markets.

The success of Dodo can rather be explained by the company's core capabilities (IT system) that enabled a sustainable competitive advantage (Prahalad and Hamel, 1990).

Discussion Question 5: How might digitalization help implement "Get-Big-Fast" strategies?

Digitalization helps to make products or deliver services faster and more conveniently for a consumer. If you are able to make things faster, sustaining the same or superior quality, it usually means that your product/service is also cheaper (due to the economies of scale). Therefore, digitalization offers a window of new opportunities for both incumbents and new market entrants while becoming a threat for established companies which do not want to change (or are too bureaucratic to change).

Digitalization favors the economy of increasing returns. As Shapiro and Varian (1999) point out, it may be rational for a firm to pursue an aggressive strategy by trying to grow faster than competitors in an industry with increasing returns effects. Sutton (1991) showed that increasing returns may eventually lead to a dominant position within the industry.

Therefore, digitalization actually *encourages* the "Get-Big-Fast" strategy. Although the fast-food market is not a typical market where "the winner-takes-it-all" as, for instance, the market of Intel or Google, Dodo's increasing returns from the IT system and big data helped the company to bust growth. Rapid expansion usually poses a threat to the company pursuing it by causing excess capacity and the risk of "overshooting and collapse." However, in the case of Dodo such a strategy does not pose a significant risk. The company was able to grow rapidly due to its franchise model. Dodo itself does not invest in new restaurants – this risk is shifted to the franchisees of the company (although Dodo helps its franchisees to mitigate the operational risks through its IT system and market forecasting skills, the investment risk is still on the franchisee).

Considering this, the "Get-Big-Fast" strategy turned out to be the right decision for Dodo. It only took the company seven years to outdo its major competitors in Russia by reinventing its key business processes with the use of digital tools.

Overall, we can conclude that digital technology might be instrumental in realizing "Get-Big-Fast" strategies. That's why it is important to study digital entrepreneurship as it differs from traditional entrepreneurship and management in terms of strategy development, market growth, business models and requirements of leadership skills.

NOTE

1.   The archive of meetings (in English) can be accessed on the company's YouTube channel. https://www.youtube.com/watch?v=NaDU0UKulyc&list=PLXOrZPAO2Ui3iyEV6C6vI5HGggHp_keri&index=7.

FURTHER READING

Achi, Z., Doman, A., Sibony, O., Sinha, J., and Witt, S. (1995). The paradox of fast growth tigers. *McKinsey Quarterly*, 3(4).

Christensen, C. M. and Raynor, M. E. (2003). *The Innovator's Solution*. Boston, MA: Harvard Business School Press.

Christensen, C. M., Raynor, M. E., and McDonald, R. (2015). What is disruptive innovation? *Harvard Business Review*. https://hbr.org/2015/12/what-is-disruptive -innovation.

Moeller, L., Hodson, N., and Sangin, M. (2018). The coming wave of digital disruption. *Strategy & Business*, 22(4), 407–419.

Porter, M. E. (1980). *Competitive Strategy*. New York: Free Press.

Prahalad, C. K. and Hamel, G. (1990). The core competencies of the corporation. *Harvard Business Review*, 68, 79–91.

Robertson, D. C. and Breen, B. (2014). *Brick by Brick: How LEGO Rewrote the Rules of Innovation and Conquered the Global Toy Industry*. New York: Random House.

Shapiro, C. and Varian, H. R. (1999). The art of standards wars. *California Management Review*, 41(2), 8–32.

Sterman, J. (2000). *Business Dynamics*. New York: McGraw-Hil.

Sterman, J., Henderson, R., Beinhocker, E. D., and Newman, L. I. (2007). Getting big too fast: Strategic dynamics with increasing returns and bounded rationality. *Management Science*, 53(4), 683–696.

Sutton, J. (1991). *Sunk Costs and Market Structure: Price Competition, Advertising, and the Evolution of Concentration*. Cambridge, MA: MIT Press.

Chapter 10: teaching notes

Gianluca Elia, Alessandro Margherita, Pasquale Del Vecchio, Giustina Secundo and Marco Valerio Izzo

CASE SUMMARY

The chapter describes the case of Buzzoole, an Italian fast-growing technology venture specializing in influencer marketing enhanced by artificial intelligence. After an overview of the industry dynamics and trends, the case illustrates how the company has developed innovative applications to help medium-large corporations to enhance customer trust and improve their overall market performance. The case of Buzzoole can be used to illustrate how the adoption of digital technologies such as social media, mobile apps, big data, and advanced analytics algorithms can trigger the experimentation of new products and services, the exploration of new markets, and the creation of new forms of customer value. The case also introduces students to key digital technologies such as text processing applications, image recognition algorithms and social networks analysis techniques, which can help companies to execute their digital marketing strategy, achieve a deeper understanding of consumers' satisfaction, and reshape the consumer–brand relationship. The case includes an introductory section on digital marketing and the new frontier of influencer marketing, an overview of Buzzoole, and a section describing the approaches adopted by the company to innovate the influencer marketing industry. Finally, the case introduces the Digital Entrepreneurship Canvas, a tool useful to design and describe a digital venture through seven key elements.

TEACHING OBJECTIVES

Through the case, students will:

- Understand the impact of digital innovation on marketing strategies and processes.
- Appreciate the importance of influencer marketing.

- Understand and apply key metrics to evaluate an influencer marketing campaign.
- Simulate the design and realization of an influencer marketing campaign going through the strategy, implementation and measurement phases.
- Conceive and design an initiative aimed at enhancing market success of an organization by leveraging digital technologies.

Target Audience

The case is recommended for senior undergraduate and graduate students on a variety of courses including digital transformation, technology entrepreneurship, innovation management, and digital marketing. Students with previous knowledge in marketing and innovation management can analyze the story from different angles, including strategy formulation, social network analysis, digital marketing, and organizational transformation. The case can attract individuals and professionals (including corporate executives) aiming to enhance their knowledge of digital marketing and influencer marketing. The main goal of the case study is to provide participants with the case of a small company able to apply the emerging digital technologies to transform one of the most crucial company processes.

DISCUSSION QUESTIONS

The students will be engaged in a discussion and classwork session articulated along the following issues:

1. Based on the definition and examples analyzed in the Buzzoole case, and using some extra research, identify and describe (from a functional point of view) the most important technologies supporting digital marketing.
2. Outline the five key points that characterize influencer marketing respect to a traditional marketing strategy.
3. Summarize and discuss the indicators you can use to assess the effectiveness of an influencer.
4. Explain the relevance of brand affinity and the factors or variables that affect or have an impact on brand affinity.
5. Using the Digital Entrepreneurship Canvas, outline a potential hi-growth start-up initiative in the field of digital marketing.

SUGGESTED TEACHING STRATEGY

The case can be delivered in a typical three-hour class, assuming students read the case in advance, according to the steps laid out in TN Table 10.1.

TN Table 10.1 Suggested instructional sequence

Step	Duration	Description
Preparatory activity (before the class)		• Students read the case • Create teams of 3 or 4 students • Select a couple of questions for the in-class discussion (remaining questions can be assigned for homework)
Introduction	10 min	Create slides with the list of steps and questions
Teamwork	60 min	Students work in teams to discuss the case, search online for additional material, and prepare the answers to the questions
Prepare the presentation	20 min	Students visualize the answers by using slides, visual maps, post-it notes, etc.
Presentation and discussion	90 min	• Each team gives a 10-min presentation of their answers • The remaining teams ask for details and clarifications, provide comments and discuss the contents

SUGGESTED ANSWERS TO DISCUSSION QUESTIONS

Discussion Question 1: Can you identify and briefly describe the five distinguishing features characterizing influencer marketing with respect to traditional marketing?

1. Emotional contents aligned to customer profiles.
2. Community-based perspective and digital marketplace orientation.
3. Larger and richer information on products.
4. More targeted campaigns on specific niches (or individuals).
5. Integrated multi-channel communication.

Discussion Question 2: Why is brand affinity so critical? What factors or variables does your brand affinity depend on? What would you recommend considering, as a consultant, for a client company that wants to improve its brand affinity?

Brand affinity refers to the emotional linkages existing between a company and its customers. It represents what a customer feels while interacting with a brand, his/her attraction and enticement towards the brand, and willingness to spend time through positively debating and communicating about the brand. Brand affinity relies on feelings and emotions that bring people to choose a brand, a company, or a product.

In relation to brand loyalty, which is essentially connected to the repeated purchasing from the same customers, brand affinity goes a step further because it is related to emotions and feelings, which are communicated in the social community and that prove crucial to building relationships with new customers and creating trust with them. In this vein, brand affinity is affected by customers' opinion, customer support service, brand identity, product quality, sales conditions, and contents communicated.

Discussion Question 3: Based on the definitions and examples analyzed in the Buzzoole case, and using some extra research, identify and describe (from a functional point of view) the most important technologies supporting digital marketing.

Digital marketing leverages digital technologies to enhance marketing activities. More specifically, the main technologies able to innovate marketing today are social media, mobile apps, business analytics, big data, artificial intelligence, and virtual/augmented reality. Each of these technologies has a potential impact of different dimensions for marketing activities, as reported in TN Table 10.2.

TN Table 10.2   Examples of uses of digital technologies for marketing applications

Digital technology	Dimensions of marketing activities impacted by technology
Social media	Communication; Virtual communities; Word of mouth
Mobile apps	Ubiquity; Immediacy; Geo-referenced services
Business analytics	Personalized offering; Targeted promotions; Insights for product enhancement
Big data	Early identification of emerging trends and behavior; Discovery of new market needs (and niches)
Artificial intelligence	Awareness about customer feedback; Discovery of relationships among products' sales and contextual conditions; Automatic customer profiling
Virtual/augmented reality	Customer lock-in; Product enhancement; Customer service innovation; Active customer involvement; Co-design and co-experimentation

Students can also perform web searches to retrieve documents, cases, and reports from which to extract further insights to complete and detail the dimensions presented in TN Table 10.2.

Discussion Question 4: Can you summarize and discuss indicators you can use to assess the effectiveness of an influencer campaign?

- *Total Engagement*, which indicates the sum of the interactions (i.e. likes, comments, shares) generated by a given content during a campaign.
- *Reach*, that is the total number of people reached by a piece of content.
- Impressions (or "views"), which refers to the number of times the content has been viewed or distributed.

- *Sentiment*, which is evaluated in terms of the number of positive, negative and neutral reactions to influencers' posts.
- *True Reach*, which indicates the number of people reached by the content produced by an influencer marketing campaign across different social media.
- *Ad Recall*, which estimates the percentage of people reached by a campaign and who remember seeing it.

Further indicators can be proposed by students during the case analysis and discussion.

Discussion Question 5: Can you ideate and design a start-up initiative in the field of digital marketing by using the Digital Entrepreneurship Canvas?

Digital Entrepreneurship Canvas is a tool useful to support the design and description of digital entrepreneurship initiatives through the definition of seven key elements, which connect technologies, processes and people with the strategic purpose to generate outputs (performance and product) while creating a positive social and environmental impact, reputation, and responsibility (planet). Table 10.1 included in the case study provides a description for each element. Based on these descriptions, students are required to work in teams with the goal to ideate a new company capable of offering innovative digital marketing services.

FURTHER READING AND ADDITIONAL RESOURCES

Parker, G., Van Alstyne, M., and Choudary, S. P. (2016). *Platform Revolution: How Networked Markets Are Transforming the Economy, and How to Make Them Work for You*. New York: W. W. Norton.

WEB SOURCES

Audience is everything™. Nielsen (2022, March 31). Retrieved April 10, 2022, from https://www.nielsen.com/it/it/.
Geyser, W. (2022, March 2). *The State of Influencer Marketing 2021: Benchmark Report*. Influencer Marketing Hub. Retrieved April 10, 2022, from https://influencermarketinghub.com/influencer-marketing-benchmark-report-2021/.
Influencers campaign case studies, rankings and reports. Buzzoole (n.d.). Retrieved April 10, 2022, from https://buzzoole.com/page/resources.
Insider Intelligence (2022, March 15). *Influencer Marketing 2022: Industry Stats & Market Research*. Insider Intelligence. Retrieved April 10, 2022, from https://www.insiderintelligence.com/insights/influencer-marketing-report/.

Chapter 11: teaching notes

Nils J. Tschoppe, Jan K. Tänzler and Paul Drews

CASE SUMMARY

This fictive case is based on the development of a real-world online marketing company that, due to its rapid growth, is in need of redesigning its IT landscape with a special focus on software to support higher integration and optimized processes. Despite regional challenges, such as the shortage of skilled workers outside of conurbations, the company Marketing Beats has grown in recent years and now has about 130 employees. This success story has led the company to be confronted with new challenges. Growing personnel structures, cross-departmental communication, and an increasingly complex IT landscape pose the risk of causing the "digital gazelle" to lose its agility. The necessary process optimization and the redesign of the IT landscape are new strategic challenges the company has to face. The loss of customer information, redundant customer data, and a high level of documentation effort present the company with the task of finding a new solution for its loosely integrated software. Students are asked to develop solution proposals for the company's IT landscape, taking into account the impact of such a redesign on the company's processes and structure.

TEACHING OBJECTIVES

The following questions will guide students to work through the case:

1. An overview of the strengths and weaknesses of the company with reference to the current IT landscape, as well as the opportunities and risks associated with its redesign, can help raise employee awareness and derive necessary measures as part of the transformation. Following this, what might a SWOT analysis look like?

2. How do the interests expressed by individual departments affect the design of the new IT landscape? Point out organizational and technical challenges that need to be taken into account in the context of redesigning

the IT landscape, and sort them according to their relevance to the upcoming transformation.

3. The transformation can range from the selective replacement or procurement of software to comprehensive integration. Which software solutions come into question here and why? Analyze their pros and cons by developing a list of features for comparison.

4. What could the transformation roadmap look like, and how would you proceed with the rollout of the new systems/software? In doing so, also consider the associated training efforts required with regard to the departments as well as the possible, temporary parallel operation of the old and new software. For this purpose, landscape models and "process support matrices," mapping departments in terms of processes and software, can be used complementarily, for example, to illustrate the as-is and to-be IT landscapes.

TEACHING STRATEGY AND ASSIGNMENT SUGGESTIONS

The case study is suitable for Master's levels, depending on the students' level of knowledge. The case study is suitable for use in the middle or at the end of a course on digital entrepreneurship. If the case is to be discussed, a time frame of between five and six hours is recommended, depending on the size of the group (see TN Table 11.1).

TN Table 11.1   Timetable

Task	Time	Total time
Familiarization with the relevant literature	60–120 minutes	60–120 minutes
Optional: as a self-study reading assignment (duration depends on each individual)	*(60–120 minutes)*	
Introduction to the case study and discussion of the learning objectives	30 minutes	60 minutes
Discussion of the facts of the case and the discussion questions	30 minutes	
Optional: introduction in a plenary	*(60 minutes)*	
Processing of the case in small groups	90 minutes	90 minutes
Optional: processing in a plenary	*(90 minutes)*	
Discussion of the results	45 minutes	90 minutes
Summary and discussion of the lessons learned	45 minutes	

THEORETICAL MODELS AND CONCEPTS RELEVANT TO THE CASE STUDY

SWOT Analysis

SWOT analysis is an instrument of strategic planning (Weihrich, 1982). It can also be used to derive strategies for IT alignment or development. With the help of the SWOT method, both an internal analysis of strengths and weaknesses, and an external analysis of opportunities and threats can be systematically carried out and visualized (TN Figure 11.1). The general approach starts with an environmental and business analysis, which can be presented in a matrix. Various strategic consequences can then be derived from the combination of the analyses.

The following strategies are available to companies:

- **Opportunities/Strengths:** Here, it is important for the company to pursue new opportunities that are a good fit with the company's strengths.
- **Opportunities/Weaknesses:** Here, it is important for the company to eliminate weaknesses in order to take advantage of new opportunities.
- **Threats/Strengths:** Here, it is important for the company to leverage strengths in order to avert risks or threats.
- **Threats/Weaknesses:** Here, it is important for the company to develop defense strategies to prevent existing weaknesses from becoming the target of threats.

		Internal factors of influence	
		Strengths	Weaknesses
External factors of influence	Opportunities	SO strategy	WO strategy
	Threats	ST strategy	WT strategy

TN Figure 11.1 Structure of a SWOT analysis

Landscape Modeling

Landscape models (see, e.g., Hanschke, 2010) are used to depict the respective states of the IT architecture. In each landscape model, a distinction can be made between the actual, the planned, and the target state. The level of detail of the landscape model decreases with the progression from the ACTUAL state through the PLANNED state to the TARGET state:

- The ACTUAL state refers to what the current IT landscape looks like and where there is potential for improvement.
- The PLANNED state is the roadmap for how to implement the desired changes. Mostly, the planned state also includes a fixed time horizon.
- The TARGET state describes what the future vision of the IT landscape looks like. In most cases, concrete steps are formulated as to how the state is to be achieved. The target state is the preferred state, which, however, cannot be implemented in every case due to various influences.

In addition, a "process support matrix" can help, among other things, to map the software used and planned to the company's processes (TN Figure 11.2).

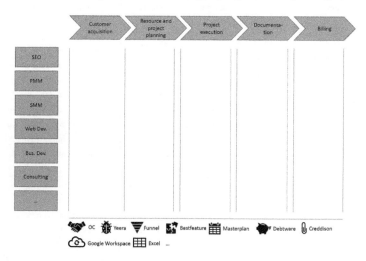

TN Figure 11.2 Process support matrix

SOLUTIONS TO DISCUSSION QUESTIONS

Discussion Question 1: An overview of the strengths and weaknesses of the company with reference to the current IT landscape, as well as the opportunities and risks associated with its redesign, can help raise employee awareness and derive necessary measures as part of the transformation. Following this, what might a SWOT analysis look like?

You can find an example of a SWOT analysis in TN Table 11.2.

TN Table 11.2　SWOT analysis with an IT focus (example)

	Strengths	**Weaknesses**
	– Industry know-how and product portfolio of the departments – Communication (agility through flat hierarchies) and networks – IT affinity of the (young) employees	– Missing software interfaces and outdated software in the IT landscape – Processes in need of optimization – No IT department
Opportunities – New software solutions on the market – New technologies (e.g., SaaS/ cloud software) – Remote work (digital leadership)	– New software solutions promote agility in the company (e.g., improved communication) – Use of new technologies (e.g., use of on-demand cloud-software) – Remote work can increase the attractiveness of the company for applicants (e.g., to penetrate new markets). – IT-savvy employees can assist with software training	– Use of cloud solutions to compensate the lack of IT know-how (e.g., backups) – Optimized workflows/process optimization through an integrated IT landscape (e.g., with better software interfaces) – New software solutions can lead to cost reductions in the long term (e.g., simplified project documentation)
Threats – Maintaining the status quo cripples performance – Wrong software selection leads to high costs (in the long run) – Rollout can lead to operational impairments	– Employees and competitors can provide helpful information in terms of software selection – Piloting of the changes in individual departments as part of the redesign of the IT landscape in order to avoid performance slumps	– External consultants can be consulted to avoid mistakes in software selection and implementation – Establishment of an internal "transformation unit" to deal intensively with software selection and implementation

Discussion Question 2: How do the interests expressed by individual departments affect the design of the new IT landscape? Point out organizational and technical challenges that need to be taken into account in the context of redesigning the IT landscape, and sort them according to their relevance to the upcoming transformation.

One way to prioritize company-wide and departmental requirements is to divide them into critical, relevant, and other factors, as shown in TN Table 11.3.

TN Table 11.3   Critical factors in the redesign of the IT landscape

	Company-wide	Online marketing departments	Web development department	F&A department	...
Critical (3 points)	– Redundant customer master data – Overview of project status and changes in cross-departmental projects	– Documentation effort/familiarization time regarding new projects is high – Google Ads requires Google Workspace	– Kanban functionality is required	– Autom. invoicing – Autom. dunning	...
Relevant (2 points)	– Statistical evaluation of the projects – Central time recording/resource planning/task assignment – Spam in cross-departmental projects	– Project management software technically obsolete – Spam in cross-departmental projects	– Invoicing effort is relatively high – Integrated resource planning	– Software interface with project management software/ integrated invoicing	...
Other (1 point)	– Knowledge management (wiki)/ central storage of passwords	– Software interface with sales/business development	– Software interface with sales/business development	– A single software program for accounts receivable and accounts payable	...

The issues that receive the highest scores should be prioritized. Business process modeling and notation (BPMN) (see, e.g., Dumas et al., 2018), can be used, for example, complementarily in the context of planning the IT landscape to obtain an overview of the relevant business processes as well as the software used within them. For example, the customer cycle from customer acquisition to project execution to customer support could be analyzed, taking into account the software solutions used therein as well as the departments involved.

Discussion Question 3: The transformation can range from the selective replacement or procurement of software to comprehensive integration. Which software solutions come into question here and why? Analyze their pros and cons by developing a list of features for comparison.

A list could include features such as interfaces to the existing IT landscape, costs, CRM and kanban functionality, project and resource planning, automatic invoicing, etc. Various tools can be used as part of the process of identifying software solutions that are potentially relevant for the company. This can be done by analyzing industry reports, interviewing specialists, or using tools such as the Gartner Magic Quadrant. As an example, the Gartner Magic Quadrant provides an overview of CRM (Gartner, 2021a) or enterprise resource planning (ERP) (Gartner, 2021b) software currently used on the market.

Discussion Question 4: What could the transformation roadmap look like, and how would you proceed with the rollout of the new systems/software? In doing so, also consider the associated training efforts required with regard to the departments as well as the possible, temporary parallel operation of the old and new software. For this purpose, landscape models and "process support matrices," mapping departments in terms of processes and software, can be used complementarily, for example, to illustrate the as-is and to-be IT landscapes.

Landscape models can help to move from an ACTUAL state to a TARGET state. Often, implementation planning is represented using a sequence of landscape diagrams. An overview of planned projects per quarter to achieve the desired IT landscape could be created here. The current IT landscape and the desired IT landscape should be visualized along with (annual) interim statuses. For example, Hanschke (2010) offers some practical examples, which could be helpful for solving this task. After the initial situation has been outlined together with the department-specific requirements for IT and external influences, such as future trends and changes in the market and competition, and a picture of the to-be IT landscape has been created together with improvements and, if necessary, risks for the next few years, the question of how this can be achieved should be answered as part of the roadmap development. This should include a visualization or list of which projects, together with their associated costs and risks, will lead to the target state being achieved, and which solutions we can already build on (pros and cons).

REFERENCES

Dumas, M., La Rosa, M., Mendling, J., and Reijers, H. A. (2018). *Fundamentals of Business Process Management*. Berlin: Springer.

Gartner (2021a). *Magic Quadrant for the CRM Customer Engagement Center*. LeBlanc, N., Davies, J., Agarwal, V., Gartner Inc., June.

Gartner (2021b). *Magic Quadrant for Cloud Core Financial Suites for Midsize, Large, and Global Enterprises*. Van Decker, J., Leiter, G., Anderson, R., Gartner Inc., May.

Hanschke, I. (2010). *Strategic IT Management: A Toolkit for Enterprise Architecture Management*. Berlin: Springer.

Weihrich, H. (1982). The TOWS Matrix: A tool for situational analysis. *Long Range Planning*, 15(2), 54–66.

Chapter 12: teaching notes

Katia Richomme-Huet and Odile De Saint Julien

CASE SUMMARY

This case study explores the construction of a Malian social and inclusive network, called Lenali, developed by Mamadou Gouro Sidibé, an IT entrepreneur and Doctor of Computer Science (see Figure 12.1). Positioned in the booming digital voice services market, Lenali is a service application that "speaks in local languages" and has been developed for the marginal market of the "digitally excluded."

For the founder, driven by an explicit social mission, access to conversational commerce via the digitalization of services is the only way to improve the quality of life of Malians and the entrepreneurial development of communities at the base of the pyramid (BoP). Far from profit maximization objectives, Lenali is a commercial and educational engine that offers large-scale economic opportunities and generates positive social impacts for the Malian population and the country's economy.

This case invites students to consider digital solutions as an entry point for this group into digital activities. It raises important questions about the impacts of digital voice technology on innovation, opportunities and technologies, on BoP entrepreneurs and on BoPs in general, in terms of exclusion and inclusion. It gives students the opportunity to think about the past, present and future of digital social business models in a country with low education levels and infrastructure problems.

TEACHING OBJECTIVES

This case study is designed to give users the opportunity to understand and analyze the evolution of the digital voice application LENALI, from its launch to the next steps. The learning objectives guide the participant in his/her reflection on the difficulties encountered by the founder, the various opportunities offered by the booming audio market and the potential evolution of Lenali's business model in order to favor its future growth and sustainability.

- LO 1 – Learn about describing and identifying viable business models for social digital ventures.
- LO 2 – Understand the difficulty of starting and growing a digital venture in countries with low levels of education and infrastructural problems.
- LO 3 – Explain the impact of digital voice technology on innovation (opportunities and technologies), on BoP entrepreneurs and on BoP people in general (exclusion and inclusion).
- LO 4 – Discuss how the business model could evolve to make Lenali a sustainable and growing venture.
- LO 5 – Identify the opportunities for the company to contribute to closing the gap of the illiteracy digital divide and to go beyond the local market of illiterate users.

TEACHING STRATEGY (OPTION 1 BASIC) AND ASSIGNMENT SUGGESTIONS

A tutorial session following the theoretical points discussed by the teacher. He/she could focus on LO 1, LO 2 and LO 3. Depending on the length of the session, instructors can use all the questions or select some. For example, for a 2h–3h session, students read the case independently (30 minutes), work in groups on the previously selected questions (1h–1h30), and finally deliver an oral presentation (30 minutes or 1 hour depending on the number of students).

LO 1 – Learn about describing and identifying viable business models for social digital ventures

Using the Social Business Model Canvas provided at the end of these teaching notes, identify the information in the text and map Lenali's current BM.

A. (Social value proposition): What are the main motivations of the founder to launch Lenali (vision)? What differences is Lenali making with existing solutions? What could be the social value proposition in one sentence? What social impact measures could Lenali use?

The founder's motivations are strongly rooted in his social mission. For him, this application must be a response to the economic and social problems he has identified.

Lenali differs from existing social networks because it is mainly based on voice technologies and on digital inclusion. Unlike Facebook, which seeks to improve relations between existing literate actors while maximizing profits obtained by monetizing users' interaction, Lenali enables the creation of links between illiterate actors in BoP communities and does not exploit these connections by selling data or supporting targeted advertising.

The social value proposition could be: Voice services offered free of charge to BoP entrepreneurs and their customers.

Social impact measures tools can be presented to the audience such as Social Accounting and Audit (SAA), Logic models, SROI (evaluative and forecast social return on investment), Theory of Change and Evaluation framework (see Rauscher et al., 2012; Zappalá and Lyons, 2009).

B. (Market): Who are the main users/customers, early adopters, etc.? What is the macroeconomic environment and what are the changes affecting the market? Who are the competitors?

The current user benefits from Lenali's inclusive and social offers but does not pay for these services: a beneficiary. In a non-profit or charitable model, focus tends to go only to serving beneficiaries, and external donors provide funding instead of customers.

It could be of interest to define the divide between a for-profit (focusing on economically sustainable models) and non-profit organization (focusing on solving social issues), and to expose the current challenge about the hybridization of the two.

Like commercial enterprises, social entrepreneurs need to be aware of the changes that occur around them. For example, the students can use the PESTEL to analyze Lenali's macro-environment in the short, medium and long term. As a mnemonic used to group macro-environment factors (Witcher and Chau, 2014), the PESTEL framework analyses the external business environment to understand the "big picture" in which the organization operates. It enables them to take advantage of the opportunities and minimize the threats faced by the organization's business activities (see the PESTEL template at the end of these teaching notes).

Other social or commercial enterprises and/or entrepreneurs, such as Viamo in Ghana, offer similar services, products or social programs to Lenali. Their social mission and beneficiaries may be similar to Lenali. The document "W4RA-FINAL BROCHURE" (see additional materials) can be presented to the audience to explain the context, environment and competitors.

C. (Implementation): What does Lenali do? What resources does Lenali have? Who helps Lenali to carry out its activities? What is its sales and marketing plan? How does Lenali reach its users/customers?

Using the elements of the case study, the students can briefly fill in the template (block by block). The answers may be validated collectively to ensure their understanding. Then students discuss the implementation phase as a whole. They can go further by answering these questions: What could have been done in other ways? Is there some missing information? How does Lenali establish these relationships with beneficiaries and how does it maintain them?

D. (Finance): What are the main costs? What are the main revenue streams? Where does Lenali intend to reinvest its surplus?

Using the elements of the case study, the students can briefly fill in the template (block by block). The answers may be validated collectively to ensure their understanding. Then students discuss the financial phase as a whole.

Social enterprises have several sources of revenue streams that ensure their sustainability such as donations, subventions, public and/or private sector contracts and eventually from marketable services. A link can be made with the hybridization model.

The surplus should define how Lenali gains and wants to/will redistribute surplus profits (self-financial margin). Instructors can mention subventions and donations, the SROI, the stakeholder and shareholder differences in expectation, the possibility or not for a personal financial benefit from surplus profits. If Lenali generates excess profits, will it invest them in the growth of the company?

E. (Impacts): What are the impacts of this social value proposition?

Several questions can be posed to the learners to guide their reasoning: for example, what are the impacts of this value proposition on the market, costs and revenues, partners and sales and marketing strategies? At what level, local, infrastructural, do Lenali's activities and services offer solutions? What influences and/or other actors could affect these impacts?

LO 2 – Understand the difficulty of starting and growing a digital venture in countries with low levels of education and infrastructural problems

A. Identify what can help or has helped Lenali to overcome low levels of education and infrastructural problems and perhaps leverage some local assets. What are the strengths and weaknesses of the company? What are the major opportunities and threats?

Answer the above questions through a SWOT analysis matrix.

It is suggested to build a SWOT matrix (see SWOT matrix template, TN Figure 12.2) to answer the above questions (TN Table 12.1).

TN Table 12.1 SWOT analysis

STRENGTHS	WEAKNESSES
S1: The founder's strong social traits and motivations	W1: Start-up company: the early stage corresponds to limited resources which could be a weakness in the seed stage of growth strategies
S2: Advanced knowledge of voice technologies and social media design and use	W2: Limited funding mostly based on "love money" contribution (family, friends, etc.)
S3: In depth knowledge of the social and economic environment and its problems	W3: High consumption of time spent on a "real" understanding of the problems and needs of BoP populations. Reorientation of the project to differentiate from existing platforms and applications
S4: BoP's human capital and locations close to resources supporting the activities of BoP communities	W4: High consumption of financial resources to develop tools with voice technologies
S5: Activities consist in creating value by transforming inputs into good and services. They aim to strengthen the capacities and skills of BoP populations in the current context of technological and digital transformation	W5: Marginal market segment with low income, little or no education
S6: Creative tools and methods to support sustainable development: enabling and facilitating access to information and digital trade for BoP through the creation of a social and inclusive network	W6: All free offers – no income from the activity
S7: Ability to provide sustained efforts to build a business community of entrepreneurs for the development of the capacities and skills of illiterate BoP users	W7: Lack of a strong brand
OPPORTUNITIES	THREATS
O1: Social enterprises are on the rise in Africa and so is the awareness of the Millennials generation to develop social impacts in society	T1: Little or no government regulation of social enterprises
O2: African governments are showing more interest in the development of social and inclusive entrepreneurship in the context of sustainable development	T2: Slow implementation of policy decisions by government, slow allocation of funds and grants, high levels of corruption
O3: Evolution of inclusive and social economic development in Malian illiterate communities: fosters the purchasing power of entrepreneurs and customers as well as their quality of life	T3: High rate of illiteracy which makes the assimilation of the use of these complex technologies difficult and slow

O4: Democratization of advanced technologies (machine learning, voice technologies, etc.)	T4: Possible increase in competition in Mali, driven by the booming audio market which offers significant commercial opportunities
O5: Booming development of the audio and voice services market	T5: Growing presence of multinationals seeking innovation in developing countries
O6: Access to low-cost smartphones and development of 4G	T6: Due to the competitive and business-centered environment (more application projects, more interests from multinationals and investors), there is a strong risk that the original social mission is transformed into a race for financial profit
O7: Strong increase in transactions and sales due to the development of digital commerce, which has an impact on the quality of life of Malians and on the economy of Mali	T7: Intellectual property is hard to protect; apps are at a high risk of being imitated

LO 3 – Explain the impact of digital voice technology on innovation (opportunities and technologies), on BoP entrepreneurs and on BoP people in general (exclusion and inclusion).

A. As audio is becoming the new frontier for user digital experience (boom of digital voice recognition and digital speech market with podcast, smart speakers, etc.), what are the opportunities for innovation?

Extend the use of the application to other sectors, such as agriculture, medical, legal advice, etc. and to the development of voice connected objects (IoTs).

B. What are the main impacts of Lenali on the Malian BoP entrepreneurs and communities?

The students should define main categories such as social, economic, financial, sociological, psychological, educational, well-being, economic development, etc. They should give at least one example in each.

TEACHING STRATEGY (OPTION 2 ADVANCED) AND ASSIGNMENT SUGGESTIONS

LO 4 and LO 5 may generate a shift toward more expert-level reasoning. They help students to take a step back from the problem at hand and make connections, but also to take steps towards greater expertise in their thinking.

This advanced modality is based on the integration of the case study into a flipped learning session. The flipped learning model is designed to move "homework" into the classroom experience while the lecture is delivered asynchronously before the in-person class.

For this case study, teachers will ask students to read the case and watch the lecture videos on their own. Class time will then be devoted to discussion and exploration of the subject. We assume that option 1 has already been performed in a previous session or that students are at an advanced level and so able to skip the more basic analysis performed for LO 1 to 3. In any case, students should be ready to think about the future of Lenali.

LO 4 – Discuss how the business model could evolve to make Lenali a sustainable and growing venture.

A. How is Lenali going to become profitable? Should its business model be changed?

First option is the evolution of the current BM from free to paying offers by extending the use of Lenali to new commercial or professional "customers" that are willing to pay for a premium offer. Students can brainstorm to generate ideas regarding what type of premium services the company could offer.

A second option is to monetize the application through advertising. This monetization is done with the broadcasting of ads or the personalization of the user experience by the integration of banners or interstitials, etc. An interstitial is a web banner (in the form of videos, photos, narratives) that attracts the user's attention for advertising purposes because it shortly covers the page visited. Students can brainstorm ideas on the forms and/or strategies of monetization, as well as personalization of advertisements and/or user experience.

B. Given its social mission, how can Lenali make the business sustainable and even profitable?

Lenali should show its ability to sustain the activities in the long term. Several revenue-generating strategies can be illustrated to students while asking them to do some extra research in thinking about ways to apply them to the case: (1) the collection of data; (2) consulting services; (3) business assistance to partners; (4) subscriptions on a monthly or yearly basis; (5) provide education and training; (6) revenue sharing or franchising; (7) organizing events.

C. Lenali is currently a not-for-profit company. Should the founder consider changing it to for-profit?

As a premise, it is important to ensure that students know the non-profit and for-profit differences. If they do not, the case offers an opportunity to introduce students to the key differences.

Thinking of transitioning depends on several criteria: (1) diversifying the user pool (from beneficiary to customer); (2) keeping the focus on the assets (successful results and great relationships); (3) including financial metrics in addition to social mission-driven metrics; (4) establishing future strategic plans using a new SWOT in line with the social mission; (5) questioning the reasons for the transition; (6) understanding the differences between a ROI and a SROI.

Students should discuss the pros and cons of the transition.

LO 5 – Identify the opportunities for the company to contribute to closing the gap of the illiteracy digital divide and to go beyond the local market of illiterate users

A. What is new with Gafé (how is it different from Lenali)? What are the main objectives of Gafé?

Lenali is focused on conversational commerce (chat commerce or conversational marketing). Gafé is oriented towards self-development (education) and solutions to illiteracy. The professor may develop elements on conversational commerce or ask the students to work on it at home (before the course).

The differences with Gafé: (1) Improving educational attainment (reduce the marked disparities in outcomes that lead to greater inequalities of all kinds); (2) increasing BoP literacy; (3) developing users' digital skills; (4) designing relevant and usable digital solutions that address a wide range of skill levels.

B. What could be other opportunities to go beyond the local market?

Lenali and Gafé connect with people on vocal social media based on their physical location. But it is also possible to be connected from international locations. While selling products can be difficult (example of Ada or Goita), online education is border-free.

Several opportunities can be proposed: (1) expand regionally (from Bamako to other towns); (2) expand internationally with specific languages (different countries with one language such as Bambara spoken in Burkina Faso, Ivory Coast, etc.); (3) transform local testimonials into global ones with the diaspora.

C. How does Lenali optimize the user experience and how may it become more attractive?

As a premise, it is important to ensure that students know some key concepts. User experience or UX is an individual's experience with a company (including everything they see, hear, and their emotional reactions).

Several optimizations can be proposed: (1) pilot the application by combining voice and visual capabilities through the voice; (2) make actions reversible; (3) increase the calls to action; (4) improve brand credibility and recognition.

REFERENCES AND FURTHER READING

Coggins, S., McCampbell, M., Sharma, A., Sharma, R., Haefele, S. M., Karki, E., and Brown, B. (2022). How have smallholder farmers used digital extension tools? Developer and user voices from Sub-Saharan Africa, South Asia and Southeast Asia. *Global Food Security*, 32, 100577. https://doi.org/10.1016/j.gfs.2021.100577.

Rauscher, O., Schober, C., and Millner, R. (2012). Social impact measurement and social return on investment (SROI)-analysis. *New Methods of Economic Evaluation*. https://socialvalueuk.org/wp-content/uploads/2016/03/Social-Impact-Measurement -and-SROI_English_Version_final_2.pdf.

Sidibé, A., Olabisi, L. S., Doumbia, H., Touré, K., and Niamba, C. A. (2021). Barriers and enablers of the use of digital technologies for sustainable agricultural development and food security: Learning from cases in Mali. *Science of the Anthropocene*, 9(1), 00106. https://doi.org/10.1525/elementa.2020.00106.

Solomon, E. M. and van Klyton, A. (2020). The impact of digital technology usage on economic growth in Africa. *Utilities Policy*, 101104. https://doi.org/10.1016/j.jup .2020.101104.

Witcher, B. J. and Chau, V. S. (2014). *Strategic Management Principles and Practice* (2nd Edition). Boston, MA: Cengage Learning.

Zappalá, G. and Lyons, M. (2009). *Addressing Disadvantage: Consideration of Models and Approaches to Measuring Social Impact*. Centre for Social Impact. https:// eval.ru/book_files/Zappala_Recent%20approaches%20to%20measuring%20social %20impact%20in%20the%20Third%20sector_135.pdf.

ADDITIONAL MATERIALS

(Necessary: many visuals, links to video materials, requiring students to combine data-driven and analytical reasoning with more creative thinking styles)

Communicate freely. Lenali (n.d.). Retrieved April 10, 2022, from http://lenali.ml/.

Document explaining the voice-based mobile services for social development in West Africa, entitled w4ra-finalbrochure: https://europa.eu/capacity4dev/file/16380/ download?token=PVYfkrYR.

Luc (1970, May 24). *Mamadou Gouro sidibé*. Afriscitech. Retrieved April 5, 2022, from https://www.afriscitech.com/en/scientists/young-scientists/846-mamadou -gouro-sidibe-a-vocal-social-network-for-africans-who-can-t-read.

Voice-based mobile services for Social Development – Europa.eu (n.d.). Retrieved April 5, 2022, from https://europa.eu/capacity4dev/file/16380/download?token= PVYfkrYR.

Wikimedia Foundation (2021, December 28). *Mamadou Gouro Sidibe*. Wikipedia. Retrieved April 5, 2022, from https://en.wikipedia.org/wiki/Mamadou_Gouro _Sidibe.

YouTube (2019, August 14). *Lenali, the Malian app empowering illiterate small-business owners.* YouTube. Retrieved April 10, 2022, from https://www .youtube.com/watch?v=H5Zt7TtUeLY.

Cases on digital entrepreneurship

IMPLEMENTATION

PARTNERS

DELIVERY

SOCIAL VALUE PROPOSITION

MARKET

USERS

MACRO ECONOMIC ENVIRONMENT

SALES + MARKETING

SOCIAL IMPACT MEASURES

COMPETITORS

COST STRUCTURE

SURPLUS

REVENUE STREAMS

INTENDED SOCIAL IMPACT AND BENEFITS

TN Figure 12.1 Social business model canvas template

	STRENGTHS	WEAKNESSES
INTERNAL	1) What are your strengths? 2) What unique capabilities do you possess? 3) What do you do better than others? 4) What do others perceive as your strengths?	1) What are your weaknesses? 2) What do your competitors do better than you?
	OPPORTUNITIES	THREATS
EXTERNAL	1) What trends may positively impact you? 2) What opportunities are available to you?	1) Do you have solid financial support? 2) What trends may negatively impact you?

TN Figure 12.2 SWOT template

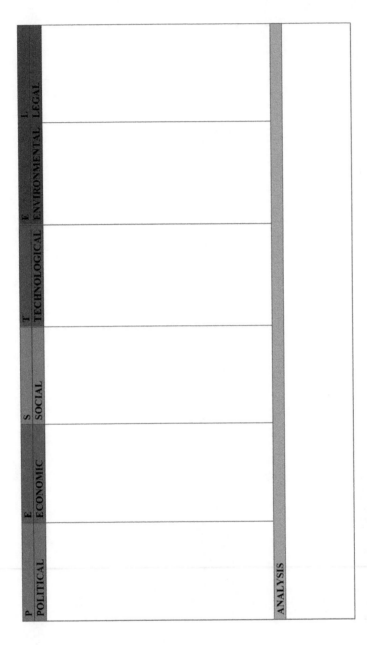

TN Figure 12.3 Pestel template

Index